Collaborating for
Comprehensive Services for
Young Children and Their Families

Collaborating for Comprehensive Services for Young Children and Their Families

The Local Interagency Coordinating Council

by

William W. Swan, Ed.D.

Department of Educational Leadership
The University of Georgia
Athens, Georgia

and

Janet L. Morgan, Ph.D.

Manatee County School District
Department of Exceptional Student Education
Bradenton, Florida

·P·A·U·L·H·
BROOKES
PUBLISHING CO.

Baltimore · London · Toronto · Sydney

Paul H. Brookes Publishing Co.
P.O. Box 10624
Baltimore, Maryland 21285-0624

Typeset by The Maple-Vail Composition Services, Binghamton, New York.
Manufactured in the United States of America by
The Maple Press Company, York, Pennsylvania.

Library of Congress Cataloging-in-Publication Data
Swan, William W.
 Collaborating for comprehensive services for young children and
their families : the local interagency coordinating council / by
William W. Swan and Janet L. Morgan.
  p.   cm.
 Includes bibliographical references and index.
 ISBN 1-55766-103-0
 1. Handicapped children—Services for—United States—States.
 2. Handicapped children—Education—United States—States.
 3. Central-local government relations—United States. I. Morgan,
Janet L. II. Title.
HV888.5.S95 1992
362.4′083—dc20   92-12381
                                                                           CIP

British Library Cataloging-in-Publication data are available from the British
Library.

Contents

About the Authors

William W. Swan, Ed.D., Associate Professor, Department of Educational Leadership, College of Education, The University of Georgia, G-10 Aderhold Hall, Athens, Georgia 30602-7171

William W. Swan completed his undergraduate work in applied psychology at the Georgia Institute of Technology and his master's degree and doctor of education in educational psychology and research design at the University of Georgia. His initial work focused on the development and evaluation of a model of services for preschoolers with emotional disturbances and their families, and the subsequent dissemination of that model nationally. Dr. Swan later joined the Bureau of Education for the Handicapped/Office of Special Education Programs (United States Department of Education) where he held leadership positions with discretionary programs. Dr. Swan returned to The University of Georgia to pursue research, instruction, and service interests in special education leadership, interagency collaboration, and regular and special education leadership collaboration. Dr. Swan consults regularly with state and local education agencies and professional organizations concerning special education leadership issues including collaboration.

Janet L. Morgan, Ph.D., Program Coordinator, Early Intervention Programs, Manatee County School District, Exceptional Student Education, P.O. Box 9069, Bradenton, Florida 34206

Janet L. Morgan received her master's degree in speech pathology at Kent State University, and educational specialist degree in administration and supervision and her doctor of philosophy in curriculum and instruction from the University of South Florida. Dr. Morgan initially worked as a speech pathologist and coordinated programs for children with speech, language, and hearing impairments; she continues to hold state licensure and certification by the American Speech-Language-Hearing Association. Dr. Morgan has served as coordinator for the Manatee County School District's early intervention programs from 1978, when she concurrently developed a local interagency coordinating council. She served as the council's coordinator until 1991. Based on the early successes of the local council in coordinating comprehensive services for children and families, Dr. Morgan received state grants to develop manuals and to provide technical assistance to other local districts to assist in the development and operation of local interagency coordinating councils. She has conducted numerous presentations and consultations with state and local education agencies and organizations concerning interagency collaboration and development and operation of local interagency councils. Dr. Morgan served as a member of the Florida Interagency Coordinating Council from 1987 to 1989.

Dr. Morgan is currently the Coordinator of the Preschool & Diagnostic Center of the Manatee County School District, a center that provides evaluative, therapeutic, and educational services for children under 5 years of age who have disabilities or who are at risk. Dr. Morgan continues to refine and expand collaborative programs for preschool children with disabilities and conditions of risk and their families in Manatee County by coordinating the district's early intervention programs.

Foreword

Collaborating for Comprehensive Services for Young Children and Their Families: The Local Interagency Coordinating Council is a timely contribution to our professional literature. It recognizes the important role of local service providers and community leaders in achieving the mission outlined under PL 99-457 to establish a "comprehensive, coordinated, multidisciplinary, interagency program of early intervention services" for all infants and toddlers with disabilities and their families. More importantly, this book is one that offers more than academic rhetoric and idealisms about interagency collaboration and coordination. It is an action book, a "how to" book that provides much-needed guidance for the dedicated people who are trying to make "interagency collaboration" and "coordinated services" really happen at the grass roots level of service delivery where the lives of children and their families are directly affected. Effective service coordination requires the partnership of many individuals across agencies, both private and public, and across both local and state levels. The involvement of so many people inevitably brings people into the planning and implementation process who differ greatly in their knowledge about:

1. Interagency systems and laws that now make cooperative interagency activities a high priority
2. Services and service agencies within their own state and community including the regulations and restrictions under which each one works
3. The complex process through which community and agency representatives must progress to plan, organize, and then implement comprehensive services systems that represent a true collaborative partnership among relevant agencies

This book provides useful information and suggestions based on the latest research results for action that can help all individuals participate more meaningfully to make interagency efforts work at the local community level.

Interagency collaboration and services coordination are topics that have had considerable attention over the past 2 decades. The late 1970s brought a recognition of the necessity for better collaboration between human services and education agencies. That decade was a time of unprecedented growth in education, health, and social services for previously underserved and unserved populations. As in any period of rapid growth, *expansion*—not consolidation or coordination—was the focus. Limited attention was given to the coordination of services within and across agencies. Problems resulting from the lack of coordination became clear: the overlapping services across agencies, duplication of agency roles, excessive costs for services duplicated across agencies, incapable bureaucracies across agencies that prevented services from being delivered in a timely way, and occurrences of service providers working with the same clients without any coordination or acknowledgment of one another. The problems directly affected families and children, reducing the effectiveness of the very services that had been designed to help them.

The 1980s were an era of advocacy for interagency collaboration. From this decade came federal policies and legislation that now move us to take action. Interagency collaboration shifted from being an intriguing topic of discussion to a perceived "necessity" for state and local agencies that traditionally worked in isolation from one another. Parents repeatedly pointed to the frustrations imposed upon them by the bureaucratic red tape they encountered when attempting to obtain services. Delayed access to services caused many parents to simply give up, leaving children and families without the assistance they needed. The time for academic and political rhetoric passed and the time for real action arrived.

The 1990s are now the decade for making coordinated interagency service delivery a reality! Congress has taken a firm stand—interagency collaboration is a requirement under federal law! PL

99-457 and its reauthorization in 1992 (PL 102-119) explicitly call for the development of a "state-wide, comprehensive, coordinated, multidisciplinary, interagency program of early intervention services" for all infants and toddlers with disabilities and their families. Furthermore, Congress required each state to create a state interagency coordinating council to assist in bringing together appropriate leaders to create the arena for planning, negotiating, and developing the mechanisms to implement this interagency agenda. Other congressional legislative actions have reflected this shift toward an interagency philosophy. The Omnibus Budget Reconciliation Act of 1989, which reauthorized Maternal and Child Health Services programs (including Medicaid, the Supplemental Food Program for Women, Infants and Children [WIC], Supplemental Security Income [SSI], and the Maternal and Child Health Block Grant Program), also included provisions emphasizing the necessity of family-centered, community-based, coordinated care and coordination of services. Policy documents from the National Commission on Children and other federal committees also call for a significant shift in services to reshape them toward more responsive, community-based, and family-oriented practices.

The reasons for the shift to collaborative service delivery among agencies are clear. First, economic realities make it imperative that excess costs from service duplications be eliminated. Second, the movement toward family-focused services necessitates that services be coordinated across agencies for the benefit of the client as opposed to practices that were used primarily for the convenience of individual agency bureaucracies and staff. Third, the reality that no single agency encompasses the resources or programs required to administer the comprehensive, multidisciplinary services now required by law for special-needs children and their families necessitates cooperation among agencies. PL 99-457 is a reflection of this paradigm shift in how agencies and their roles and responsibilities are being viewed as we move toward the year 2000.

So, what does a local interagency coordinating council (LICC) have to do with all this? Swan and Morgan make their point clearly: It is at the local, community level where the ultimate test of the interagency concept occurs. It is here that collaboration in service delivery among agencies will either happen or fail to happen. Many states are encouraging communities to create a LICC as the means for organizing their working interagency system at the grass roots level. Federal and state interagency work will either facilitate or deter local citizens from creating an effective interagency system. However, the real test of this concept rests in what happens among people who work directly with children and families and who are responsible for connecting appropriate services to their intended clientele.

Swan and Morgan make many critical points, several of which merit emphasis here. First, they emphasize that legislation or mandates alone cannot make interagency collaboration occur. In addressing the question, "So, will effective interagency collaboration be created?", Swan and Morgan suggest that while the initiative has been clearly established by the federal government through joint policy statements and at the state level through cooperative agreements between agencies, there *must* be a concrete plan or model to assist in the development of coordinated service delivery at the *local or community level*. They suggest that loose, poorly defined systems will not work.

Second, Swan and Morgan note that the task of reducing fragmentation in services, eliminating wasteful duplication, streamlining the system for families, and ensuring quality services for all young children with disabilities or who are at risk can again only be achieved at the local, community level! Therefore, the LICC offers a means for doing this. The level where interagency coordination affects children and families the most and where it will happen or will fail to happen is at the grass roots community level. This is where the real test of implementation lies and this is where effort must be placed and support must be given. As Swan and Morgan so graphically state, the key is effective implementation at the local level—at the "ground or street level where the rubber hits the road."

Third, Swan and Morgan stress that if community agencies, educational programs, and human services organizations are sincere in their intent to create the full continuum of educational, parent–family, medical, therapy, and social services for young children with disabilities and their families, then *ongoing coordination of the primary services of the various community agencies is vital*. Thus, local service providers are most likely to engage in this ongoing coordination if they are to create the plan and the model for their own interagency activities.

This book will be a superb resource and guide for many individuals who are working on this complex and critical task of creating more coordinated, collaborative interagency service delivery systems for children with at-risk conditions and disabilities and their parents. What a wonderful guide and resource for new members of LICCs and for learning about what states are trying to accomplish on behalf of infants and toddlers and what local interagency coordinating councils can do to facilitate that process!

As Chairperson of the Kansas Interagency Coordinating Council for Early Childhood Developmental Services and member of my own LICC, this book is one I definitely want to share with my colleagues. It is undoubtedly a most informative, insightful, and grand information resource that will help people as they tackle this important national, state, and local agenda.

Nancy L. Peterson, Ph.D.
Professor of Special Education
University of Kansas
and
Chairperson, Kansas Interagency
Coordinating Council for Early
Childhood Developmental Services

Preface

The legislative and regulatory requirements for state interagency coordinating councils (ICCs) under Part H of PL 99-457 have guided councils' development since 1986. While the state ICCs focus on statewide policy issues, the emphasis for local interagency coordinating councils is distinctly different. Recognizing these differences provides important clues to councils' organization, membership, and operations.

Collaborating for Comprehensive Services for Young Children and Their Families: The Local Interagency Coordinating Council focuses on the collaborative development and implementation of local interagency coordinating councils based on the most relevant literature, most current research, and best practices. It is a guide for all those at the local level, in both the public and the private sectors, who wish to ensure that a comprehensive continuum of services exists to serve children and their families. While the state ICC emphasizes broad policy development, the local emphasis requires consideration of both local policy and provision of direct services. The provision of direct services is the acid test for policy development—a test that requires that the abstract be translated effectively into the concrete world of meeting the varied needs of unique individuals and families.

This book is designed as a handbook for those who wish to develop or enhance local interagency councils. A combination of theoretical bases and practical applications provide the user with the rationale as well as a means to achieve the array of comprehensive services needed for children and their families. While the examples and activities are based on actual experiences at the local, state, and federal levels, the reader is encouraged to adapt these materials for local use. Consistent with the individualization of programs for children with disabilities or children at risk and their families, the reader needs to individualize the application of this book to maximize the impact based on the unique combination of qualities and conditions in each community.

Section I, Foundations for Interagency Collaboration, includes five chapters that provide the basis for effective interagency collaboration. Chapter 1 reviews collaboration as a part of shifting paradigms, the legislation and history of interagency collaboration with programs for individuals with disabilities, and local interagency council objectives. Chapter 2 specifies the means to assess the readiness of local groups to collaborate. Chapter 3 defines the stages of cooperation, coordination, and collaboration with emphasis on collaboration. Chapters 4 and 5 present a model for local interagency councils including critical characteristics, elements of effectiveness, and stages of development.

Section II, Creating a Local Interagency Council, focuses on the importance of the human factor in the operation of local interagency councils. Chapter 6 reviews varied leadership parameters and provides a paradigm for leadership by a council coordinator emphasizing the concept of shared decision making. Chapter 7 describes the nature of group processes, the role of council members, successful meeting practices, and the influence of such practices on the productivity of the local interagency council. Chapter 8 uses the leadership and process parameters in the earlier chapters to provide a step-by-step outline for the creation of a new local interagency council.

Section III, Council Activities and Outcomes, is the longest section of the book. This is consistent with the emphasis on translating theoretical bases (the abstract) into concrete applications and the combined foci for the local council on both policy development and direct service. Chapter 9 specifies organizational and procedural activities including analyses of existing services, developing a local council philosophy, meeting schedules and agenda, and council composition. Sample procedural guidelines are included. Chapter 10 focuses on information-sharing activities. Chapter 11 presents an analysis of the existing service delivery system, including a community agency services matrix and a continuum of services matrix with completed samples. Chapter 12 contains guidelines and examples of coordination of agency services including council structure and membership, child identification and assessment, referral services, screening services, evaluation services, and transition services. Chapter 13 focuses on coordinating parent services and staff development based on specific assessment of parent needs and assessment of agency personnel needs. Chapter 14 emphasizes the new perspectives on case management, service coordination at the community and family levels, the array of coordination activities, and an interagency child tracking system (sample procedures for a child tracking system are provided). Chapter 15 focuses on interagency collaboration including such areas as an interagency intake team, consistent policies across agencies, collaboration on grant development and budgets, collaboration on parent programs, standardization of forms including IEPs and IFSPs, and transition procedures. Chapter 16 provides specific examples of the evaluation of the interagency councils including an approach with specific examples.

Section IV, Financing Early Intervention Services, emphasizes the financial strategies to support the array of comprehensive services needed by children with disabilities or children who are at risk and their families. Chapter 17 provides specifics on local financing of early intervention services emphasizing flexibility and innovative use of available resources in the most effective ways. Chapter 18 focuses on contracts and written agreements including both procedures and specific examples.

It is our hope that this description of the local interagency council and the numerous activities described will stimulate local problem solving, effective interagency relationships, and, especially, quality and comprehensive services. It is also our hope that development of these local councils does not occur as an end in itself, but that the councils create observable outcomes that intimately touch the lives of children and their families and that are valued based on their ability to do so.

Acknowledgments

Portions of this book are based on resource manuals developed by the Manatee District Schools (Florida) through the Prekindergarten Handicapped Interagency Project, funded by the State of Florida, Department of Education, Division of Public Schools, Bureau of Education for Exceptional Students, under Federal Assistance for the Education of the Handicapped (PL 91-230, Part B, as amended by PL 99-457). The content of the manuals does not necessarily reflect the view of the Bureau of Education for Exceptional Students, the Department of Education, or any other agency of the United States Government.

Appreciation is expressed to those who facilitated the devleopment of these materials including project staff, members of the Manatee County Interagency Council, and staff from the Bureau of Education for Exceptional Students. Particular appreciation is expressed to the School Board of Manatee County: C. Gene Witt, Superintendent of Schools; Virgil Mills, Assistant Superintendent; and Raymond S. Ciemniecki, Exceptional Student Education Director.

Special thanks are extended to the following persons whose involvement or participation assisted in creating a better understanding of the concept of local interagency collaboration: Jane Bambace, HRS Developmental Services; Phil Blankenship, Easter Seal Society; Colleen Bloom, Children's Haven and Adult Center; Ruby Byrd, School Board of Manatee County; Barbara Brownell, Child Find; Suzanne Ford, HRS Developmental Services; Ray Foster, Therapeutic Concepts, Inc.; Olive Gatke, Health and Rehabilitative Services; Gay Hawk, United Cerebral Palsy; Kathie Haag, Child Find; Crystal Herold, Manatee County Schools; Edwina Jones, HRS Developmental Services; Karin Jones, HCA L. W. Blake Hospital; Marjorie Kinnan, Manatee County School Board; Diane Kornse, Palm Beach County Schools; Nancy Marsh, United Cerebral Palsy; Rebecca Pruett, Gadsden County Schools; Myriam Reyes, Parent to Parent; MariAnn Shannon, Manatee County Public Health Department; Jean Shoemaker, Manatee County Public Health Department; Ruth Spillman, Manatee County Head Start; Carolyn Steele, Child Migrant Program; Susan Terry, Easter Seal Society; Allene Vega, HCA L. W. Blake Hospital; Alice Weaver, Children's Medical Services; and Lucy Young, Glen Cove Child & Family Center.

Foundations for Interagency Collaboration

The foundation required for effective interagency collaboration in providing services to young children with disabilities and those at risk and their families is defined and demonstrated in this section's five chapters. Chapter 1 reviews the current emphasis on improving collaborative efforts as a part of changing paradigms, the goals and objectives of the Education of the Handicapped Act Amendments of 1986 (PL 99-457) with emphasis on financial responsibility for services, past efforts at interagency collaboration, and objectives for local interagency councils. Chapter 2 describes the steps needed to stimulate and realize the motivation and readiness of agencies to collaborate. It also discusses eight premises underlying collaboration and provides a sample checklist for evaluating the need to collaborate. Chapter 3 defines the three stages of cooperation, coordination, and collaboration among agencies; differentiates between state and local collaboration; and provides the key concepts of collaboration.

Chapters 4 and 5 present a model for local interagency councils. Chapter 4 specifies the critical characteristics of a local council—definition, mission, contrasts to other types of groups, and the elements of effectiveness. Chapter 5 describes the three stages of a council as it grows to maturity and discusses the nature and development of groups. Examples of specific strategies and activities, such as development, child identification, public awareness, evaluation, and service delivery, are noted for each stage of council development: 1) cooperation, 2) coordination, and 3) collaboration.

Chapter 5 marks the transition from the foundation and initial strategies presented in this section to a more specific focus in Section II on the human factors involved in creating a local interagency council.

Chapter 1

Foundations of Local Interagency Council Development

Local interagency councils are the focus of considerable interest. Their potential as a successful strategy in accomplishing the goals and objectives of federal and state legislation related to early intervention services has become apparent. The interest in achieving effective development and implementation of local councils is related to three factors: 1) the complexity and fragmentation in the existing service delivery system, 2) interagency coordination requirements specified in the Education of the Handicapped Act Amendments of 1986 (PL 99-457), and 3) the current emphasis on problem solving at the local level.

Frustration has increased in the fields of education and human services over the system's complexity and fragmentation that ultimately act to the disadvantage of both agency and client. Since the Education for All Handicapped Children Act (PL 94-142) was passed in 1975, both public and non-public programs have experienced an increased demand for services. This expansion, however, has been paired with increased requirements for cost efficiency, often in the face of budget reductions. In addition, there is a noticeable mistrust of government and public programs and a belief that the programs are not sufficiently responsive to their clients' needs.

The results of a Rand Corporation study on services to people with disabilities (Brewer & Kakalik, 1982) documented that both providers and consumers of the services were often denied access to them because of the complexity and disorganization of the delivery system. These agencies, originally designed to serve this specific population, have experienced a process of institutional change that has reduced their responsiveness to the needs of their clients. It has been hypothesized that agencies, organizations, and institutions change in a definite predictable sequence (Shapiro, 1985). Organizations tend, with growth and expansion, to become more complex and multipurposed. With such growth, managers and administrators devote increasing amounts of time to the internal organization and procedures of the bureaucracy itself. A rigid hierarchy emerges with a system of rules and procedures designed to maintain operations, organizational routines, and goals. Rank takes precedence over ideas; dogma, ritual, red tape, and routine proliferate. As more time is devoted to the organization's operation, less time is available for responding to clients' needs. As the organization's structural elements become more differentiated and complex, the organization becomes less and less adaptive (McNulty, 1989).

The majority of government organizations still operate under a classic pyramidal, bureaucratic model (McNulty, 1989). This model explains why an agency or organization experiences difficulty adapting to a changing environment. Case management personnel must be employed to assist in the complex task of navigating the service delivery system, satisfying paperwork requirements, and meeting the organization's needs. Education and social service programs have become masterful at protecting their resources rather than providing them to clients. Families have experienced the service delivery system as both fragmented and dehumanizing (Gerry & McWhorter, 1991). This situation is critically in need of a remedy.

PL 99-457 confirms the realistic notion that one agency, organization, program, or discipline cannot accommodate all of the diverse needs of young children with special needs and their families. Congress called for the development of a comprehensive system of service delivery by incorporating new innovations into the strengths of existing programs and services. Furthermore, Congress required that all providers work with one another, as well as with families, to enhance the development of young children with disabilities and provide necessary support to help families make intelligent choices and manage resources in the best interest of their children.

Through the enactment of PL 99-457, Congress established a new national initiative: The expansion of opportunities for all eligible young children and their families in the United States to receive the benefits of early intervention and preschool services. To accomplish this task, coordination and collaboration among many agencies and organizations are required and a mandatory base for interagency program planning is established. The law offers a significant challenge to a complex and fragmented service delivery system.

To assist in addressing the issue of coordination, PL 99-457 requires the establishment of a state interagency coordinating council (ICC). The ICC provides a mechanism for discussion of issues and implementation of necessary services among groups of parents, lawmakers, educators, and policymakers. States typically report that three or four agencies have primary and overlapping responsibilities for providing services to children, birth through 5 years of age, and their families (Meisels, Harbin, Modigliani, & Olson, 1988). Interestingly, the creation of state ICCs, in accordance with the legal requirement, has often followed much earlier and voluntary creation of local ICCs that resulted from the complexity and

fragmentation of the service delivery system and the dissatisfaction with the quality and extent of services to children and families.

The emphasis on problem solving at the local level is consistent with the networking and individual trends seen in the culture (Naisbitt, 1982) and the federal and state emphasis on public services funding and priority setting initiated by the Reagan Administration in 1981. This emphasis is supported by funding patterns, political rhetoric, and the current attitudes of voters in maintaining local control. The basic premise is to solve problems as close to the client as possible by effectively responding to real needs in flexible ways that are based on local strengths and needs.

GOALS AND OBJECTIVES OF PL 99-457

Part H, Services to Birth Through 2 Years

The primary goal of Part H is "to develop and implement a statewide, comprehensive, coordinated, multidisciplinary, interagency program of early intervention services for disabled infants and toddlers and their families" (Section 671[b] [1]). A theme involving linkage and coordination is conveyed in the requirements for coordinated service delivery, case management, and implementation of individualized family service plans (IFSPs). Case management is designed to preclude difficulty or inability in gaining access to services and to repair the fragmentation that has occurred in the service delivery system. It is also designed to avoid instances where children "fall through the cracks," families are referred to agency programs in a circular fashion, and multiple agencies each proclaim that it is the "payor of last report." Other goals of Part H include: "to facilitate the coordination of payment for early intervention services from Federal, State, local, and private services (including public and private insurance coverage)" (Section 671[b] [1]) and "to enhance their capacity to provide quality early intervention services and expand and improve existing intervention services being provided to disabled infants, toddlers, and their families" (Section 671[b] [1]).

Eligible children served under PL 99-457 are defined as those who experience developmental delays or have a diagnosed physical or mental condition that has a high probability of a later associated delay in one or more of the following areas: cognitive, physical, speech-language, self-help, and psychosocial development.

The statewide comprehensive system must include services that are:

Provided under public supervision
Provided at no cost, except when federal or state laws permit
Designated to meet the developmental needs of young children across all five delay areas
Inclusive of, but not limited to, family training and counseling, special instruction, speech pathology, occupational therapy, physical therapy, case management, medical evaluation and diagnosis, and screening
Delivered consistent with the IFSP
Consistent with state standards as well as new federal standards
Provided by qualified personnel

Also, development of the comprehensive system of early intervention is guided by the components described in the IFSP. These required components include:

Multidisciplinary assessment and identification of appropriate services
Description of early intervention services to be provided, including frequency, intensity, and method of delivery
Expected major outcomes for the child
Expected major outcomes for the family
Projected dated for services, within a 45-day time period following referral
Identification of a case manager from the most immediately relevant profession

Transition plan to Part B services on the child's third birthday

PL 99-457 contains a variety of programs, including Title I—Program for Infants and Toddlers with Handicaps (birth through 2 years inclusive), and is an entirely new section of the Education of the Handicapped Act (EHA). This discretionary program to assist the states required 14 minimum components that comprise the statewide system (Table 1).

Section 619, Services to 3- Through 5-Year-Old Children

Section 619, the Preschool Incentive Grants of the EHA, was amended to create enhanced incentives for states to provide a free, appropriate, public education (FAPE) to all eligible disabled children between the ages of 3 through 5 by the school year

Table 1. Minimum components under Part H, a program for infants and toddlers with disabilities

1. Definition of developmental delay
2. Timetable for availability of services to all children in the state in need of services
3. Comprehensive multidisciplinary evaluation of needs of children and families
4. Individualized family service plan and case management services
5. Comprehensive child find and referral system
6. Public awareness activities
7. Central directory of services, resources, experts, research, and demonstration projects in the state
8. Comprehensive system of personnel development
9. Single line of authority to a lead agency responsible for general administration and supervision, identification and coordination of available resources, assignment of financial responsibility to the appropriate agency, procedures to ensure the provision of services, procedures for resolution of interagency disputes, formal interagency agreements
10. Policy for contracting or making arrangements with local service providers
11. Procedure for timely reimbursement of funds
12. Procedural safeguards
13. Policies and procedures for personnel standards
14. System for compiling data on the early intervention program

1991–1992. Provisions of FAPE include the individualized education program (IEP), due process, confidentiality, and most inclusive environment.

Community services to provide FAPE can be implemented in many ways. Section 203 of the bill clarifies the relationship among public agencies for providing or paying for services set out in a child's IEP. This issue was the subject of a report titled "Special Education—Financing Health and Education Services for Handicapped Children," prepared by the United States General Accounting Office (GAO) (Special Education, 1986). The GAO report concluded that Congress, in enacting PL 94-142, established a single line of authority and placed this authority with educational agencies. This meant that, in the event of disputes among agencies regarding responsibility for payment of a particular service, the educational agency must ensure that the child with disabilities received the services described in the IEP during the resolution of the dispute. The policy was intended to prevent buck-passing among agencies.

Although PL 94-142 designated the state educational agency to be responsible for ensuring FAPE, GAO reported that it did not make the educational agency solely financially responsible for all services. Congress intended that the services be funded from various sources. These include appropriations under PL 94-142 and state and local education funds, as well as funds from other federal, state, and local sources, such as Medicaid, for which children with disabilities qualify.

Congress established a legal framework under which one agency (the educational agency) is ultimately accountable, and multiple agencies (educational, health, welfare, and other social service agencies) are expected to pay for appropriate services. Although this framework was not sufficiently understood and implemented under PL 94-142, the congressional intent of securing interagency collaboration and shared responsibility for services to children with disabilities was clarified and strengthened in the language of PL 99-457.

Interagency Collaboration To Finance Services

The Part H program is a payor of last resort. As a result, financing a system of comprehensive services requires identification and coordination of multiple federal, state, and local public and private funding sources. The identification and coordination of all these sources—including constantly changing priorities and funding authorities—constitute a challenging task at the local level. For example, considering only federal programs, Thiele and Hamilton (1991) identified 16 programs (e.g., Medicaid) that could provide funds for at least one type of early intervention services (Table 2).

School districts may provide home- or center-based programs directly or indirectly through agreements or contracts with other qualified service agencies or providers. Provisions for sharing the costs of FAPE among appropriate state agencies (not limited to educational agencies) include:

1. Sharing of costs by multiple agencies
2. Supplementing and not supplanting costs to ensure that funds under Part B are not used to satisfy a financial commitment for services that would have been paid for by other federal, state, and local agencies (including health agencies)
3. Requiring development and implementation of interagency agreements to define the financial responsibility of each agency
4. Developing procedures by which educational agencies may initiate proceedings for resolving disputes under the interagency agreement in order to secure reimbursement from other agencies or otherwise implement the provisions of the agreement
5. Disallowing reduction or exclusion of medical (including Medicaid) or other assistance available or to alter eligibility under Title V or Title XIX of the Social

Table 2. Federal programs that could provide funds for at least one type of early intervention services in 1991

1. Handicapped Infants and Toddlers Program (Education of the Handicapped Act)
2. Deaf-Blind Children and Youth (Education of the Handicapped Act—Part C)
3. Chapter 1 Handicapped Program (Education Consolidation and Improvement Act of 1981—, Title 1, Chapter 1)
4. Assistance for Education of All Handicapped Children (Education of the Handicapped Act—Part B, Part C)
5. Head Start Program (Head Start Act)
6. Medicaid (Social Security Act, Title XIX)
7. Maternal and Child Health Block Grants (Social Security Act Title V)
8. Child Welfare Services Program (Social Security Act, Title IV-B)
9. Developmental Disabilities Basic State Grants Program (Developmental Disabilities Assistance—Bill of Rights)
10. Alcohol, Drug Abuse and Mental Health Block Grant Programs (Public Health Service Act)
11. Community Health Service Program (Public Health Service Act)
12. Indian Health Service Program (Indian Health Care Improvement Act)
13. Migrant Health Services Program (Public Health Service Act)
14. Preventive Health and Health Services Block Grant (Health Block Grant)
15. Health Care for the Homeless Program (Homeless Assistance Act—Health for the Homeless)
16. Social Services Block Grant (Social Security Act)

Adapted from Florida State Application for Fiscal Year 1990 Funds for Part H of the Individuals with Disabilities Education Act (1991), p. 160, and Thiele and Hamilton (1991), p. 12.

Security Act for services that would have been provided for but are required in the IEP

6. Requiring development of the IFSP in a manner that permits parents and a variety of local providers to identify the respective roles and financial responsibilities with respect to a given child and family

Individuals with Disabilities Education Act

The Individuals with Disabilities Education Act (IDEA, 1990) reauthorized and amended PL 94-142. IDEA reflected the preference for the term *disabled*, rather than *handicapped*, throughout the act and in the revised rules and regulations. Priorities for early education of infants, toddlers, and preschool children with disabilities and those at risk include improving the early identification of these children, facilitating their transition from medical care to early intervention services and from early intervention to preschool, promoting the use of assistive technology devices, and addressing the early intervention needs of children exposed prenatally to drugs. A stronger emphasis is given to integration of infants and toddlers with disabilities into nondisabled peer groups.

Discretionary grant programs (e.g., personnel preparation, programs for children with severe disabilities, research and demonstration projects) have been expanded to include priorities on programs and services for infants and toddlers with disabilities. With the new emphasis on meeting the needs of traditionally neglected populations, IDEA defines *underrepresented*—a common legal term—as minority, poor, and limited English–proficient individuals. These aspects of IDEA support the continued development of collaborative efforts among a variety of agencies to meet the diverse educational needs of infants, toddlers, and preschool children with disabilities and their families. Because of the many services required, interagency collaboration appears to be the only viable solution.

PAST EFFORTS AT INTERAGENCY COLLABORATION

The concept of interagency collaboration has existed for some time in the areas of human services and education for people with disabilities. Interagency efforts have been referred to by such terms as *interagency cooperation, service coordination, service integration, networking,* and *linkages.* Whatever term is used, the importance of interagency efforts among public and private providers, as well as local and state agencies, who serve preschool children with disabilities and those at risk and their families has been long recognized. The nature of the required services and multiple needs of this extremely heterogeneous group of children will continue to require the involvement of multiple agencies to meet their complex educational, parent/family, medical, therapy, and social services needs. To be effective, however, these services must be coordinated.

Because of the continuum from birth through 5 years, many agencies, programs, and organizations have the potential to be affected by the implementation of PL 99-457. These include organizations with different professional orientations and beliefs. The unique mix of services needed for each child and his or her family requires the commitment of a variety of professionals from a variety of agencies. Furthermore, the unique mix of needed services will require frequent periodic review and ongoing revision to remain appropriate and responsive.

In addition to the need for comprehensive services, the elimination of unnecessary duplication of services must be addressed (*A Rationale for Interagency Collaboration*, 1989). In any community, several service providers may be responsible for identical or overlapping populations of children with disabilities. Competition and "turf guarding" may be apparent. There must be a realization, however, that the public cannot afford the luxury of independent and parallel systems that obviously provide duplicative services. As early intervention programs for children, both those with disabilities and those at risk, encounter budget restrictions, the programs will be challenged to identify successful strategies for collaboration that ensure improvement and expansion of services without multiplying costs.

Although the cooperative approach to serving children and families has been encouraged and even required, interagency collaboration seldom has been achieved to the desired degree. Unfortunately, the previous lack of success may result in the reluctance of school districts, human services agencies, and community programs to make

further attempts at collaboration despite legislated requirements. Educational agencies have historically served the 5- to 18-year-old population independently without emphasizing interagency collaboration. Given this operational history, there is danger that a similar operating procedure is likely to occur for the infant, toddler, and preschool population. The interagency coordinating requirements of the program for infants and toddlers with disabilities are specific, but the strategies for accomplishing coordination are not clear. The vague notion of how interagency coordination and collaboration are defined may plague implementation of PL 99-457, as it has done for PL 94-142.

FUTURE REQUIREMENTS OF INTERAGENCY COLLABORATION

Legislation or mandates alone simply cannot force interagency collaboration (Hodge, 1984; Morgan & Swan, 1988; *A Rationale for Interagency Collaboration*, 1989). Many written agreements have been only promises to cooperate, and few successful outcomes have occurred.

How will effective interagency collaboration be created? The answer must be found at the local level. Although the initiative has been established by the federal government through joint policy statements and at the state level through cooperative agreements between agencies, there must be a concrete plan or model to assist in the development of coordinated service delivery at the local or community level. It is clear that a loose structure of coordination does not work. The multiple programs and support services required by families of young infants and toddlers with disabilities and those at risk require systematic coordination. But, it is also clear that reducing fragmentation, eliminating wasteful duplication, streamlining the system for families, and ensuring quality services for all of these young children can be done only at the local or community level.

The local interagency coordinating council provides a model to establish effective, coordinated service delivery. Moreover, the local council is the only way to recognize and accommodate the unique characteristics of each community and the particular needs of the children and families to be served. Specific needs and resources vary significantly from community to community and over time. Working relationships among service providers also vary. There is no single prescription for all communities to follow in a lock-step fashion. Each community has its own characteristics, cultural values, beliefs, history, stigmas, problems, needs, expectations, and agency relationships. A local interagency council is capable of considering these varied characteristics and developing the most appropriate and efficient system of early intervention services for the community's unique blend of conditions.

Agency commitment to genuine service coordination is logical and rational, and it results in sound planning. Implementation of interagency collaborative strategies becomes a wise investment for all participants. If community agencies, educational programs, and human services organizations are sincere in the intent to create the full continuum of educational, parent/family, medical, therapy, and social services for preschool children with disabilities and their families, ongoing coordination among the primary service providers is vital. Fragmentation and unnecessary duplication of services must be eliminated; a system must be developed that maximizes appropriateness, quality, and cost effectiveness, including accountability. These goals can be accomplished in part by emphasizing successful practices when new or refined ventures are initiated in local interagency collaboration, with the net result of improved services for children and families. One such model is the local interagency coordinating council.

LOCAL INTERAGENCY OBJECTIVES

The frustration expressed by parents and providers of early intervention services creates a powerful motivator to implement the concept of interagency collaboration set forth in PL 99-457. Statewide program requirements translate into objectives for interagency efforts at the local level. The statewide system of comprehensive services will be built from a "grass roots" or bottom-up approach. It will utilize the knowledge of local agency personnel and parents who most accurately understand the shortcomings of the current system and who can provide the leadership to increase its response to the needs of preschool children with disabilities and their families.

By directing its activities to include coordination and collaboration of the unique characteristics of community providers, a local interagency council can achieve the following 11 results:

1. Ensure the delivery of all needed early intervention services to children and families in a timely manner.
2. Coordinate various eligibility requirements, including the definition of developmental delay.
3. Develop a comprehensive multidisciplinary evaluation procedure.
4. Develop and implement the IFSP across the community providers.
5. Develop a comprehensive child-find and referral system.
6. Develop a public awareness program to focus on the importance and availability of early intervention services.
7. Develop and disseminate a local central directory in addition to disseminating the state central directory.
8. Develop and implement a system of personnel development, in-service education, and adoption of personnel standards.
9. Identify and facilitate contracts and written agreements among providers to expand and improve existing services.
10. Identify methods to increase generation of revenue.
11. Identify and implement data collection and child tracking systems to evaluate the early intervention system.

The key to successful implementation of a statewide comprehensive service delivery system is effective implementation at the local level—the ground or "street level" where the rubber hits the road (Dokecki & Heflinger, 1989; Lipsky, 1980). The opportunity exists for implementation of the legislation at the local level in a manner that allows parents and service providers to work together as partners within the system. Parents and family members must be recognized as capable caregivers; their judgments and preferences must be trusted and honored. A well-coordinated service delivery system considers the unique resources and strengths of the community and encourages collaboration among the various providers to attain a "futuristic" view of the system. They have the opportunity to break away from previous top-down machinations of service delivery and develop a responsive and sensitive system that is exemplified in the concept of the individualized family service plan. The local interagency council, existing at the ground level, can provide a magical mix of organizational capability and maintain an individual focus, as opposed to the organizational or bureaucratic focus that has historically dominated much of the service delivery system.

REFERENCES

Brewer, G.D., & Kakalik, J.S. (1982). *Handicapped children: Strategies for improving services.* New York: McGraw-Hill.

Dokecki, P.R., & Heflinger, C.A. (1989). Strengthening families of young children with handicapping conditions: Mapping backward from the street level. In J.J. Gallagher, P.L. Trohanis, & R.M. Clifford (Eds.), *Policy implementation and PL 99-467: Planning for young children with special needs* (pp. 59–84). Baltimore: Paul H. Brookes Publishing Co.

Education for All Handicapped Children Act of 1975, PL 94-142 (August 23, 1977). 20 U.S.C. 1401, et seq: *Federal Register, 42*(163), 42474–42518.

Education of the Handicapped Act Amendments of 1986, PL 99-457 (September 22, 1986). 20 U.S.C. Sec. 1400, et seq: *Congressional Record, 132*(125), H 7893–7912.

Florida State Application for Fiscal Year 1990 Funds for Part H of the Individuals with Disabilities Education Act. (1991). Tallahassee: Florida Department of Education, Bureau of Education for Exceptional Students.

Gerry, M.H., & McWhorter, C.M. (1991). A comprehensive analysis of federal statutes and programs for persons with severe disabilities. In L.H. Meyers, C.A. Peck, & L. Brown (Eds.), *Critical issues in the lives of people with severe disabilities* (pp. 495–525). Baltimore: Paul H. Brookes Publishing Co.

Hodge, R. (1984). *Interagency cooperation: Related issues and concerns.* Bloomington: Indiana University, School of Education, A CASE Research Committee Report (Division of the Council for Exceptional Children).

Individuals with Disabilities Education Act of 1990, PL 101–476 (The 1990 Education of the Handicapped Act Amendments, October 30, 1990.) 20 U.S.C. SS 1400–1485.

Lipsky, J. (1980). *Street-level bureaucracy.* New York: Russell Sage.

McNulty, B.A. (1989). Leadership and policy strategies for interagency planning. Meeting the early childhood mandate. In J.J. Gallagher, P.L. Trohanis, & R.M. Clifford (Eds.), *Policy implementation and PL 99-457: Planning for young children with special needs* (pp. 147–167). Baltimore: Paul H. Brookes Publishing Co.

Meisels, S.J., Harbin, G., Modigliani, K., & Olson, K. (1988). Formulating optimal state early childhood intervention policies. *Exceptional Children, 55*(2), 159–165.

Morgan, J.L., & Swan, W.W. (1988). *Local interagency councils for preschool handicapped programs: An effective strategy to implement the mandate.* Bloomington: Indiana University, Council for Administrators of Special Education, Inc. (CASE) (Division of the Council for Exceptional Children).

Naisbitt, J. (1982). *Megatrends: Ten new directions transforming our lives.* New York: Warner Books, Inc.

A rationale for interagency collaboration. (1989). Tallahassee: Florida Department of Education, Bureau of Education for Exceptional Students.

Shapiro, A. (1985). *A theory of institutional change and control: Tri-partite power.* Paper presented at the annual meeting of Association of Supervision & Curriculum Development, Chicago.

Special Education—Financing health and educational services for handicapped children (GAO/HRD–86–62BR). (1986). Washington, DC: United States General Accounting Office.

Thiele, J.E., & Hamilton, J.L. (1991). Implementing the early childhood formula: Programs under PL 99-457. *Journal of Early Intervention, 15*(1), 5–12.

Chapter 2

Motivation and Readiness To Collaborate

An effective and ongoing collaboration among community agencies requires an awareness of the need, a belief in its importance, and a realization of its potential impact. Collaboration does not automatically occur; legislative mandates alone are not sufficient to achieve interagency collaboration. Local and state agencies often fail to work cooperatively to improve and expand the service delivery system because of a lack of motivation, readiness, or belief that coordination is essential. An agency staff may view the world from the perspective of only its own agency and fail to obtain a *gestalt* of the community service system. It is far easier to work alone.

Human services and education personnel frequently feel overwhelmed with the number and complexity of daily agency tasks and directives they are required to manage. With insufficient hours to accomplish the work that must be done, agency personnel are forced to prioritize the goals of their organization so they may perceive there is no time for innovative endeavors with other agencies. Under such time constraints, the need for effective interagency collaboration must be apparent and must generate a motivation to collaborate and a belief that efforts will be productive. Personnel should regard collaboration as a strategy to solve problems, not as a requirement that creates new problems.

MOTIVATING AGENCY PERSONNEL

Interagency coordination is a primary issue in the implementation of the Education of

the Handicapped Act Amendments of 1986 (PL 99-457), particularly the Part H program for the states. The key is to find a successful strategy that achieves this coordination across the various local programs funding early intervention services. Thiele and Hamilton (1991) reviewed 16 federal resources that provide funding for early intervention services under the Department of Health and Human Services and the Department of Education. Only one program, Part H, was designed to coordinate and provide comprehensive services to infants and toddlers with disabilities and those at risk and to their families.

Motivating voluntary collaboration by agency personnel who lack a mandate may prove to be one of the great challenges of PL 99-457. Personnel responsible for the delivery of these direct services to young children and families may be critically aware of the flaws within the system but feel powerless to correct them. Voluntary collaboration will result only from a belief in interagency efforts and from a belief in the necessity for a structured system of collaboration.

Working together within the structure and form of a local interagency coordinating council, the personnel of the various agencies can strengthen the system of services and eliminate the gaps. Three steps will stimulate efforts in this direction.

Heighten Awareness

Heightening awareness involves expressing how collaboration through an effective interagency coordinating council can assist: 1) children and families, and 2) the agencies

11

providing the services. This first step in the creation of an effective council is the recognition that interagency collaboration is crucial and that collaboration among the various providers can result in a stronger and more viable system. Case management, or service coordination, must occur on the institutional level as well as for the individual child. The interagency coordinating council provides this coordination. Services for individual children and families may not have maximum impact unless agencies develop formal interagency agreements that define new ways in which they will work together (Kingsley, 1989).

Interagency collaboration also assists agencies, even though their resources, funds, personnel capabilities, and time remain limited. Agencies need assurance that their resources are being expended in the best possible manner. Without this assurance, they may place severe restrictions to protect the resources of the agency at the expense of children and families. If an agency lacks confidence that program expenditures are being used to the best advantage, it may assert its role as the payor of last resort and proclaim that other agencies must assume the first financial responsibility.

The questionnaire, "Do You Need To Collaborate?" (Figure 1) can assist in creating an awareness of the need for interagency collaboration. The specificity of the items can stimulate discussion and serve as the first step in defining goals, eventual activities, outcome statements, and action plans for the interagency council.

Identify Existing Barriers to Comprehensive Local Service Delivery

When the need for interagency collaboration has been established, local agency representatives can identify service delivery requirements, barriers that exist, and strategic steps required to overcome these barriers. In order to develop a comprehensive service delivery system, precise outcomes that are desirable and essential must be clarified.

Representatives from the various agencies providing early intervention should engage in a group planning process during this second step. Mutual planning fosters a cohesive sense of purpose and an awareness that each agency and program has similar goals, commitment to children and families, and limitations and problems. By creating a sense of "sameness" and cohesiveness within the group of isolated players, the planning process can eventually bring them together as an effective and functioning team. Group process strategies are important and facilitate effective working relationships among participants, including professionals and parents, and encourage joint ownership of both the problems and the solutions.

At this initial planning stage, agency representatives closely examine the comprehensiveness and adequacy of the local service delivery system. They consider the range of local services and identify the barriers that prevent provision of a comprehensive array of early intervention services to meet the needs of children and families.

The majority of these barriers are common to communities of all sizes and types (Table 1). In addition to this common core of barriers, each community can identify unique barriers related to geographic, economic, and cultural characteristics. Outcomes for collaborative activities are then suited precisely to specific community needs.

When agency personnel are provided an opportunity to focus on their mutual problems in service delivery, the application of a systematic group process technique assists in defining the focus and describing specific local needs. For example, using the technique of brainstorming (Daniels, 1986) or the nominal group process (Ford, 1975) enables the team to identify the unique factors or barriers in its community that interfere with the provision of quality, comprehensive, and effective service in accordance with the cultural, familial, and other needs of children and families (see Chapter 9). Barriers are clarified as a result of this group activity and can be translated into goals and an action plan.

DO YOU NEED TO COLLABORATE?

	YES	NO
Do agency programs have limited funding and resources with which to operate?	—	—
Is there insufficient facility space for needed classrooms, programs, and expansion?	—	—
Are children receiving duplicated assessment and evaluation services?	—	—
Is there an unwillingness on the part of agency programs to accept evaluations from other agencies, thereby requiring duplication of testing?	—	—
Do problems and time delays exist in requests of records and reports?	—	—
Do differences in program/agency eligibility requirements result in children falling through the cracks?	—	—
Is there difficulty securing needed medical recommendations and prescriptions in order to provide therapy and treatment in a timely manner?	—	—
Are personnel shortages (speech, occupational, and physical therapy) limiting the provision of services?	—	—
Do personnel lack understanding of social services (i.e., food stamps, WIC, SSI, food commodities, AFDC, counseling, child support enforcement) in the community?	—	—
Is there a lack of awareness about the location of various programs (i.e., UCP, speech and hearing clinic, Head Start, Arc, Easter Seal Society, school programs, parent lending libraries)?	—	—
Is there a lack of understanding of referral and eligibility procedures for other agency programs?	—	—
Do agencies compete for the same population of children or fund sources? Does turf guarding exist?	—	—
Do agencies and programs complain, criticize, devalue, and mistrust one another?	—	—
Are there gaps in the service delivery system? Are needed educational, medical, therapeutic, case management, or social services insufficient?	—	—
Are services to children fragmented between several agencies?	—	—
Are parents confused about the roles of agencies, eligibilities, and how to secure services for their child?	—	—
Is there a lack of free, effortless, and natural communication and information exchange between agencies?	—	—
Is there an absence of an established and systematic transition procedure between programs?	—	—
Is there a lack of coordination and transition between 0–2 programs and 3–5 programs?	—	—
Is there a lack of communication between programs for children with disabilities or at risk?	—	—
Is it difficult to secure placement in the least restrictive environment, in mainstreamed settings, or in integrated settings?	—	—
Is there duplication in parent education and training services?	—	—
Do limited financial and organizational resources limit staff development activities?	—	—

Figure 1. Sample checklist for evaluation of the need for collaboration. (WIC, Women, Infants, and Children; SSI, Supplemental Security Income; AFDC, Aid to Families with Dependent Children; UCP, United Cerebral Palsy; ARC, Association of Retarded Citizens) (Adapted with Permission of the Florida Department of Education, Bureau of Education for Exceptional Students, from *A rationale for interagency collaboration*, [1989], p. 21)

Achieve Group Consensus on Basic Premises that Foster Collaboration

Successful collaboration among personnel from different, sometimes opposing, agencies requires modification of existing perceptions. A dramatic change is needed in the paradigms (Barker & Christensen, 1989) within which community agencies operate.

Table 1.   Common barriers to comprehensive local service delivery

Transportation limitations	Lack of facilities
Unfamiliarity with eligibility criteria	Shortage of therapists
Competition for funding	Insufficient occupational and physical therapy
Insufficient staff development	Insufficient speech therapy
Refusal to accept evaluations	Difficulty in obtaining records
Different definitions and vocabulary	Turf guarding
High cost of contracted therapy	Multiple IEPs/IFSPs
Unfamiliarity with services	Waiting lists
Inadequate decision making	Insufficient trained staff
Concern for confidentiality	Poor information exchange
Public attitudes and lack of support	Transient families
Low Medicaid reimbursement rates	Strict eligibility criteria
Failure of physicians to refer	Overprotection of resources
Inadequate understanding of PL 99-457	Different agency forms
Agency-specific procedures	Poorly informed public
Church preschools/religious instruction	Different philosophies
Different standards and certification	Agency competition
Lack of experience in coordination	

These paradigms establish the roles that agency personnel perceive they hold, the activities in which they engage, the procedures they employ, and their relationships with other agencies.

Agency focus—generally placed on program operation and procedures (independent of the roles of other agencies)—must dramatically switch to a child and family focus. A change from process-driven and program-driven goals to child-driven or family-driven goals must occur. This results in a radical departure from the manner in which personnel generally evaluate programs, determine activities, and identify priorities.

This change requires "stepping back" from one's own agency and viewing it from an outside perspective. It requires separating from entrenched procedures and substituting a vision of the entire community system of services, of which each agency is only one small part. With this change in perspective, agency personnel can begin to make decisions based on the overall needs of the children and families they serve. Each agency must visualize its role as it relates to the community and other community providers.

Effective interagency collaboration and success of the local interagency council depends on the establishment of new perceptions by agency representatives concerning the roles of their agencies and the relationships among them. Success also depends on their ability to prioritize the needs of children and families and their willingness to adjust existing roles, policies, and procedures to the newly created interrelationship of the agencies. Ultimately, this success is based on trust.

Consensus must be reached on eight basic premises (Table 2) that form the foundation of successful interagency efforts. These premises convey the attitudinal change that is a prerequisite for team work. Agency personnel must be guided through a process of confronting, discussing, and eventually reaching consensus on these premises. Without consensus and changes in previous perceptions, collaboration may be difficult and superficial. What occurs during this critical period of interagency planning and assessment determines whether the collaborative system is firmly built into the basic community framework or is eventually undermined or diverted.

Table 2. Basic premises that underlie collaboration

1. One agency alone cannot provide all of the services needed by the young child with disabilities or at high risk and his or her family.
2. With limited resources and categorical focus, agency programs must coordinate efforts to avoid waste, unnecessary duplication, and service gaps.
3. There is nothing to be gained by competition. The agency that provides the service is not as important as the fact that the child and family are appropriately served.
4. The differences across agency programs represent a strength, not a weakness or problem to be eliminated.
5. The service delivery system must consist of a wide variety of options from which families may choose.
6. Agency programs are "equal" in importance.
7. Agencies must provide mutual support and assistance to one another. Favorable trade-offs exist.
8. A structured system of interagency collaboration must exist.

(Adapted with Permission of the Florida Department of Education, Bureau of Education for Exceptional Students, from *Developing interagency councils,* [1989], p. 10)

Premise One One agency alone cannot provide all of the services needed by a young child with disabilities or at high risk and his or her family.

The young child who has disabilities or is at risk has numerous and complex medical, educational, and therapeutic needs. These needs are paired with the needs of the family (e.g., information about the child's condition, expectations, referral to community services, parent and family support). The community service delivery system consists of agencies that have categorical programs, designated functions, prescribed services, and narrowly or precisely defined eligibility criteria. No one agency can serve all of the complex needs of the child and family (Hazel et al., 1988; Linder, 1983; Magrab & Schmidt, 1980; Morgan & Swan, 1988). The complexity of a child's changing needs, as well as those of the family, requires a planning and decision-making process beyond the scope of any single case manager or professional.

The Part H program, early intervention services for infants and toddlers, is described as an interagency program. This underscores congressional intent for the program

to cross agency lines and involve all relevant public and private agencies. As a result, workable interagency systems must be built at the local level.

Premise Two With limited resources and categorical focus, agency programs must coordinate efforts to avoid waste, unnecessary duplication, and service gaps.

Although needs clearly exist for children and families, agencies and programs also have needs. Resources, funds, personnel capabilities, and time are always limited. This reality must be accepted. Agencies need assurance that they are expending resources in the most effective manner and that services provide maximum benefit. Identifying the best use for allocation of limited resources is difficult when many needs are evident. Only when agency personnel compare their available funds, sources of revenue, and funding capabilities can they determine whether funds are being spent most wisely. Duplication of services, failure to generate potential funds through federal and state child counts, and policies that result in needless waste of resources must be identified. Program personnel find that planning and fiscal collaboration for staff training and in-service activities, parent education and support, child identification, screening, and evaluation activities can result in a significant savings to program budgets. In addition to cost-effectiveness, other results of collaboration can include higher quality and a more expansive range of services.

Premise Three There is nothing to be gained by competition. The agency providing the service is not as important as the fact that the child and family are appropriately served.

Turf guarding and attempting to be the exclusive provider of services to preschool children with disabilities and those at risk are often characteristic of community agencies. Turf guarding creates criticism among providers, unwillingness to engage in joint planning, and generation of waiting lists of children because personnel resist making referrals to other agencies. Children may receive fragmented and inappropriate services when they are not referred to another provider. Competition for clientele is acceptable in the business arena, and the financial well-being of a company may depend on outselling competitors. Competition maintains pressure on companies to maintain high levels of product quality and sales. Both the situation and the product differ, however, for services provided to infants, toddlers, and preschool children. When these services are considered, competition should be placed within organizations—not between them—in order to ensure high quality. The needs of the child and the family and the promise to provide the most appropriate services are the priorities. Families often experience frustration and confusion when they attempt to locate services. Instead, they need the security of a system of community agencies that work together and support each other. The agency or organization that assists a child and family is not important; the only important factor is that the child and family receive high-quality, appropriate services. Community agencies should cooperate in building a system of strong programs and providers.

Premise Four The differences across agency programs represent a strength—not a weakness or problem to be eliminated.

The service delivery system is composed of an array of diversified agencies providing educational, medical, therapeutic, social, economic, and family services. Because of their categorical nature, service programs differ in eligibility criteria, funding sources, guidelines, regulations, capabilities, philosophies, constraints, and target populations. What one agency cannot do, another can. Alone, their services are limited. Together, they provide a rich array of service options for families. A positive perception of this variety in community agencies and programs is an advantage; when coordinated, they may provide a nearly complete continuum of service options.

Premise Five The service delivery system must consist of a wide variety of options from which families may choose.

The assortment of community programs providing early intervention services creates many options for children and their families. Diversity in delivery models, distribution of programs in convenient geographic locations, and a variety of programs can offer families a choice of providers. As the needs of children and families change, parents should have the flexibility of selecting different providers based on the appropriateness of the services, preference, and accessibility. Home-based services, center-based programs, therapy, integrated settings—all should be available to meet the unique needs of each child and family, along with agency personnel to assist the family in making rational choices.

Premise Six Agency programs are "equal" in importance.

From the perspective of the child and the family, the size of the agency is irrelevant compared with the appropriateness of the delivery model and the ability of the program to meet the unique needs of the family. A small speech and language clinic that comprises three speech-language pathologists is as important as a large school district program. For the child and family needing a specific service or delivery model, the program's importance is undeniable. All types of programs are equally needed, whether large or small, public or private, home based or center based.

Premise Seven Agencies must provide mutual support and assistance to one another. Favorable trade-offs exist.

Early intervention programs share a common bond—provision of services at the earliest point in an attempt to prevent or minimize negative effects on the lives of young children. Mutual trust among agencies can be fostered if each recognizes the achievements of the others and the importance of a strong communitywide system of services. Threats by one agency to the programs of another agency are unnecessary and avoidable. Respect for the interests and needs of each agency is required for a strong foundation that will accomplish the goals of PL 99-457 and the Part H program.

Inflation and shrinking resources, paired with competing priorities across agencies serving preschool children, place increasing demands on available financial resources. Establishing collaborative programs can provide functional and cost-effective ways to enhance programs for children and families, as well as the agencies themselves. Shortages in therapy staff, difficulty with transportation services, or insufficient facility space or location can be remedied through the development of written agreements and contracts among the various agencies.

Premise Eight A structured system of interagency collaboration must exist.

Interagency collaborative efforts at the state level are irrelevant if local implementation is not addressed (Rogers & Farrow, 1983). Although collaboration can facilitate interagency efforts at the local level, there are no guarantees that local interagency systems will automatically develop (Peterson, 1991). Extensive collaborative planning by local agency personnel is needed to establish interagency systems and activities that will have significant impact on the day-to-day provision of services.

ROLE OF THE LOCAL INTERAGENCY COUNCIL

The local preschool interagency coordinating council is one model for successful interagency collaboration. The impact of the council is directly related to its composition, underlying philosophy, and purpose. The success and viability of the council will be in direct proportion to the beliefs of the members, their commitment to interagency collaboration, and the authority given by administrators and managers of the participating agencies.

Education and human services agencies serving young children with disabilities have a history of operating in a parallel and isolated fashion. The development of a local interagency coordinating council has received considerable attention as a means of achieving sustained coordination (Peterson, 1991).

Used as a strategy to create an arena for ongoing planning and communication among agencies that provide early intervention services, the interagency council can facilitate the emergence of such ventures as collaborative programs, written agreements, and contracts for services. It can provide an alternative organizational framework for the development and provision of comprehensive services for children, from birth through age 5, who are disabled, developmentally delayed, or at high risk, and for their families. A carefully assembled council has the potential to identify, coordinate, and mobilize the efforts and resources of community agencies serving these children. The council is a "master-planning" and problem-solving group (Morgan & Swan, 1988; *A rationale for interagency collaboration*, 1989). A small, committed group of management-level personnel can assess existing services and gaps in service delivery and follow up with direct and systematic planning to improve and expand the services.

REFERENCES

Barker, J.A., & Christensen, R.J. (1989). *The business of paradigms: Discovering the future*. Burnsville, MN: Charthouse Learning Corporation.

Daniels, W.R. (1986). *Group power: A manager's guide to using meetings*. San Diego: University Associates.

Developing interagency councils. (1989). Tallahassee: Florida Department of Education, Bureau of Education for Exceptional Students.

Ford, D.L. (1975). Nominal group technique: An applied group problem-solving activity. *The 1975 annual handbook for group facilitators*. San Diego: University Associates.

Hazel, R., Barber, P.A., Roberts, S., Behr, S.K, Helm-stetter, E., & Guess. D. (1988) *A community approach to an integrated service system for children with special needs*. Baltimore: Paul H. Brookes Publishing Co.

Kingsley, C. (1989). *A guide to case management for at-risk youth*. Waltham, MA: Brandeis University, Center for Human Resources.

Linder, T.W. (1983). *Early childhood special education: Program development and administration*. Baltimore: Paul H. Brookes Publishing Co.

Magrab, P.R., & Schmidt, L.M. (1980). Interagency collaboration: A prelude to coordinated service delivery. In J.O. Elder & P.R. Magrab (Eds.), *Coordinating service to handicapped children: A handbook of interagency collaboration* (pp. 13–24). Baltimore: Paul H. Brookes Publishing Co.

Morgan, J.L., & Swan, W.W. (1988). *Local interagency councils for preschool handicapped programs: An effective strategy to implement the mandate.* Bloomington: Indiana University, Council for Administrators of Special Education, Inc. (CASE) (A Division of the Council for Exceptional Children).

Peterson, N.L. (1991). Interagency collaboration under Part H: The key to comprehensive, multidisciplinary, coordinated infant/toddler intervention services. *Journal of Early Intervention, 15*(1), 89–105.

A rationale for interagency collaboration. (1989). Tallahassee: Florida Department of Education, Bureau of Education for Exceptional Students.

Rogers, C., & Farrow, F. (1983). *Effective state strategies to promote interagency collaboration. A report of the handicapped public policy analysis project* (Vol. 1–4; Contract No. 300-82-0829). Center for the Study of Social Policy, 236 Massachusetts Avenue, N.E., Washington, DC 20002 (ERIC Document Reproduction Service No. ED 245 467; EC 162 746).

Thiele, J.E., & Hamilton, J.L. (1991). Implementing the early childhood formula: Programs under PL 99-457. *Journal of Early Intervention, 15*(1), 5–12.

Chapter 3

The Meaning of Collaboration

Collaboration, labeled today's "buzzword" (Benard, 1989), appears to be thriving in America (Gardner, 1990; Rogers, Anthony, & Danley, 1989). Collaboration has been cited widely in the educational, mental health, and human services literature and has been discussed and recommended in countless national and state reports. The word has appeared in state and federal legislation, such as the Education of the Handicapped Act Amendments of 1986 (PL 99-457) and of 1990 (PL 101-476), the latter of which renamed the law the Individuals with Disabilities Education Act (IDEA). Some interagency relationships that have emerged were mandated by legislation; others were voluntary. The wide range of efforts described in the literature vary from superficial or informal linkages to comprehensive networks.

Despite the rising popularity of collaboration, scholars and practitioners continue to debate the meaning and search for a functional definition (Kagan, Rivera, & Parker, 1991). The literature suggests that little consistency is found in collaborative undertakings and even less consensus is noted regarding the essential ingredients of interagency collaboration (Baumheier, Welch, & Cook, 1976; Cohen 1981; Kagan et al., 1991). Furthermore, insufficient research has been undertaken to determine the most effective types or models of interagency collaboration.

Basically, collaboration describes efforts to unite organizations and people for the purpose of achieving common goals that could not be accomplished by any single organization or individual acting alone. As collaboration in education and human ser-vices has emerged, four factors have combined to form its base: 1) effectiveness of collaboration in business and industry, 2) recognition of the need to integrate child and family services that were previously separated, 3) cost containment and restructuring necessitated by the scarcity of human services resources, and 4) program expansion (Kagan et al., 1991). Collaboration has been described as informal or formal (Morse, 1981). The participants in informal collaboration rely on mutual desire and commitment for the improvement of services; control rests with the participants as they determine procedures for interagency communication, responsibilities, and activities. Formal collaboration involves written agreements, administrative policies, and regulations. Control rests more with a central authority who delegates responsibilities downward, as opposed to the shared authority of less formal collaborative processes. Workable definitions and frameworks are important guides in developing strategies that will produce effective and measurable outcomes through agency collaboration.

DEFINITION OF TERMS

Common terms in the literature include interagency cooperation, interagency coordination, collaboration, linkages, networking, and services integration. Interagency activities in the area of early childhood services have evolved since the 1970s. The term *services integration* was formally mentioned first in 1971 in a policy memorandum by Eliot Richardson, Secretary of Health, Education, and Welfare (Humm-Delgado, 1980). Gans and Horton (1975) used the term *social services integration* to refer to "the linking together by various means of the services of two or more service providers to allow treatment of an individual's or family's needs in a more coordinated and comprehensive manner" (p. 3). In the human services area, Pryzwansky (1977) noted that collaboration includes joint responsibility and the mutual development of intervention. As new programs and services for children with disabilities and those at risk developed, interagency collaboration became exceedingly important.

The various terms have been carelessly used and occasionally misapplied; they may remain vague and nebulous to the practitioner. Alone, the terms fail to prescribe how these interagency efforts are conducted. Personnel from early intervention agencies are aware of the complexity of the service delivery system and the inability of a single agency to provide all of the services needed by the child with disabilities or at risk, and his or her family. Although agency personnel may be aware that they should interact with other agencies, too often they are at a loss about what to do and how to do it. A definitive framework for local interagency collaboration and effective strategies to achieve and maintain it are necessary.

The most prevalent view suggests that *cooperation, coordination,* and *collaboration* constitute a hierarchical progression (Figure 1) within local interagency efforts. These terms are often used interchangeably, but they should be perceived as describing different levels of sophistication of interagency activities (Black & Kase, 1963, Hord, 1986; Kagan et al., 1991; Morgan & Swan, 1988; Peterson, 1991; Stafford, Camp, & Vander Meer, 1984).

At the lowest level of the hierarchy, co-

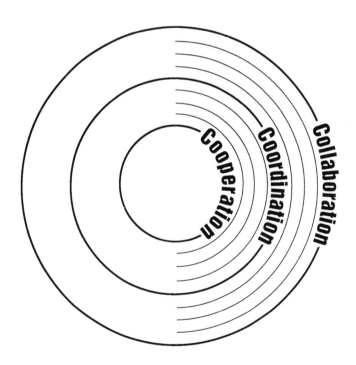

Stages in a Developmental Sequence

Figure 1. Three levels of interagency efforts.

operation is the least complex. Cooperation and even coordination between agencies can occur without proceeding to more intricate activities that characterize interagency collaboration. Collaboration, however, best describes the interagency teamwork required to address the complexities inherent in the Part H program and PL 99-457 (Peterson, 1991).

Interagency Cooperation

Interagency cooperation is a process of working together informally to achieve the day-to-day goals of the organization (Black & Kase, 1963). It represents a superficial level of agency interaction. The term implies that agencies are aware of one another and interact to provide general information, support, or referrals. Some specific examples of cooperation include adding outside agency personnel to mailing lists, forwarding or exchanging program newsletters, disseminating program information, sharing agency brochures, and extending invitations to meetings and staff development activities. Agency personnel may participate in committee activities and other community coalitions that are advisory or informational in nature. Agency procedures, policies, and activities remain distinct and separate and are determined without reference to the procedures and policies of the other agencies. The agencies are autonomous, function independently in parallel fashion, and work toward the identified goals of their respective programs. Interagency cooperation can be likened to the parallel play of children. It demonstrates a peaceful co-existence, but it is neither genuinely interactive nor interdependent.

Most agency personnel have experienced this superficial level of agency exchange. Unfortunately, it represents the primary perception of what constitutes interagency relationships. Agency personnel too often mistakenly believe that they are effectively collaborating when they are engaging in this rudimentary sharing of information. Their efforts lack depth and have little impact on

the service delivery system for children and families.

Agency personnel must do more than simply talk to one another, share information, and raise issues and concerns. They must go beyond this superficial cooperative stage and proceed to solve the problems they identify. They must change the way they work together to create new and effective ways of organizing the service delivery system.

Interagency Coordination

Interagency coordination differs slightly from cooperation, but represents a more sophisticated level of interagency interaction. The term has been defined by several authors. Morris and Lescohier (1978) defined coordination as a process of engaging in various efforts that alter or smooth the relationships of independent organizations, staffs, or resources. Agency personnel recognize that their agencies share commonalities, particularly a responsibility for providing services to young children with disabilities. They describe and clarify their respective programs and services so that the community service delivery system can be seen as a whole rather than as independent parts. With this total view of the various programs, the agencies are able to coordinate their services by establishing a common understanding of the services committed to and provided by each agency and by determining each agency's accountability and its responsibility to specific groups. Unnecessary duplication is identified and eliminated; resources are shifted and reallocated to fill voids and gaps in the service system.

Black and Kase (1963) described coordination as a more formalized process of adjustment or utilization of existing resources than cooperation. At this level, agencies initiate change to accommodate the procedures and activities of other agencies. Personnel adopt procedures for joint planning and scheduling of such events as conferences and staff development activities. They identify mutually agreeable meeting times and goals in contrast to unilateral scheduling and notification to other agencies. Information is exchanged in order to streamline referrals, forward records efficiently, and facilitate services to the clients. Activities become more interactive than parallel, although the agencies continue to remain autonomous relative to formal policies and procedures and agency goals.

Coordination involves substitution of procedural accommodation for the superficial information-sharing activities characteristic of interagency cooperation. Reorganization begins to occur with shifting procedures, shifting resources, and mutual planning.

Interagency Collaboration

Interagency collaboration, the most sophisticated level of agency relationships, has been discussed by several authors. Black and Kase (1963) described collaboration as a more intensive and jointly planned effort by organizations over a mutual concern that results in a mutually desired outcome. Morris and Lescohier (1978) described collaboration as action that brings previously separated and independent functions and organizations into a new unitary structure.

Bartel (1977) provided the most comprehensive description of collaboration by defining it as a relationship between two or more agencies in which the parties share common goals, mutual commitments, resources, decision making, and evaluation responsibilities. Collaboration involves a common goal with a clearly articulated and shared commitment that is within the scope of the general goals of the collaborating agencies. An investment of agency resources must exist through mutual contributions of time, personnel, materials, funds, and facilities because the agencies must do more than simply endorse an idea. With shared decision making and leadership, each agency maintains control of its own contributions and does not perceive any negative loss of power vis-à-vis the others. Agency personnel realize, however, that some agency au-

tonomy must be relinquished through the process of shared decision making. In collaborative relationships, the notion of sharing expertise and relying on others on an ongoing basis is essential. Collaboration implies that individuals and programs with differing expertise work together to maximize each agency's strengths and minimize each agency's weaknesses. No one agency possesses all of the expertise; that is why other agencies are involved. The greatest challenge in collaborative undertakings of joint planning and problem solving is the assurance that each agency has a role in the implementation of recommendations and that the best interests of children and families represent the driving force behind these changes. Genuine collaboration also implies joint evaluation in which each party has an equal prerogative to judge the effectiveness of the project and the quality of the collaboration.

Interagency collaboration, a radical departure from the traditional functions of independent and parallel agencies, is characterized by teamwork, mutual planning, shared ownership of problems, shared vision of goals, adjustment of policies and procedures, integration of ideas, synchronization of activities and timelines, contribution of resources, joint evaluation, and mutual satisfaction and pride of accomplishment in providing quality and a comprehensive service delivery system. Collaboration includes shared financial responsibility, written agreements, and contracts. New programs are created—joint programs co-owned and co-operated by two or more agencies. These new entities provide creative service options that could not exist without the willingness of agencies to pool their resources and expertise.

The great challenge for the local interagency coordinating council is to guide the coalition of community agencies through this process of maturation of interagency efforts. The local council must continually reinforce, realign, and strengthen the working relationships of the various agencies in order to accomplish the desired outcomes for preschool children with disabilities and those at risk and for their families.

STATE VERSUS LOCAL COLLABORATION

When long-term changes in the service delivery system are needed, particularly those related to policy and funding issues, collaboration must be a major activity at the state level that represents a wide range of early childhood constituents (Kagan et al., 1991). State-level collaboration produces change slowly because of the sensitive nature of these policy changes and the time required for interagency negotiation.

Conversely, targeting immediate improvement in services at the program level may be most effective when agencies are local and form distinct, one-to-one relationships addressing specific needs and problems. Most collaborative efforts at the local level have a direct and observable impact on the extent and quality of services offered to children and families. Impact at both state and local levels is imperative for successful collaboration; however, interagency collaborative efforts at the state level are irrelevant if local implementation is not addressed (Rogers & Farrow, 1983). Long-term resources and staff allocations must be committed to perpetuate collaboration. If agency staffs do not follow through at the local level, little progress may occur and long-term collaboration may ultimately fail (Peterson, 1991).

One of the most difficult aspects of state-level interagency coordination is deciding which agencies will be responsible for the various aspects of the program. The lead responsibility for both Part H and Section 619 has been established by law, but the mechanism for accomplishing effective cooperation has been outlined only in broad terms. For example, under Section 619 (Education of the Handicapped Act Amendments of 1986), the state educational agency is charged with the responsibility to:

set forth policies and procedures for developing and implementing interagency agreements between the State Educational Agency and other appropriate state and local agencies to (a) define the financial responsibility of each agency for providing disabled children and youth with free appropriate education, (b) resolve interagency disputes, including procedures under which local educational agencies may initiate proceedings under the agreement in order to secure reimbursement from other agencies or otherwise implement the provisions of the agreement.

The difficulty of this task is reflected by the progress of the states in implementing Part H. Progress was reported by Harbin, Gallagher, Lillie, and Eckland (1990) through the Carolina Policy Studies Program. Progress in four procedures lagged behind: 1) assignment of financial responsibility, 2) interagency agreements, 3) timely reimbursement, and 4) development of statewide data systems.

A critical test of collaboration rests with the lead agency. How that agency and its staff address the tasks detailed in Part H and Section 619 sets the stage for the collaborative attitude, or lack of it, that will dominate. Management styles for planning and developing services also set precedents that shape how the program will be managed in succeeding years. Although such messages may not be deliberately intended, they can influence the perceptions of other agencies' staffs regarding the attitude of the lead agency and affect how these agencies respond when asked to invest their staff time and resources in the early intervention program.

The state interagency council activities offer a major mechanism for bringing together on common ground the representatives of key agencies, service providers, and other important state groups. Interagency collaboration at the state level facilitates interagency work at the local level. This does not guarantee that local interagency systems will automatically develop. Extensive collaborative planning by local agencies and their personnel must occur to establish interagency systems that affect day-to-day service delivery to children and families. The real test of the interagency philosophy ultimately rests with personnel from local service agencies who make collaboration work.

KEY CONCEPTS IN COLLABORATION

Collaboration Cannot Be Mandated

Legislation or mandates alone do not result in effective collaboration. People cannot be forced to use a collaborative interaction style with others. Congress may mandate it, states may pass legislation requiring it, school districts may develop policy and procedure describing it, and program administrators may report that they engage in it. But, true collaboration occurs only when agency personnel believe in it. Success stories have been too few in the past, and the instances of "paper cooperation" have been too many (Hodge, 1984). Despite mandatory legislation, genuine collaboration results only when children's and families' needs and service issues are seen from a broader perspective than that available to individual agencies, programs, and disciplines. Open and effective communication, trust, and a spirit of team problem solving must exist. Furthermore, leadership and administrative support are crucial in establishing an environment that endorses, encourages, and reinforces interagency efforts. These efforts will not occur on a lasting basis without firm leadership and direction (Rogers & Farrow, 1983).

Collaboration Is Both a Process and an Attitude

Collaboration can be defined in terms of various interagency efforts and activities that bring together various organizations to create what none of them can accomplish independently. The process and the resulting outcomes, however, cannot occur without the beliefs and attitudes on the part of agency leaders and staffs that collaboration is not

only important but essential. Collaboration is not just a process. It represents an attitude and a different perspective relative to the manner in which agencies mutually plan, provide, and evaluate the range of community services designed to meet the needs of young children with disabilities and their families. Collaboration requires powerful commitments to change and operates within a system that is child and family directed, rather than program directed.

The spirit of collaboration does not occur spontaneously (Magrab & Schmidt, 1980). It must be encouraged and modeled. Carefully designed and orchestrated planning is necessary to bring an independent group of agency representatives to consensus that no real advantage to competition, or turf guarding, among agencies exists. Community agency personnel and providers must agree that all identified children deserve to receive prompt and appropriate services. The level of trust and respect must be developed to the degree that the agencies ensure that all children are properly served, regardless of the program providing the service. Issues of power and authority can be lethal to the spirit of collaboration.

Collaboration Takes Time

Time is a precious commodity. As mandates and responsibilities increase and resources limit or reduce staff, meeting the daily demands of any program may appear impossible. Lack of time is always cited as a primary barrier to the development of effective interagency efforts. Successful leaders, however, promote the belief that they must make time for important activities. They are also aware that success does not occur rapidly and immediately. Lasting and meaningful outcomes are achieved only when change is allowed to evolve slowly over a period of time.

The time spent today in creating effective interagency collaborative efforts will pay off when time-efficient, problem-solving group activities result. Effective interagency strategies save time for both professionals and parents. The real barriers may be impatience and the demand people express for immediate results. People who are always in a hurry may expect instant results and be unwilling to engage in activities that require long-term commitments, attention to detail, and substantial effort. Even though the time required to accomplish collaboration may be significant, agency personnel must recognize that the eventual outcome will be more effective than if the task had been completed by a single agency.

Collaboration Does Not Develop Evenly

The pace and direction of community collaborative efforts are influenced dramatically by such factors as local politics, values and philosophy, geography, previous collaboration attempts, and agency stability. Interagency collaboration is neither neatly linear nor consistently progressive. External events and influences, including fluctuation in or loss of funding, changes in leadership, turnover of interagency council membership, and changes in program mission at the state or local level, may result in reverting to an earlier stage in order to regroup and conceptualize new goals and direction. Community agencies may also interact differently with respect to agency functions and demonstrate multiple developmental stages (cooperation, coordination, and collaboration) simultaneously. Although the agencies may find it safe to enter into collaborative parent education and support activities, they may not yet be ready to create collaborative classroom programs based on shared funds and

agency resources as described in a written agreement.

Collaboration Must Be Nurtured

After effective interagency collaboration has been achieved, it needs high levels of continued support, nurturing, guidance, and direction. Leadership of the interagency council must be strong and consistent; otherwise, long-term follow-up and continuation of early efforts may fade and ultimately cease. Participants from various agencies have differing perspectives that affect how everyone melds into a cohesive working group. Turnover of members requires constant orientation and transition into the working group. The council coordinator must exert substantial effort in maintaining a cross-agency perspective as agencies and personnel periodically shift.

Collaboration Must Have Clear Goals

Goal setting is crucial to the development and efficient operation of a local council. The definition of collaboration includes the interaction among parties as they voluntarily engage in shared decision making and work toward common goals. Clear articulation of the goals motivates and mobilizes the group to action. The group must engage in extensive effort to reach consensus on a clear set of goals and outcomes. The method of approach in uniting disparate entities around common goals may be just as important as the goals themselves (Kagan et al., 1991).

REFERENCES

Bartel, J.M. (1977). The collaborative process for service integration. In *The service integration project: Final report*. Durham, NC: Lloyd Shore.

Baumheier, E.C., Welch, H.H., & Cook, C.C. (1976). *Interagency linkages in vocational rehabilitation*. Denver, CO: Regional Rehabilitation Research Institute Center for Social Research and Development, Denver Research Institute/University of Denver.

Benard, B. (1989). Working together: Principles of effective collaboration. *Prevention Forum, 10*(1), 4–9.

Black, J., & Kase, M. (1963). Interagency cooperation in rehabilitation and mental health. *Social Service Review, 37*(1), 26–32.

Cohen, M. (1981). *Improving interagency collaboration between mental health and vocational rehabilitation services: Conference summary report*. Boston: Boston University Center for Rehabilitation Research and Training in Mental Health.

Education of the Handicapped Act Amendments of 1986, PL 99-457 (September 22, 1986), Sec. 675(b), (c) 20 U.S.C. Sec. 1475, 100 STAT 1145-1177.

Gans, S.P., & Horton, G.T. (1975). *Integration of human services: The state and municipal levels.* New York: Praeger.

Gardner, S. (1990). Failure by fragmentation. *Equity and Choice, 6*(2), 4–12.

Harbin, G., Gallagher, J., Lillie, T., & Eckland, J. (1990). *Status of states' progress in implementing Part H of PL 99-457: Report #2.* Chapel Hill: University of North Carolina at Chapel Hill, Carolina Institute for Child and Family Policy, Frank Porter Graham Child Development Center, Carolina Policy Studies Program.

Hodge, R. (1984). *Interagency cooperation: Related issues and concerns.* A CASE Research Committee Report. Bloomington: Indiana University, CASE (A Division of the Council for Exceptional Children).

Hord, S.M. (1986). A synthesis of research on organizational collaboration. *Educational Leadership, 43*(5), 22–26.

Humm-Delgado, D. (1980). Planning issues in local interagency collaboration. In J.O. Elder & P.R. Magrab (Eds.), *Coordinating services to handicapped children: A handbook for interagency collaboration* (pp. 163–178). Baltimore: Paul H. Brookes Publishing Co.

Individuals with Disabilities Education Act of 1990, PL 101–476 (The 1990 Education of the Handicapped Act Amendments, October 30, 1990) 20 USC SS 1400-1485.

Kagan, S.L, Rivera, A.M., & Parker, F.L. (1991). *Collaborations in action: Reshaping services to young children and their families* (Executive Summary). Yale University: The Bush Center in Child Development and Social Policy.

Magrab, P.R., & Schmidt, L.M. (1980). Interdisciplinary collaboration: A prelude to coordinated service delivery. In J.O. Elder & P.R. Magrab (Eds.), *Coordinating services to handicapped children: A handbook for interagency collaboration* (pp. 13–24). Baltimore: Paul H. Brookes Publishing Co.

Morgan, J.L., & Swan W.W. (1988). *Local interagency councils for preschool handicapped programs: An effective strategy to implement the mandate.* Bloomington: Indiana University; Council for Administrators of Special Education, Inc., Division of the Council for Exceptional Children.

Morris, R., & Lescohier, I.H. (1978). Service integration: Real versus illusory solutions to welfare dilemmas. In R.C. Sarri & Y. Hansenfeld (Eds.), *The management of human services* (pp. 21–50). New York: Columbia University Press.

Morse, M.T. (1981). Interagency coordination: An overview. In S. Threet and P. Hattenger, *Interagency coordination: A necessity in rural programs. Making it work in rural communities. A Rural Network Monograph* (pp. 1–6). Washington, DC: Office of Special Education.

Peterson, N.L. (1991). Interagency collaboration under Part H: The key to comprehensive, multidisciplinary, coordinated infant/toddler intervention services. *Journal of Early Intervention, 15*(1), 89–105.

Pryzwansky, W.B. (1977). Collaboration or consultation: Is there a difference? *Journal of Special Education, 11,* 179–182.

Rogers, C., & Farrow, F. (1983). *Effective state strategies to promote interagency collaboration. A report of the handicapped public policy analysis project* (Vol. 1–4; Contract No. 300-82-0829). Center for the Study of Social Policy, 236 Massachusetts Avenue, N.E., Washington, DC 20002 (ERIC Document Reproduction Service No. ED 245 467; EC 162 746).

Rogers, E.S., Anthony, W.A., & Danley, K.S. (1989). The impact of interagency collaboration on system and client outcomes. *Rehabilitation Counseling Bulletin, 33*(2), 100–109.

Stafford, B.G., Camp, J.C., & Vander Meer, P. (1984). *Final Evaluation Report of the Care Linkages Project.* Nashville, TN: Report funded through a demonstration grant from the U.S. Department of Health and Human Services, Head Start, Administration for Children, Youth, and Families (Grant #90CW685/01).

Chapter 4

Model of a Local
Interagency Coordinating Council

A local interagency council is defined as a master planning group of community agency representatives (10–12 people) of the primary programs serving children with disabilities or at risk, birth through 5 years, with the authority to create changes in the programs. The council operates on an ongoing basis to define roles and responsibilities of agencies, coordinate existing agency services, identify and fill service gaps, and develop a full continuum of services. It engages in both policy-making and case management functions.

THE COUNCIL AS A STRATEGY

The local interagency coordinating council model (Morgan, Guetzloe, & Swan, 1991; Morgan & Swan, 1988) is designed as a strategy to provide a framework for continual coordination of agency programs, as well as the use of collaboration in problem solving. It is an effective model because it focuses on the development of a formal, working team of agency representatives who have authority within their programs. The representatives meet regularly for the purpose of achieving eight goals:

1. To develop a common information base and communication
2. To eliminate unnecessary duplication of services
3. To coordinate existing agency programs
4. To identify gaps in services
5. To determine agency roles and responsibilities

6. To shift resources to create a complete continuum of services
7. To develop an interagency case management function
8. To ensure appropriate services to all identified children

Compensation for a Categorical and Fragmented System

The local interagency coordinating council compensates for the increasingly complex nature of the service delivery system that currently provides for infants, toddlers, and preschool children with disabilities and those at high risk and their families. The system is composed of diversified agencies offering educational, medical, therapy, and social services. The delivery system is highly categorical in nature; the various programs have developed as a result of legislation and specific initiatives. They have been typically designed and funded to serve narrow target populations defined by strict eligibility criteria. Some programs, for example, are targeted to serve only children with disabilities; others serve only at-risk children. Some programs are designed to serve only children from migrant or agricultural families; others serve economically disadvantaged children within a narrowly specified age range. Some programs serve the chronically ill or medically fragile; others are designed to provide only primary care; yet others target a specific medical condition, such as epilepsy or spina bifida. The result is an assortment of highly categorical community agency programs that are program and eligibility driven. Children, however, do not

Portions of this chapter are used with Permission of the Florida Department of Education, Bureau of Education for Exceptional Students, from *Developing interagency councils,* (1989), pp. 3–20.

come in the neat and precise categories described in the various regulations, eligibility criteria, and program guidelines. Children are unique and demonstrate overlapping multiples of these criteria. As a result, many children fail to fit the programs that have been developed and are left unserved, underserved, or inappropriately served.

As a strategy for bringing together the categorical programs in a community, the local interagency council encourages program personnel to cross the invisible barriers existing among agencies in order to create the broad scope of coordinated services needed by individual children and families. The council strategy provides a forum for planning across agency lines, putting pieces of the service delivery system back together again, and assisting one another in providing the most efficient and effective service.

Because agencies typically have different eligibility criteria, guidelines, capabilities, constraints, funding sources, and overlapping populations of children and families; their personnel often have little understanding of the procedures, characteristics, and functions of other agencies. The results are fragmentation of services to families, inappropriate referrals, duplication of services, and significant frustration. Parents of children with disabilities experience confusion and frustration in their attempts to navigate through the maze of community agencies in order to obtain appropriate services. The interagency coordinating council provides an effective strategy by helping agencies to understand, communicate, and work with each other in better serving these clients.

Clarification and Promotion of the Mission

The mission of the local interagency council is to develop and ensure the provision of a comprehensive array of services for children, from birth through 5 years of age, who have disabilities or who are at risk and their families. The council exists only as a strategy or a vehicle to meet this objective. The council—in and by itself—is not important. The interagency council is important only to the extent that it creates a responsive system to serve the needs of these children and their families (*A rationale for interagency collaboration*, 1989).

Developing and providing a comprehensive array of services (Table 1) require that the services be available for preschool children with disabilities or at high risk regardless of their ages or types of impairment. Various service delivery models are needed because no one model is appropriate for all

Table 1. Comprehensive array of services

Developmental screening	Case management
Multidisciplinary evaluation	Counseling services
Specific-discipline evaluation	Medical services
Individualized planning	Nursing services
Special education (classroom)	Home nursing care
Special education (home-based)	Nutrition services
Speech-language therapy	Vision services
Occupational therapy	Mobility training
Physical therapy	Audiology services
Integrated classroom	Transportation
Consultation	Respite care
Parent education	Day care
Parent support services	Residential services
Psychological services	Specialized equipment
Social work services	Recreation services
Psychiatric services	Economic services

children and families. An assortment of full-time, part-time, integrated, itinerant, home-based, consultative, and parent training options is required. Furthermore, a variety of services—educational, medical, social, and related services—must be identified and be accessible. All council objectives, activities, and resources are directed toward this purpose. Through participation in the local interagency council, each agency can identify the rich assortment of local programs and services that exist and how they can operate to complement one another.

The local interagency council must synchronize the efforts of independent agencies with varied functions and roles in order to generate a full continuum of services. The strength of the council is its orientation to tasks that focus on the energies of the agencies and promote a spirit of collaboration among them. The effectiveness of the council, however, requires the full commitment of the individual agencies and their representatives to the ultimate goal of providing appropriate and coordinated services to each eligible child and family.

The concerns of agency personnel parallel the concerns of parents. Administrators, supervisors, social workers, teachers, therapists, medical personnel, and others need assurances that their efforts with children and their families are synchronized with those of other agencies so that the various efforts are not counterproductive. They must work closely with other professions in order to avoid duplications and sometimes conflicting treatment approaches. Most personnel are interested in streamlining procedures to improve their services and searching for more effective ways to provide the services.

Agencies also have needs. Resources, funds, personnel capabilities, and time are real limitations that must be considered. Agencies must have assurance that their resources are being expended in the most efficacious manner. Prioritizing, selecting, refining, and even eliminating services that can be provided by others make up a complex process for each agency. For example,

an agency may provide screening and evaluation, social work services, direct intervention with children and families, public awareness and public relations activities, related services, parent education and training, staff development activities, program and curriculum development and refinement, and program evaluation. Because many of these efforts may be common among agencies, competition for children and families, protectionism, turf guarding, and a tendency to devalue other agency programs can result. A smaller agency may be unable to devote resources to staff development or social services. Other services, such as comprehensive parent programs, may not be possible because of funding and staff limitations. On the other hand, an agency's services may be underutilized if its target population is small.

The local interagency council can provide an effective and powerful strategy for coordination of services and collaboration among agencies. If properly organized and supported, the council allows for the needs of the children and their families and the needs of the agencies to be met effectively and simultaneously; it is a powerful and functional administrative tool. The council is usually composed of a team of mid-level management representatives from the primary agencies that serve children with disabilities and those at high risk from birth through 5 years of age. It meets at least monthly to address both policy issues and direct services to these children. The council directly and internally creates needed changes, improvement, and expansion of services to individual children, as well as to entire populations or programs.

Establishment of an Organizational Framework

The council provides an organizational framework for facilitating delivery of services and coordinating every aspect of the delivery system across agencies. The results are shared services and clarification of the respective roles and responsibilities of the various agencies in order to avoid competition and duplication and to minimize costs. As a strategy, this framework offers significant advantages to the agencies themselves, including efficient use of funds, focused services, and better quality.

The bottom line, however, is that the council provides a strategy for coordination of agency resources to ensure that all children in need of services are identified and receive the services they need. The primary goal of the strategy is to synchronize programs of the various agencies so as to provide a complete array of services, maximize progress, and streamline the delivery process. This child-oriented goal must be foremost in the minds of agency personnel. It is the underlying rationale and raison d'être for the council and the agencies themselves.

Development of a
Case Management Function

The local interagency coordinating council can serve as a forum for collaboration of service delivery programs, as exemplified in the case described below. This family is at high risk for fragmented and uncoordinated service delivery. The complexity of the child's needs, as well as those of the family, requires a decision-making process that is beyond the scope of a single case manager or professional. Such cases are not unusual. The interagency council agenda, with a focus on direct services and coordination, can include time for discussion of specific children for whom case coordination is critical.

Jennifer, now 28 months old, was born prematurely at 3 pounds, 4 ounces to a 15-year-old single mother. Two months after her birth, Jennifer was discharged to her grandmother when her mother refused to assume the responsibility. Within a month, Jennifer was admitted to the emergency room in distress and was immediately transferred to an intensive care center in a regional hospital with pneumonia, seizures, dehydration, and failure to thrive. Following her hospitalization, she continued to be seen for primary medical care both at the local health department and by a private pediatrician.

Referrals were made to the Department of Human Resources for social service assistance to the family, to Children's Medical Services, and

then to Developmental Services for screening and evaluation when developmental delays became apparent. Ongoing parent training and social services were provided to assist the grandmother in caring for Jennifer, now diagnosed with vision and hearing impairments, cerebral palsy, and severe retardation. Her grandmother continued to work two jobs to support the large and dependent family. She was angry and resentful because she was left with the care of this complex youngster.

While her grandmother worked the evening shift at a nursing home, Jennifer was left in the care of a 12-year-old aunt. The family did not own a car, and medical appointments were too frequently missed. Medical services through Children's Medical Services were provided at a location 20 miles from the child's home, and arranging Medicaid transportation for each appointment was difficult.

At 16 months of age, Jennifer was enrolled in a center-based program at The Arc Center. Parent training and social services continued to be provided. The grandparent's work schedule, confusion with medical providers, transportation problems, distance from the preschool program, and other family and personal pressures continued to complicate provision of services. The family was often confused over differing opinions and instructions. The complex needs of the child, the number of agencies involved, and the limitations of the family created a difficult case management situation.

Determination of Agency
Roles and Responsibilities

The interagency council provides a system for determining the respective roles and responsibilities of the agencies so that services of one agency are not depleted on complicated cases. Agency personnel can discuss and mutually decide, in conjunction with the parents, how the various services (e.g., educational, therapy, equipment, parent training, transportation, social, medical, and related services) can be most appropriately, efficiently, and economically provided. Written agreements and policy directives can provide a formal means of sharing the cost for services, as well as identifying procedures for resolving disputes.

Establishment of Interagency Systems

As individual schools function in a coordinated manner within a school system and individual departments function in a coordinated manner within an organization, the interagency council provides a strategy to facilitate coordination and collaboration among independent agency programs within a community. Agencies can function as a team, with the focus on the needs of the child and family, rather than as independent, parallel programs.

The concept of interagency coordination and collaboration provides a new perspective on the manner in which agencies work and relate. When agencies become part of a larger community system in which they play critical and interdependent roles, they must depend on others to play the required complementary roles. Agency personnel begin to perceive the *gestalt*—the entire scope of services needed by the children and their families—and their roles and relationships with one another within the context of the community. They adjust these roles and relationships for the benefit of the children and families they serve.

The council provides a strategy for the development, coordination, and provision of the components of the preschool programs. It organizes the efforts of all community agencies to develop the following systems in a coordinated manner:

Comprehensive service delivery
Child location and identification
Information exchange
Referral and transition
Case management
Personnel development
Parent services
Data collection and tracking
Evaluation of interagency efforts

Although these systems operate within most community agencies, they are agency-specific, duplicative in nature, and often independent of similar services provided by other agencies. As a result, costs may be unusually high for underutilized services as agency programs compete for the same population. Collaboration among agencies significantly expands and improves the ability of the various agencies to meet the needs of children, families, staff, and agencies alike.

Therefore, collaboration meets two objectives: 1) to improve the delivery of services to children and families, and 2) to improve the efficiency and effectiveness of the service delivery system (Zeller, 1980). A local interagency council may be a valuable strategy for the development, coordination, and provision of all aspects of preschool services within a geographical area.

CONTRAST TO OTHER TYPES OF GROUPS

In defining an interagency coordinating council, it can be helpful to describe what it is not. Comparing it with similar groups can clarify terms and reveal the most effective manner for the council's mode of operation and composition. The interagency coordinating council:

Is not an advisory group
Is not a task force
Is not a learning or information group
Is not an advocacy group

Each type of group listed above has unique characteristics and is designed for a particular purpose (Deighton, 1971; Husen & Postlethwaite, 1985). The interagency council includes the functions of all of these types to some degree, but it is not limited to any specific function.

The purpose of an advisory group, for example, is to provide feedback to an organization, a department, a program, or an administrative entity. This input may affect change only indirectly and chances are that it may be ignored. The advisory committee can only advise—the recommendations are not bound to be followed. In contrast to the advisory group, the local interagency council directly affects policy and procedure. It can create change and devise solutions to the problems it identifies. The interagency council does not advise administrative personnel who hold the power to create change but is composed of that administrative level of personnel. Therein lies the strength of the council.

A task force is a temporary committee

responsible for investigating a particular issue or problem in depth. It is generally funded by sponsoring groups and is well connected to power holders. The task force operates within a designated time frame. Recommendations are made at the conclusion of the study, at which time the group disbands. Like the advisory group, the task force provides information and input. It is capable of recommending change, but it is not responsible for causing it.

Learning and information groups are common. They are generally informal and often large. There is no well-defined membership, and the participants may change from meeting to meeting. The meetings are generally open and are conducted for the purposes of presenting topical speakers, creating awareness of community programs, sharing information, exchanging ideas, and discussing issues. Learning groups rely heavily on media contact, public hearings, and meetings to disseminate information. The membership often consists of relatively well-educated, middle-class people, but such groups generally have no connection to the power holders. They have no defined missions or specific goals other than to facilitate the exchange of information and to encourage informal networking. Learning and information groups usually meet monthly or quarterly. Some are social in nature and may include a restaurant meal or a brown-bag lunch.

Advocacy groups are formal but largely volunteer organizations whose membership subscribes to common beliefs. They are governed by constitutions and bylaws and are usually supported by a statewide coalition of community action groups. These groups rely heavily on such tactics as press releases, public meetings, and testimony at public hearings. They conduct constant lobbying efforts at state and federal levels.

CHARACTERISTICS OF EFFECTIVE COUNCILS

The local interagency council provides an organizational framework within which the independent but similar functions of various agencies are structured. It eliminates fragmentation and duplication of services, allows for more effective utilization of personnel and resources, and ensures the provision of a full array of services within the community. It streamlines the service delivery system for families and eliminates the sense of territoriality that too often plagues services to children. Acting as a community team, the agencies can focus on a broader sense of organization to ensure that all preschool children with disabilities receive appropriate intervention services.

The characteristics of effective interagency councils have been determined through review of the literature, analysis of existing councils, survey of best practices, personal experience with operating an interagency council in a school district, and feedback gained through group discussion in state and national professional meetings and conference sessions (*Developing interagency councils*, 1989; Foster, 1986). Table 2 lists these characteristics.

Dual Focus of Policy and Direct Services

Olsen (1983) described the experiences of 15 local special education administrators in providing related services through collaboration with other agencies. He found that interagency committees at the local level appeared to be of two types:

Table 2. Characteristics of effective local interagency councils

Dual focus of policy and direct services
Problem-solving, action, or task orientation
Small group of 10–12 members
Primary service providers
Middle-management representatives
Consistent representation
Commitment to collaboration and innovation
Equal partnership
Immediate service area
Consistent leadership
Agency-neutral coordinator
Well-defined goals
Trust and group cohesiveness
Established operational procedures

(Adapted with Permission of the Florida Department of Education, Bureau of Education for Exceptional Students, from *Developing interagency councils*, [1989], p. 12.)

1. *Policy:* These committees comprised administrative representatives who developed interagency agreements, established general frameworks within which agencies would operate, and took the initiative in establishing new interagency programs and facilities. Priority needs were discussed and mutually acceptable solutions were defined.
2. *Direct services:* These committees focused on individual children, served by more than one agency, for whom problems or conflicts had arisen. The committees reviewed cases, discussed the needs of children and families and service alternatives, and developed plans of action.

Olsen found that the most successful groups incorporated both components. They tracked individual children until the problems were resolved, thus serving a case management function. Representatives were generally middle-management personnel and committee functions included role clarification, increased understanding of agency capabilities and procedures, case reviews, joint funding, and resource pooling. The interagency council model incorporates both policy and direct services.

Problem-Solving, Action, or Task Orientation

Although the early stages of council development are characterized by informational and awareness activities, it is critical for the council to perceive its main role as a problem-solving and action-taking group. If the council is limited to "learning" about other agencies and programs without identifying service needs and proposing solutions, it will not accomplish its purpose. The problem-solving nature and high degree of task orientation are essential elements in the expansion of preschool programs and services.

Small Group of 8–12 Members

The chances of succeeding in effective collaboration are significantly improved if the effort is limited to a specific age group, such as birth through 5 years, and to a manageable geographic area, such as the local community. The fewer agencies involved in the council, the more likely it is that effective lines of communication and working relationships can be established and maintained (Elder, 1980). Gilbert and Specht (1977) found that interagency coordination projects involving fewer than 12 agencies were more likely to achieve positive results. They found that a large number of participating agencies was negatively related to the success of coordination. These results suggest that collaboration attempts in large urban areas should be divided into efforts of smaller subgroups.

Because the intent of a council is to engage in discussion related to policy issues, problem solving, and service delivery for children and families, its size is a critical variable. Successful problem solving and task-oriented behavior are most effectively accomplished in a group where small-group dynamics exist. The most effective group may be one that does not exceed 8–12 members (Ferrini, Matthews, Foster, & Workman, 1980). Beyond this size, the members' ability to discuss issues freely and reach consensus is significantly reduced. If the group increases in size, more time is spent protecting one's territory, greater threat is perceived, less discussion occurs, cohesion may not develop, and further stabilization of the group's role structure becomes increasingly difficult.

Primary Service Providers

Involvement in the council of every community group that is in some way related to preschool children with disabilities and their families is unreasonable and impractical. To do so would result in an excessively large group of personnel, many of whom would sense only a tangential purpose in attending meetings and would eventually withdraw.

It is critical to identify the primary service providers within the community for local interagency council participation. They compose the main group that serves the defined population. The local council must include representatives of the primary providers of education, medical, therapy, parent, and social services to allow for coordination of the services needed by a child and a family.

The primary providers vary from district to district. Crippled children's services or children's medical services may be the primary medical provider in one county, whereas the local public health department may provide most of the services in another. Migrant preschool programs may be found in rural and agricultural counties but not in largely urban areas. The primary providers in each district must be carefully determined.

Primary service providers generally include the local school system, crippled children's services, developmental disabilities, parent training programs, health department, The Arc (formerly known as The Association for Retarded Citizens), United Cerebral Palsy, parent resource programs, Title XX daycare, local speech and hearing clinics, hospital rehabilitation units, perinatal programs, Head Start, migrant preschool programs, and mental health centers.

The local interagency council should form linkages with such community services as March of Dimes, Council on Epilepsy, Division of Blind Services, and other smaller programs. However, it should not be compelled to include them on the council if they are not directly providing services to the majority of the children who will be the focus of problem solving and discussion. Doing so will make the group size excessive, involve representatives who will sense little purpose in being there, and diffuse the action capability of the group. The council should be aware of these programs and work with them as needed.

Middle-Management Representatives

One pitfall encountered in developing interagency agreements is the tendency to communicate too low or too high in the organizational structure. Council membership characterized by teachers or nonadministrative personnel may be self-defeating in policy areas. However, top level administrators may not be sufficiently close to the actual implementation of policy decisions to realize problems with feasibility (Hall, 1980).

Olsen (1983) reported that a middle manager is the most appropriate representative on an interagency council that focuses on direct services to children. The middle manager is aware of line functions, works closely with administrators, is open to change, and can create change.

Also, middle managers usually maintain sufficiently close proximity to the children and families, are accountable for provision of services, and are able to influence high-level policymakers to create needed change (Kazuk, 1980; Olsen, 1983).

Councils composed largely of nonmanagement-level personnel who cannot commit the agency resources or speak on behalf of the agency are likely to be doomed to terminal nonproductiveness and to function only as awareness or learning groups. As time passes, these groups become increasingly frustrated and aware of their lack of productiveness. The membership loses its stability as participants are forced to prioritize their time on tasks most critical to their job demands.

Consistent Representation

An important requirement of this model is commitment of agencies and personnel (Peterson, 1991). Commitment to the concept requires the designation of a middle-management staff member who will attend meetings consistently. It is essential that the representatives attend all meetings (Ferrini et al., 1980). Consistent attendance provides for continuity of perspective and problem solving and the development of a cohesive interagency team that addresses the needs of the children and of the service delivery system on a long-term basis. This element is critical for productivity. Frequent turnover in membership creates a barrier that interferes with the ability to form a knowledgeable, cohesive, and accountable work group. Substitute or rotational representation is unacceptable because it disrupts the collaborative planning process.

Hall and Williams (1966) found that established groups are more effective than ad hoc groups in the solution of problems, the use of member resources, and the handling of conflict. Systematic variation of member turnover in problem-solving groups has revealed that performance effectiveness of groups decreased with the increase in rate of turnover (Rogers, Ford, & Tassone, 1961; Trow, 1960).

Commitment to Collaboration and Innovation

The membership of an interagency council is the most significant factor in the success of local collaborative efforts. For this reason, members must be carefully selected. Their ability to recognize and acknowledge mutual problems, paired with their creativity and capacity for devising innovations in service delivery, is the lifeblood of a council. They must be risk takers and agents for change. They must display a steadfast commitment, first, to the well-being of the children and families they serve and, second, to proposing the changes and procedural reforms needed within the bureaucracy. This willingness to seek and propose change comes most readily to middle-management and supervisory personnel. Top-level managers, such as program directors, have the greatest need to defend the organization, maintain the status quo, and avoid taking risks. Because they are usually more conservative and may fear establishing precedents that could have repercussions, agency directors are often not the best choices for a local interagency council.

Council members must genuinely believe in collaboration and must be willing to suffer the pain and awkward moments encountered during the change process. They must believe that the eventual gains to the agencies, children, and families will be sufficient

to warrant the risks and to attempt innovation and change. Without this willingness and ability to promote change, a local interagency council may succeed only in creating an additional level of the existing bureaucracy.

Equal Partnership

The council must operate as an independent coalition of agency representatives, with each perceived as equally important regardless of size of the agency or program. Although one or two members must assume the responsibility for facilitation and guidance of the council activities, all members must sense that they have equal partnership in the group (Ferrini et al., 1980).

The council must not create another level of bureaucracy and should not be regarded as an extension of any single agency (Mulvenon, 1980). Under no circumstances should any agency sense or express "ownership" of the council. Ownership creates an imbalance; it jeopardizes interagency efforts and fosters suspicion that one agency benefits at the expense of others. Furthermore, no agency has the power to impose its control over other agencies or to mandate participation, commitment, or compliance of other agencies or outside programs.

Caution also should be exercised in developing a council hierarchy by establishing officers. This practice implies greater responsibility and control by certain members. Problems of power, control, and authority within a council can create significant friction and mistrust among members and impair the group's productivity. Stogdill (1948) found that discussion and negotiations among group members are most effectively implemented when representatives are equal in status.

Interagency council letterhead stationery and a council logo help to establish the council as an independent coalition. The stationery of a participating agency should not be used. Rotating monthly meeting locations among the community agency sites also reinforces mutual and equal participation and ownership of the activities and beliefs of the council. Establishing a unitary meeting place at one agency site may inappropriately indicate that agency's ownership or control and must be avoided.

Immediate Service Area

The council should focus on the local or main administrative area served by the agencies. This area may be a single county, a segment of a large county that has been administratively subdivided, or several small counties in an educational collaborative system. Because of the complexity of regions or multicounty areas containing districts or counties that function independently to provide services, the districts might combine cooperatively before working with other agencies for council activities.

The council's focus on the immediate service area enables members to establish meaningful goals, objectives, and activities that will meet the needs of children and their families, as well as the needs of the agencies. The result is an increased commitment to the council and the stabilization of membership. Council members must observe a direct relationship between participation in the council and solutions to their service delivery problems.

Consistent Leadership

During the initiation of council development, membership stabilizes as an understanding of the process increases and adjustments in agency representation occur. Likewise, council leadership emerges and stabilizes as the competencies and skills of the council coordinator become apparent.

Productiveness of the council depends on the stability of both the leadership and membership. This stability generates group cohesion, differentiation of roles, sensitivity to agency needs, continuity of goals, and problem solving. Pryer, Flint, and Bass (1962) reported that groups tend to remain effective as long as they do not change leaders. Furthermore, the performance of a group has been found contingent on both

the motivational system of the leaders and the degree to which the leader has control and influence in a particular situation (Fiedler & Chemers, 1974). In a study involving collaborations in three states, Kagan, Rivera, and Parker (1991) confirmed that a strong, objective, and effective leader is an important ingredient in collaborative success. Although leadership may develop informally, the authors found that usually one individual is recognized as the primary possessor of power and authority. The leader tends to be a seasoned professional who guides the collaboration's work with vision, passion, and knowledge.

The council coordinator must assume the responsibility of providing guidance, direction, and motivation. He or she can accomplish this only through a firm understanding of the programs and administrative problems at hand. The coordinator must also motivate, organize, and mobilize the group to achieve solutions to identified problems and continually reinforce the cohesiveness of the group.

Lack of continuity and instability of the group may occur if the council coordinator changes periodically. There may be less motivation to achieve goals when temporary council coordinators lack long-term investment and accountability. Rotating the role of council coordinator may compensate for the lack of commitment on the part of any one individual to assume responsibility for coordination, but it is bound to create a disadvantage over the long term.

Agency-Neutral Coordinator

The interagency council coordinator may be an employee of one of the participating agencies, but it is important that an agency-neutral role be established so that the council is not used for better advantage of one agency. Fairness, equal support for the needs and concerns of all agencies, and a commitment to the needs of the children and families as a whole must be the focus. The coordinator should work from a child-centered base, rather than from any specific agency or program base (Elder, 1980), should serve as an advocate for the children instead of the agencies, and should facilitate member participation. Rotation of meeting sites among agency facilities also reinforces this notion of agency neutrality.

The coordinator must be able to deal effectively with the human factors involved, understand group dynamics, demonstrate skills in developing interpersonal relationships, possess conflict resolution skills, have a sense of community history, and be committed to the goal and process of the council. In addition to these qualities, an understanding of the coordinated service delivery system and the collaborative efforts that must be created is necessary.

Well-Defined Goals

Well-defined goals are another vital aspect of an effective interagency council (Kagan et al., 1991; Morgan & Swan, 1988). Ensuring the existence of a comprehensive continuum of services to these children and their families is a central focus required of all council participants. Without a clear focus, the participants are confused and their attempts are ineffective. The results are disappointment, disillusionment, and dissatisfaction. The council coordinator must facilitate the development of well-defined goals to achieve an effective local interagency council.

Trust and Group Cohesiveness

Group cohesiveness can be defined as attraction of the members to the group (Bass, 1960), level of group morale, and coordination among members (Shaw, 1976). This quality (or its lack) may "make" (or "break") the group and is largely responsible for the level of productivity. It serves as a type of dynamic tension that binds the group together and generates a spirit of support and assistance across agencies. Cohesiveness is dependent on the consistency of representation, the members' commitment to similar goals, and the trust level of the group.

Established Operational Procedures

To ensure consistent representation and a sense of stability within the group, council meetings should follow established meeting procedures. Meetings should be scheduled monthly at a mutually agreeable day and time. Establishing a regular meeting time, for example, the third Thursday of each month, enables members to block out that time period for their attendance. Meetings held less often than once a month do not allow for development of a cohesive interagency team or sufficient time for problem solving. In the beginning, interagency teams may even wish to meet on a more frequent basis in order to maintain interest and momentum and to establish working relationships and council goals. Agency personnel undoubtedly have had unproductive experiences with committees and task force groups in the past. As a result, during the early stages of operation the council members may need to sense the accomplishment of several tasks. They then have the necessary confirmation of the benefits available through participation in the group.

A monthly meeting schedule at rotating agency sites is an effective strategy for maintaining neutrality of the council, fostering improved understanding of the various agency programs, and strengthening rapport among the members. Creating a high level of comfort with all of the agency programs and staffs should be a primary goal. Communication and working relationships among council members can be enhanced significantly through their acquaintance with secretaries and other staff members who are frequently on the other end of telephone conversations.

Responsibility must be decided for distributing meeting notices, drafting the meeting agenda, and determining whether formal, written meeting minutes will be maintained. These housekeeping functions take time, resources, and consistency and should be assumed by the council coordinator. Attempts to rotate such responsibilities generally meet with poor results and friction among council members. All council members are not equally proficient at these functions, and some may not wish to risk failure in front of other members. The resulting friction and discontent may be counterproductive to the spirit of cooperation required of the council.

Leadership of the council is a key issue.

The productivity of the group is directly proportional to the quality and stability of leadership. The leader must have a thorough knowledge of the community, display expertise in preschool program areas, understand the group process, be capable of generating followership, and mobilize the group to accomplish its goals.

REFERENCES

Bass, B.M. (1960). *Leadership, psychology, and organizational behavior.* New York: Harper & Row.

Deighton, L.C. (Ed.). (1971). *The encyclopedia of education* (Vols. 1–8). New York: Macmillan and Free Press.

Developing interagency councils. (1989). Tallahassee: Florida Department of Education, Bureau of Education for Exceptional Students.

Elder, J.O. (1980). Essential components in development of interagency collaboration. In J.O. Elder & P.R. Magrab (Eds.), *Coordinating services to handicapped children: A handbook for interagency collaboration* (pp. 181–201). Baltimore: Paul H. Brookes Publishing Co.

Ferrini, P., Matthews, B.L., Foster, J., & Workman, J. (1980). *The interdependent community: Collaborative planning for handicapped youth.* Cambridge, MA: Technical Education Research Centers.

Fiedler, F.E., & Chemers, M.M. (1974). *Leadership and effective management.* Glenview, IL: Scott, Foresman.

Foster, R.E. (1986). *An evaluation report on the state plan grant project to improve pre-kindergarten services to handicapped children in Florida.* Tallahassee: Florida Department of Education, Bureau of Education for Exceptional Students.

Gilbert, N., & Specht, H. (1977). Qualitative aspects of social service coordination efforts: Is more better? *Administration of Social Work, 1,* 53–61.

Hall, H.B. (1980). The intangible human factor. In J.O. Elder & P.R. Magrab (Eds.), *Coordinating services to handicapped children: A handbook for interagency collaboration* (pp. 45–62). Baltimore: Paul H. Brookes Publishing Co.

Hall, J., & Williams, M.S. (1966). A comparison of decision-making performances in established and ad hoc groups. *Journal of Personal-Social Psychology, 3,* 214–222.

Husen, T., & Postlethwaite, T. (Eds.). (1985). *The international encyclopedia of education.* Oxford: Pergamon.

Kagan, S.L., Rivera, A.M., & Parker, F.L. (1991). *Collaborations in action: Reshaping services to young children and their families* (Executive Summary). Yale University: The Bush Center in Child Development and Social Policy.

Kazuk, E. (1980). Development of a community-based interagency model. In J.O. Elder & P.R. Magrab (Eds.). *Coordinating services to handicapped children: A handbook for interagency collaboration* (pp. 99–

131). Baltimore: Paul H. Brookes Publishing Co.

Morgan, J.L., Guetzloe, E.C., & Swan, W.W. (1991). Leadership for local interagency councils. *Journal of Early Intervention, 15*(3), 255–267.

Morgan, J.L., & Swan, W.W. (1988). *Local interagency councils for preschool handicapped programs: An effective strategy to implement the mandate.* Bloomington: Indiana University, Council for Administrators of Special Education, Inc. (CASE) (A Division of the Council for Exceptional Children).

Mulvenon, J. (1980). Development of preschool interagency teams. In J.O. Elder & P.R. McGrab (Eds.). *Coordinating services to handicapped children: A handbook for interagency collaboration* (pp. 133–162). Baltimore: Paul H. Brookes Publishing Co.

Olsen, K.R. (1983). *Obtaining related services through local interagency collaboration.* Lexington, Kentucky: Mid-South Regional Resource Center. Report funded by the Office of Special Education and Rehabilitative Services, Washington, DC (Report #300-80-0722) (ED 239-439).

Peterson, N.L. (1991). Interagency collaboration under Part H: The key to comprehensive, multidisciplinary, coordinated infant/toddler intervention services. *Journal of Early Intervention, 15*(1), 89–105.

Pryer, M.W., Flint, A.W., & Bass, B.M. (1962). Group effectiveness and consistency of leadership. *Sociometry, 25,* 391–397.

A rationale for interagency collaboration. (1989). Tallahassee: Florida Department of Education, Bureau of Education for Exceptional Students.

Rogers, M.S., Ford, J.D., & Tassone, J.A. (1961). The effects of personnel replacement on an information-processing crew. *Journal of Applied Psychology, 45,* 91–96.

Shaw, C.E. (1976). *A comparative study of organizational climate and job satisfaction at selected public and Catholic secondary schools in Connecticut.* Unpublished doctoral dissertation, University of Connecticut, Storrs.

Stogdill, R.M. (1948). Personal factors associated with leadership: A survey of the literature. *Journal of Psychology, 25,* 35–71.

Trow, D.B. (1960). Membership succession and team performance. *Human Relations, 13,* 259–269.

Zeller, R.W. (1980). Direction service: Collaboration one case at a time. In J.O. Elder and P.R. Magrab (Eds.), *Coordinating services to handicapped children: A handbook for interagency collaboration* (pp. 65–97). Baltimore: Paul H. Brookes Publishing Co.

Chapter 5

Developmental Stages of a Local Interagency Council

The success of a local interagency coordinating council depends on its members' understanding the nature of an interactive group, the dynamics that influence productivity, and the impact of group process. Council meetings are the primary strategy for engaging agency representatives in effective collaboration. An effective council coordinator must understand various types of meetings and choose the type that will be most productive in achieving the council's goals.

NATURE OF GROUPS

A major problem often encountered by interagency councils is a failure to take concrete and decisive action. The initial development of a local council may have been stimulated by a common need of community agencies to define and discuss problems in the delivery of services to young children with disabilities and those at high risk and their families. Unless a systematic, goal-directed, action-oriented process is undertaken, the interagency team will flounder and slip further into inaction (Magrab, Elder, Kazuk, Pelosi, & Wiegerink, 1982). Inaction negatively affects future council development. If agency representatives do not feel a sense of accomplishment within a reasonable time period, they may question the necessity of their commitment and the group may steadily deteriorate. This possibility highlights the importance of the meeting process and the critical facilitation role of the coordinator. The coordinator must have an understanding of the nature of:

1) meetings, 2) leadership, and 3) group process.

The interagency council must be committed to function as a problem-solving, task-oriented group, rather than limit its activities to simple information sharing (*Developing interagency councils*, 1989). Because of this commitment, the council meeting is a powerful tool for change; the council coordinator must avoid using such a tool simply to disseminate information. Meetings are most commonly used to bring people together for the purpose of disseminating information. This kind of meeting is called a briefing (Daniels, 1986). Unfortunately, it is never brief enough. This type of meeting, if held periodically, can have only one result: boredom. Information alone is useless but becomes useful when it compels people to solve a problem, make a decision, or devise a plan.

Unproductive meetings create skepticism about the potential usefulness of newly developed groups, such as an interagency council. Previous negative experiences in unproductive briefings and information-sharing groups cause concern when additional meetings are required for people with already overburdened schedules. Pulling people together solely for the purpose of information sharing is asking for failure (Daniels, 1986).

The council's ability to function successfully after initial development is influenced by several critical factors, including the role of the coordinator, group interaction and dynamics, team cohesiveness, understanding of the nature of change, and effective

Portions of this chapter are used with Permission of the Florida Department of Education, Bureau of Education for Exceptional Students, from *Developing interagency councils*, (1989), pp. 21–26.

planning and implementation. Each factor relates directly to the dynamics and maintenance of the interagency team. The correct combination of factors can result in a cohesive and productive group that not only discusses concerns and problems but also solves them.

GROUP DEVELOPMENT

The development and growth of any group, including the interagency council, is fairly predictable and progresses through a logical sequence of stages that result in maturation and effective action. An understanding of the developmental stages focuses the council coordinator and members on the critical factors that facilitate group process (Corey, 1990). The effective group leader maximizes efforts to help council members reach stated goals. By understanding the problems and potential crises of each stage, the leader knows when and how to intervene and becomes aware of the tasks that must be successfully completed before the council can move to the next stage.

Several authors have discussed stages of group process development. Specific content and terminology vary, but these authors describe similar trends and processes. Yalom (1975) named three stages of development. The initial stage is characterized by orientation, hesitant participation, and a search for meaning and the second stage by conflict, dominance, and rebellion. The third stage, the stage of cohesion, is marked by an increase in morale, trust, and self-disclosure. Schultz (1973) also described three stages: inclusion, control, and affection. Gazda (1978) listed four stages: exploration, transition, action, and termination. Mahler (1969) described five stages: formation, involvement, transition, working, and ending. Hansen, Warner, and Smith (1980) indicated five stages: initiation of the group, conflict and confrontation, development of cohesiveness, productivity, and termination. Finally, Corey (1990) divided

group process development into four stages. Stage 1 is the orientation phase—a time of exploration during the initial sessions. Stage 2 is the transition stage and deals with examination of conflict, defensiveness, and resistance. Stage 3, called the working stage, is characterized by cohesion necessary to engage in productive exploration and is marked by action. Stage 4, the consolidation stage, is characterized by consolidating and applying what has been learned in the group and putting it to practice in everyday life.

Consistent with these stages in group formation, a predictable pattern of organizational development characterizes the local preschool interagency council as shown in Tables 1 and 2 (*Developing interagency councils,* 1989; Foster, 1986; Kagan, Rivera, & Parker, 1991; Morgan & Swan, 1988). This pattern of organizational development—cooperation, coordination, collaboration—was described by Foster (1986) (Figures 1 and 2). As development progresses through these three stages, an increase in sophistication is represented by the quality of the interagency activities. At each stage, group process and levels of trust, cohesion, and working relationships require different approaches to program functions. Examples of activities at each stage are contained in Table 3. Although the pace and sequence of events vary, 2–4 years are usually required for a local interagency coordinating council to mature and reach an effective operational level.

The characteristics and pattern of progression through these stages must be understood by the coordinator, who serves as the group facilitator. The level of development directly corresponds to the activities the council undertakes and influences the potential for success. An appreciation of the nature of systematic evolution of groups prepares the coordinator for the required developmental tasks at each stage, the problems to overcome, and the adjustments that must occur. An effective group does not simply happen. It is created by a group leader who has identifiable skills and who

Table 1. Stages of group development

Stage	Description
1. Cooperation	Orientation stage—the council engages in a period of orientation and formation of the group, characterized by rather superficial introductory sharing of selves *(forming)*. This is a time of exploration and learning. Members get acquainted and begin to define goals and boundaries. Council members are hesitant to make commitments and attempt to identify their roles and expectations for their participation.
2. Coordination	Transition and working stage—conflicts and differences are identified *(storming)* as the group examines the current service delivery options to children and the policies and procedures that may present constraints to the delivery of those services. The roles of members become clear as adaptation and negotiation occur. Power struggles may surface as members attempt to find their place. The structure of the council and the leaders allow members to differ, confront, and negotiate. Roles are specified, and tasks are identified. In this stage, council members attempt to reach consensus on often sensitive issues. A sense of unity begins to emerge.
3. Collaboration	Consolidation stage—this stage is reached as the group develops cohesion based on high morale, trust, and self-disclosure. The group has now developed into a true team and takes action. Conflicts reach resolution and common goals are acknowledged *(norming)*. Concrete action is initiated *(performing)*.

Table 2. Examples of levels in interagency activities

Cooperation	Coordination	Collaboration
The school district sends notices to other agencies to inform them of teacher in-service activities.	The Arc and UCP schedule joint staff training activities with mutually agreed-upon days and times.	Arrangements are made for a consultant to do training in music therapy. The schools pay the consultant fee, Head Start provides printing, UCP provides the facility, and the Easter Seal Society provides coffee and refreshments.
The local UCP center refers children to the school district as children turn 3 years old.	Community agencies develop procedures for determining changes in placement for children who turn 3 years old to avoid lack of continuity in programming.	
A general meeting is held to inform agency personnel about other programs. Agencies distribute their brochures and policy manuals to each other for informational purposes.	Agency leaders meet and determine the roles and responsibilities of each agency with respect to the different kinds and ages of preschool children with disabilities. Procedures are developed to refer children for services in the least restrictive environment.	The local rehabilitation center and the Sertoma Club jointly develop, plan, and fund a Saturday morning childcare program for infants and toddlers with disabilities.
Outside agency personnel are asked to serve on the advisory committee. Input is considered in program and grant development.		The school district and UCP enter into a written agreement to jointly develop a program for children under 3 years old. UCP provides the facility and transportation. The school district provides the teacher and purchases OT/PT/speech therapy for those children not Medicaid-eligible.
The school district considers input from outside agencies in the development of the Preschool Entitlement Grant.	IFSP and IEP meetings include all relevant agency personnel and parents; meetings are scheduled at mutually agreed-upon times and places.	
Outside agency personnel are invited to IFSP meetings.	Local transition activities, procedures, and timelines are developed by a committee comprised of various agency representatives.	The school district, health department, and children's medical services develop a policy agreement for shared responsibility for payment of OT and PT services for children with medically related therapy needs.
The health department forwards records to agencies as requested and as the proper authorization for release of confidential information is received.	Agencies mutually establish and define evaluation standards and develop procedures for accepting another agency's evaluation results and reports.	
Agencies share information about the screening and evaluation services they provide. Agencies provide copies of their referral and application forms to each other to facilitate referrals.	Agencies identify similar forms and accept other agency forms to avoid duplication and time delays.	Several agencies each contribute one staff member to create an interagency evaluation team designed to assess preschool children served by the agencies.

(continued)

Table 2. *(continued)*

Cooperation	Coordination	Collaboration
Title XX daycare programs refer children to the school district's psychologist for evaluations when indicated.	Agency programs coordinate their program calendars. Procedures are developed for reserving day-care slots for children with disabilities during the summer when school is not in session.	Agencies pool time and funds to jointly develop and disseminate a local directory describing all community preschool services. Copies are used by all programs. Joint funds support a mass mailing to pediatricians, social workers, specialists, hospitals, and others to increase public awareness and referrals.
		The school district provides speech therapy services to Title XX daycare programs under a written agreement, generating state funds to cover the cost.
		Agencies replace individual program forms with one standardized set to be used by all agencies.
		Agencies pool funds to employ a parent educator who develops a list of specialists and coordinates services across agencies.
		Therapists from the school district, UCP, and the Easter Seal Society contribute weekly time at the health department primary care clinic to conduct screening.
		Children's medical services and the school district implement an evening clinic in school for easy access by families. The school district provides an interpreter for Hispanic families.

UCP, United Cerebral Palsy; IFSP, individualized family service plan; IEP, individualized education program; OT, occupational therapy; PT, physical therapy.

understands the significant implications of his or her role as council coordinator.

Characteristics and activities corresponding to each stage of council development can be identified (*Developing interagency councils,* 1989). Graphic representation of council development is shown in Figures 1 and 2. An important feature to note is the irregularity of the line in Figure 2 that represents the periodic and expected growth, plateaus, and regression experienced by all groups. Expectation of irregular growth can prevent undue frustration on the part of council leaders and members who otherwise might look forward to unrealistically linear and steady maturation without interruptions and problems.

STAGES OF DEVELOPMENT

Stage 1—Cooperation

The initial stage of a group allows orientation and exploration (Corey, 1990). Members get acquainted, determine the structure of the group, anticipate the expectations of the other members, and define their goals. At the initial sessions, members maintain a public image and present a side of them-

ORGANIZATIONAL DEVELOPMENT STAGES

STAGE 1: COOPERATION	STAGE 2: COORDINATION	STAGE 3: COLLABORATION
□ focus of formal structure • meeting schedules • meeting locations • role and function • program specific concerns	□ turnovers followed by smaller more stable group	□ success leads to trust
	□ new members have authority to commit resources	□ council members learn to "cut deals" to "make the system work"
□ personnel limitations • isolated in positions • no experience with group • insecure, take no risks • no informal networking • council functions in name, not in practice • share information, not resources • suspicious of others	□ 1st case reviews lead to focus on kids, not programs	□ informal networking supplants formal structure for action
	□ group organizes around case-specific problems	□ hidden leadership emerges, roles established, trust, intimacy formed
□ operating style • formal, get acquainted • focused on programs, not on common clients • cautious cooperation • learning about structure of other programs	□ informal networking & teamwork develops, problems defined differently	□ resources held in common, goal is optimal mix of services for kids using a "game board" strategy
	□ group risk-taking low, but developing, $$ mixed	□ tracking & case management emerge as essential parts of the service coordination process
	□ success in cases leads to trust in group members & council progress	

Figure 1. The three stages of organizational development. (From Foster, R. E. [1986]. *An evaluation report on the state plan grant project to improve pre-kindergarten services to handicapped children in Florida.* Tallahassee: Florida Department of Education, Bureau of Education for Exceptional Students.)

selves that is cautious and socially acceptable. They may sense a certain anxiety and insecurity about the structure of the group and their respective roles.

The group creates a formal operating structure for the local interagency council (Foster, 1986). Formal cooperation is evidenced by focusing on meeting schedules, agenda items, and meeting sites. In order for members to become acquainted, information sharing is the natural and central content of early meetings and helps members to develop a more complete understanding of agency roles, capabilities, and limitations.

Clarification of the purposes of the interagency council in the form of goal statements then follows. During the early part of stage 1, members have only vague ideas about what they want from the group. Trust has not yet developed, and members operate formally as representatives of their agencies. Little informal networking may exist at this

point; members are not yet sufficiently secure in their roles to commit program resources. Establishing trust is critical in this stage. Without trust, group interaction will be superficial, constructive deliberation will not occur, and the group will operate under the handicap of instability. The interagency council coordinator must play an active role in the establishment of group trust.

Leadership is a critical component of this initial stage and is particularly necessary for the group to mature into stage 2. If the leader can establish new visions and meet the needs of agency representatives, he or she will develop a following and inspire the group to proceed with confidence. The greatest possibility of dynamics for change exists when the leader also has personal magnetism, or charisma. Members become attached to the leader because of the attractive nature of his or her personality and because the leader's ideas represent the often

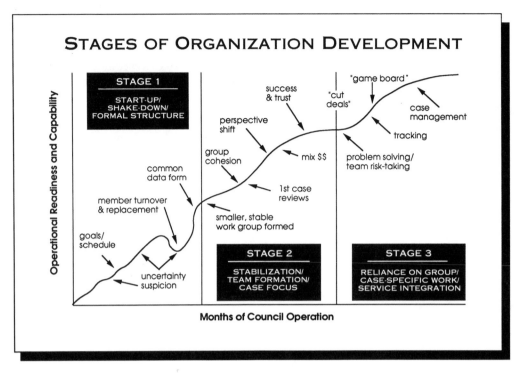

Figure 2.   Progression of the stages of organizational development. (From Foster, R. E. [1986]. *An evaluation report on the state plan grant project to improve pre-kindergarten services to handicapped children in Florida*. Tallahassee: Florida Department of Education, Bureau of Education for Exceptional Students.)

unspoken feelings and needs of group members.

Initial organizers of local councils are often personnel who serve as agency liaisons (e.g., social workers, child find specialists, case managers) and work with agencies in search of services for their clients. They are often instrumental in conveying the need for an interagency coordinating council and in bringing together agency personnel. Although they serve in the role of organizer, they may not possess the necessary skills or authority to coordinate the council on a long-term basis. If they are not management-level personnel, they may encounter difficulty in attempting to lead a group whose credentials far surpass their own.

Two distinct forms of leadership behavior emerge in the facilitation of councils: 1) goal achievement—the achievement of specific group goals, and 2) group maintenance—the maintenance or strengthening of the group itself (Morgan, Guetzloe, &

Swan, 1991). In stage 1, where the task is ambiguous, highly directive behavior serves to increase satisfaction by clarification of the task (House, 1971). To accomplish this, the coordinator must demonstrate solid knowledge of program administration and competency in group skills.

In summary, the cooperation stage is characterized by a willingness of council members to work together and to increase their understanding of the various programs and services. It is a time of exploration and learning. Communication increases and members begin to share information of mutual interest and benefit as they become better acquainted; however, adjustments to agency procedures are not yet being made. Agency representatives continue to work in parallel fashion. The initial organizers have motivated the group to action, but they may not possess the skills or authority needed to guide the council on a long-term basis. Task orientation, at this stage, must be high to

Table 3. Activity levels of interagency efforts

Activity	Cooperation	Coordination	Collaboration
Staff development	Agencies plan and conduct independent staff development activities. The content and date for the training are based on the needs of their own personnel and are program related. Notification may be given to other agency personnel along with an invitation to attend, but mutual scheduling or planning does not exist.	Recognition that staff development needs are similar across agencies. Personnel discuss mutual needs and try to schedule them at mutually convenient times. Training sessions are promoted as interagency in nature. Content may also include cross-training to increase knowledge of procedures and skills of other agency personnel.	Interagency needs assessment identifies overall priorities. Agencies mutually determine the content, schedule, and range of in-service activities. Cost is shared based on abilities; some pay for consultants/trainers, others provide materials, space, printing, and refreshments.
Parent education and support activities	Agencies develop program-specific parent education, training, groups, or support activities. Duplication of cost and effort exists as each agency develops independent parent groups or meetings.	Attempt to identify the array of parent services across the different programs, organize them into a continuum, and reduce duplication. Different agencies identify their strengths and take responsibility for certain activities.	Develop interagency plan for services based on ability and expertise. Conduct a needs assessment; identify needs; agree upon roles and responsibilities of the agencies; combine staff, funds, and resources to provide a complete array of services.
Lending libraries	Agencies have program-specific parent lending libraries (reading materials or toys); costly duplication of the same materials.	Coordinate purchase of items to avoid duplicated costs. Programs specialize in types of materials.	Combine efforts and funds to establish a central or regional parent lending libraries.
Child identification and public awareness	Agencies conduct independent and similar/duplicative activities to locate children. Newsletters, mailings, brochures, and other public awareness activities target individual agency programs.	Identify the range of activities, target population, and methods. Identify gaps and determine other activities and agency roles. Conduct joint mailings; eliminate duplication.	Consolidate newsletters into one community-wide newsletter. Combine funds and staff time to share the cost of public awareness activities, media events, television ads, and newspaper articles.
Screening	Developmental, vision, and hearing screening is provided; often duplicates screening done by other programs. Agencies rescreen children; ignore other screening done but share results.	Identify various activities, target populations, and range. Identify gaps and shift resources. Eliminate duplication. Agree on standards to allow acceptance of each other's results.	Pool personnel and resources to conduct joint screening activities.
Evaluation	Program-directed evaluations are conducted to determine eligibility. Personnel duplicate previous evaluations and may not accept those done by other agencies or professionals. Procedures, standards, and instruments used vary based on the program.	Establish community standards and procedures for evaluation. Standardize use of instruments, format, and other items. Coordinate procedures for exchange and acceptance of outside agency results. May purchase evaluation services.	Programs identify one specialized team to conduct evaluations. Programs may develop an interagency team by contributing various members.

(continued)

Table 3. (*continued*)

Activity	Cooperation	Coordination	Collaboration
Service delivery	Agency programs operate independent of other programs. Services provided, policies, and procedures are based on the needs as determined by each agency. There is competition for children; waiting lists are maintained rather than systematic referral of unserved children to other programs.	Agencies identify and coordinate roles with respect to various services and target populations. Fill gaps by shifting efforts and resources. Eliminate sources of duplication.	Agencies combine resources through contracts and written agreements to develop new programs, increase therapy services, add after-school childcare to programs, and other services.
Transition	Some agencies attempt to notify receiving programs; limited communication, forward records, provide parents with some information. May hold orientation meetings. Agency representatives may meet to exchange names of children and discuss procedures.	Coordinate transfer of records; establish timelines and personnel responsible. May schedule visitations to receiving program and mutually schedule staffings.	Develop interagency transition plan, timeline, case file exchange, and parent meetings. Use consistent format for meetings via written agreement.
Program forms	Agency programs explain and share copies of their respective forms. Forms are agency- and program-specific. Parents sign duplicate forms.	Agencies become familiar with each other's forms. Exchange and file forms, such as individualized education programs, but continue to use own forms. May use similar format.	Agencies develop standardized forms and eliminate duplicates.

maintain group momentum. The leader must be direct, dynamic, and capable of generating followership.

Stage 2—Coordination

During this second stage of development, council members increase their trust in other members. The coordinator becomes better able to share information, and roles of the members become clear. From the increased openness, however, anxiety and defensiveness may emerge as representatives and agencies are exposed on a level that is more intimate than the public image. Over time, this anxiety is replaced by genuine openness, intimacy, and trust that lead to eventual development of a cohesive working group.

During this stage, members learn to accept constraints of the agency programs without blame and to acknowledge that children cannot be served comprehensively by any single agency program. They begin to provide mutual support, assistance, and discussion of complex cases where coordination is essential.

Interagency council members begin to improve coordination of services within the limits of prevailing rules and regulations. The perspective shifts away from individual programs to the complex problems of individual children and families. Council members discover creative ways to mix resources from their respective programs to meet the challenging problems of children with disabilities (Foster, 1986). They begin to engage in mutual planning instead of superficial sharing of information. Individualized family service plan (IFSP) and individualized education program (IEP) meetings are scheduled by agencies at mutually agreeable times, rather than simply inviting others to attend the meetings. The agencies make adjustments in their work methods and planning. Personnel begin to coordinate their roles and functions while considering others' needs and constraints.

During the coordination stage, turnover in membership occurs as the roles and competencies of the participants become clear. Power struggles may surface as individual members attempt to find their places in the group. A smaller, more stable, committed group emerges, and members discover whether the group is a safe place to disagree, ask for support, and offer assistance. Discussions about procedures, division of responsibility, and strategies for problem solving are necessary. The smaller structure of the council and neutrality of the leadership allow members to differ, contrast, negotiate, and solve problems. The group engages in building a solid foundation for later resolution of problems in service delivery. The role of the coordinator continues to be critical, and the leadership may change if a more experienced and task-oriented coordinator is required.

Stage 3—Collaboration

By this working stage, the interagency council has reached the level of maturity required to organize services for children with complex needs. Members of the council have developed into a true team that is capable of realizing unitary goals and objectives and working in a collaborative manner. The trust level of the group is sufficient to allow for exploration of significant problems and effective action. Group cohesion becomes a key element of the group process at this stage. Cohesion refers to the attractiveness of the group for the participants and to a sense of belonging, inclusion, and solidarity (Corey, 1990). Council members are able to accept risks involving shortcuts in procedures and flexibility in rules that otherwise might prevent a child from receiving a needed service in a timely manner.

Informal networking supplants formal program structure as a basis for action in individual cases. New agency roles, based on trust and intimacy in working relationships, result in improved case management. A well-developed and functional child tracking system is finalized to solidify a system where children cease to "fall between the cracks" of agencies and eligibilities.

The interagency council has reached a stage where trust and solid working relationships enable creation of new collaborative programs, written agreements, agency contracts, joint efforts at service delivery, and policy adjustments in an attempt to streamline the procedure for the benefit of young children and their families. The establishment of these working relationships results in the continuous functioning of a coordinated interagency team that is capable of meeting the challenge of ever-changing resources, constraints, regulations, funding levels, and community needs.

REFERENCES

Corey, G. (1990). *Theory and practice of group counseling* (3rd ed.). Pacific Grove, CA: Brooks/Cole Publishing Co.

Daniels, W.R. (1986). *Group power: A manager's guide to using meetings.* San Diego: University Associates.

Developing interagency councils. (1989). Tallahassee: Florida Department of Education, Bureau of Education for Exceptional Students.

Foster, R.E. (1986). *An evaluation report on the state plan grant project to improve pre-kindergarten services to handicapped children in Florida.* Tallahassee: Florida Department of Education, Bureau of Education for Exceptional Students.

Gazda, G.M. (1978). *Group counseling: A developmental approach* (2nd ed.). Newton, MA: Allyn & Bacon.

Hansen, J.C., Warner, R.W., & Smith, E.M. (1980). *Group counseling: Theory and process* (2nd ed.). Chicago: Rand McNally.

House, R.J. (1971). A path-goal theory of leadership effectiveness. *Administrative Science Quarterly, 16,* 321–338.

Kagan, S.L., Rivera, A.M., & Parker, F.L. (1991). *Collaborations in action: Reshaping services to young children and their families* (Executive Summary). Yale University: The Bush Center in Child Development and Social Policy.

Magrab, P.R., Elder, J.O., Kazuk, E., Pelosi, J., & Wiegerink, P. (1982). *Developing a community team.* American Association of University Affiliated Programs. (Prepared for Department of Health, Education, and Welfare, Interagency Task Force, under Grant #54-P-71476/3-02).

Mahler, C.A. (1969). *Group counseling in the schools.* Boston: Houghton Mifflin.

Morgan, J.L., Guetzloe, E.C., & Swan, W.W. (1991). Leadership for local interagency coordinating councils. *Journal of Early Intervention, 15*(3), 255–267.

Morgan, J.L., & Swan, W.W. (1988). *Local interagency councils for preschool handicapped programs: An effective strategy to implement the mandate.* Bloomington: Indiana University: Council for Administrators of Special Education, Inc. (CASE) (A Division of the Council for Exceptional Children).

Schultz, W. (1973). *Element of encounter.* Big Sur, CA: Joy Press.

Yalom, I.D. (1975). *The theory and practice of group psychotherapy.* New York: Basic Books.

Creating a
Local Interagency Council

The first section of this book relates to the foundations and legislative initiatives that require effective interagency collaboration in the provision of services to young children and describes a model for the local interagency coordinating council. This model provides a systematic strategy for achieving and maintaining local interagency collaboration as required under PL 99-457 (as amended).

Chapters 6, 7, and 8 discuss the importance of the human factor in the operation of local interagency councils and its influence on outcomes. Chapter 6 provides an overview of leadership, the role of the council coordinator, critical success factors, and a paradigm for local council leadership consistent with the concept of shared decision making.

Chapter 7 describes the nature of group process, the role of council members, successful meeting practices, and the influence of each practice on the productiveness of the local interagency council. The voluntary nature of participation and collaboration, paired with the composition of the council (administrative equals rather than superior/subordinate relationships), creates a unique team that is dependent on the presence of motivation rather than direction.

Chapter 8 utilizes the leadership and process parameters presented in the earlier chapters to provide a step-by-step outline for creation of a new interagency council.

Chapter 6

Leadership and
the Council Coordinator

This chapter presents an overview of research on leadership, perspectives for considering leadership in human services programs, a paradigm for local interagency council leadership, and leadership styles and roles for the council coordinator.

Maturation of the local interagency council from cooperation through collaboration requires leadership from the council coordinator. This leadership is essential to the council's success (*Building interagency teams,* 1990) in achieving the council goal:

> To develop a continuum of coordinated services (medical, social, educational, therapy, family) with the community to ensure that appropriate services are available to every disabled and high-risk child identified and his family. (*Interagency program solving,* 1989, p. 2)

RESEARCH ON LEADERSHIP

The leader of an interagency coordinating council requires generic knowledge and leadership skills, as well as specific knowledge and skills unique to preschool programs for children with disabilities and those at risk. Three topics emerge from leadership research: 1) historical perspective, 2) definitions of leadership, and 3) leadership for interagency councils.

Historical Perspective

Early classic studies focused on theoretical issues and the identification of traits or attributes that differentiated leaders from nonleaders (Bass, 1981). Trait theory, also known as the great man theory, was the focus of most empirical work (Fiedler & Chemers, 1974). Traits often investigated included intelligence, masculinity, insight, scholarship, dominance, aggressiveness, judgment, and decision making. Contradictory findings in this research cast doubt on the great man approach.

During the 1940s, the complex interaction among personal traits and situational factors seemed to be more significant than the traits of leaders (Byrd, 1948; Jenkins, 1947; Stogdill, 1948). For example, Stogdill (1948) reviewed more than 100 studies that resulted in two major findings. First, the average leader exceeded the average follower in intelligence, scholarship, dependability in exercising responsibility, activity and social participation, and socioeconomic status. Second, the characteristics and skills required of a leader were determined significantly by the parameters of the situation in which the leader functioned.

Subsequent research has indicated that no single leadership style is universally effective. The majority of current leadership models involve a contingency approach that specifies the situational variables moderating the relationship between leader traits or behaviors and some outputs. Such approaches include House's path-goal theory, Fiedler's contingency model, and Fiedler's cognitive resource theory (Hoy & Miskel, 1991). Hoy and Miskel (1991) concluded that the question as to what kind of leader maximizes outputs in what kind of situations remains largely unanswered.

The situational leadership theory (Hersey & Blanchard, 1988) is an effective and accepted method used for analyzing and guiding leadership behavior. Although this theory is not a guide for research, it provides a means to obtain insights into leader and follower behaviors and to diagnose the situation and develop strategies to adapt leadership behavior to meet the demands of the situation (Hoy & Miskel, 1991). Hersey and Blanchard (1988) paired the task and the relationship orientation behaviors of leaders with the maturation of the followers in a dynamic interaction. Task behaviors include the extent to which behaviors are likely to organize and define the roles of the group members; to explain the activities; and to determine when, where, and how tasks are to be accomplished (e.g., analysis of needs for existing programs, analysis and reduction of unnecessary duplication among programs, implementation of interagency staff development activities). Relationship behaviors include the extent to which leaders are likely to maintain personal friendships among group members by opening channels of communication, providing socioemotional support, and facilitating behaviors (e.g., ensuring that all council members perceive that their opinions are heard, ensuring council members that they can trust the group, ensuring agencies that the council is sensitive to the strengths and needs of agency programs and personnel).

Definitions of Leadership

Definitions of leadership have revealed two consistent themes: 1) leadership is an interaction between or among people, and 2) leadership is an effort to direct the behavior of others toward a particular goal (*Building interagency teams*, 1990). These themes are contained in the following representative definitions:

> To lead is to engage in an act which initiates a structure in interaction with others, and [to administer] is to follow or engage in an act which maintains a structure initiated by another. (Getzels, Lipham, & Campbell, 1968, p. 145)

> Leadership entails the capacity to assume responsibility and to manage. Effective leadership implies the ability to foresee necessary changes, to solve problems creatively, and to guide and influence the thinking of others. (Linder, 1983, p. 45)

> Leadership is the process of influencing the activities of an individual or group toward the goal achievement in a given situation. (Hersey & Blanchard, 1988, p. 86)

These three definitions suggest that the council coordinator must be both an administrator and a leader. An administrator acts to maintain a structure initiated by another (Getzels et al., 1968). The coordinator must assist in maintaining existing programs that provide effective services, as well as systems to support those programs. Additionally, the coordinator must be a leader by initiating new structures (e.g., a new council, a new program) and by influencing the activities of an individual or a group through effective interactions (Getzels et al., 1968; Hersey & Blanchard, 1988).

The implementation of The Education of the Handicapped Act Amendments (PL 99-457) specifically requires a *lead* agency, not an administrative agency. According to Peterson (1991), the lead agency acts as a facilitator, coordinator, initiator, and negotiator that organizes the necessary cross-agency activities to put the program into place. The lead agency must model collaboration and be informed about all community programs; it must recognize and build on the achievements of other agencies. The coordinator must facilitate the council's support of problem-solving and program development activities through effective administrative actions. Thus, the coordinator must be not only an administrator but also a leader.

Leadership of Interagency Councils

The research on local interagency council leaders and situational leadership for councils has been extremely limited. Few models have existed for comparison. Operational local councils only recently have developed under the mandate of PL 99-457. A few related studies, however, provide suggestions for leading local councils (*Building interagency teams,* 1990).

Fiedler (1958) found that some tasks, such as leadership on a board of directors, appear to require accepting, permissive attitudes that enable all participants to express their ideas freely. Doyle (1971) found that egalitarian leadership is most effective in the analysis phase of problem solving, whereas in the synthesizing phase where coordination is more important, a group with a powerful leader is particularly effective.

Several studies suggest preferred traits for council coordinators. Although some traits may be relatively superficial, they provide indicators for leadership behaviors. Mulvenon (1980) suggested the selection of a council chair who is an assertive and energetic leader with excellent public relations abilities. Elder (1980) stated that the coordinator should be knowledgeable about the total service delivery system, work from a client-centered base, be an advocate for the client, and be able to deal effectively with interpersonal relationships and group dynamics. Kazuk (1980) described a community-based interagency council with a paid coordinator selected for organizational abilities and skills in developing procedures in order to provide the group with structure and direction. Johnson, McLaughlin, and Christensen (1982) found that success of an interagency collaborative effort is related to interpersonal factors and recommended employing a facilitator trained in group dynamics.

A more recent study (Morgan, 1989) examined the perceptions of leadership style and behavior of preschool interagency council coordinators and members. A situational leadership approach was employed to identify the prevalent styles exhibited by coordinators and the perceptions of members regarding the most appropriate styles. Coordinators perceive their dominant leadership style as a balanced high-task/high-relationship, or "selling" style. Similarly,

members perceive this style to be the most appropriate for coordinators. No differences exist across small, medium, or large school districts. Regardless of the council's maturity, situational demands of interagency collaboration appear to require high levels of both task and relationship orientation. As council membership is voluntary, continued member involvement may depend on high levels of task orientation (e.g., problem solving, development of needed services) to maintain involvement, as well as high levels of socioemotional support to maintain a productive and comfortable group process.

PARADIGM SHIFT IN HUMAN SERVICES LEADERSHIP

Barker and Christensen (1989) defined a paradigm as a set of rules and regulations that define boundaries and filter incoming information so that one is able to take action. Paradigms help to solve problems and direct focus to relevant information. If one's paradigm fails to adapt or shift on the basis of new information, however, one suffers "paradigm paralysis" and is unable to act effectively in changing situations. The authors suggested that each leader continually try to answer a key paradigm shift question: Although considered impossible today, if it were possible, what would fundamentally change in the future?

The leadership of local interagency councils is faced with at least four areas constituting fundamental change or paradigm shifts: 1) responsiveness of human services agencies to clients, 2) leadership approaches, 3) inclusion of individuals with disabilities among the nondisabled population, and 4) program-driven to child-driven/family-focused services.

Responsiveness of Human Services Agencies

Human services providers, especially those involved with interagency coordination, need skills that will help them to manage the process of change (McNulty, 1989). Mc-

Nulty stated that the classic pyramidal, bureaucratic model characterizing most governmental organizations contributes significantly to the difficulty in adapting to change. A significant paradigm shift was suggested in which multiple diverse perceptions and realities are integrated into organizations that become more responsive to client needs. PL 99-457 is one example of this paradigm shift. It redefines the roles and functions of organizations as they provide services to preschool children with disabilities and those at risk and their families. The shift stresses the collaborative responsibilities of all community agencies (Peterson, 1991; Thiele & Hamilton, 1991) in using a combination of federal, state, and local funds and programs to meet the needs.

The interagency council can be the most viable vehicle to implement this paradigm shift at the community level. Although significant support for interagency collaboration has been apparent at all levels of government, few models have been available to implement the concept with real and measurable impact on services to children and their families. The goal of local interagency coordinating councils articulated by the authors reflects this paradigm shift and focuses on maximum responsiveness of agencies and personnel to the needs of these children and families.

Leadership

The traditional bureaucratic paradigm of leadership is shifting to emphasize participatory management (Hoy & Miskel, 1991), shared decision making (Hoy & Miskel, 1991), restructuring (e.g., Lamotey & Swanson, 1989), shared governance (e.g., Glickman, 1990), and backward mapping for policy development (Dokecki & Heflinger, 1989). Three common characteristics appear in the new paradigm:

1. Each person is treated as an individual of worth.
2. Individuals trust each other and the organization.
3. The process focuses on results.

These shifts and characteristics suggest that although a general set of principles can be used across programs, leaders must individualize the application of the paradigm to each unique set of program strengths and weaknesses for maximum effectiveness in particular situations.

The council is a vehicle for members to participate collaboratively to maximize the community resources available for children and their families. The coordinator must ensure that each person is treated as an individual of worth, that trust exists among all members, and that the process is modeled and continued as new opportunities for problem solving and program refinement become available.

Inclusion of Individuals with Disabilities Among the General Population

A third important paradigm shift focuses on including individuals who have disabilities with those who are nondisabled. The Education for All Handicapped Children Act (PL 94-142) defines special education as unique but includes it as a part of regular education (e.g., least restrictive environment). Implementation, however, has resulted in special education that is separate from regular education. The Individuals with Disabilities Education Act (PL 101-476) (1990), formerly PL 94-142 (as amended), reflects the paradigm shift from identification as handicapped to identification as disabled and from exclusion to inclusion of an individual with a disability among the individual's nondisabled peers. Although the least restrictive environment requirement of PL 94-142 has been in effect since 1977, the emphasis on inclusion has been heightened by the change in the name of the law, the emphasis on inclusion in the literature, the results of limited student achievement in relatively isolated settings, the dismal track record of students with disabilities in getting jobs subsequent to completion of school, and the demonstrated effectiveness of integrated programs (e.g., Madison Metropolitan School District, Wisconsin; Project LEAP, Pittsburgh, Pennsylvania).

The interagency council provides the vehicle for incorporating this change within the community. The inclusion of preschool children with disabilities and those at risk with their nondisabled peers has been a central purpose of many preschool programs (e.g., Head Start). Because its members are aware of the variety of community programs available, the council can provide the opportunity to achieve this purpose. The coordinator must consider this change as a means to maximize the value of services to preschool children with disabilities and those at risk and their families.

Program-Driven to Child-Driven/Family-Focused Services

The fourth shift reflects the emphasis of The Education of the Handicapped Amendments of 1986 (PL 99-457), the Individuals with Disabilities Education Act of 1990 (PL 101-476), and the Individuals with Disabilities Education Amendments of 1991 (PL 102-119) from program-driven to child-driven/family-focused services. The individualized family service plan (IFSP) and emphases on the roles of parents and families articulated in these legislative actions reflect this paradigm shift. The local interagency council and the council coordinator can assist the inclusion of this shift by emphasizing the correct use of the IFSP by all agencies for all children with disabilities or at risk and their families.

PARADIGM FOR LOCAL COUNCIL LEADERSHIP

In view of the current perspective and paradigm shifts, a paradigm indicating the knowledge and skills needed by a coordinator can be a guide for council leadership. The one presented here is based on a paradigm for the instructional leadership for principals (Dwyer et al., 1985) and the adaptation of that paradigm to include special education (Burrello, Schrup, & Barnett,

1989). A review of prior research and development, a discussion of the rationale for selecting this paradigm for use with local interagency coordinating councils, and a description of the enhanced paradigm follow.

Review of Prior Research and Development

Bossert, Dwyer, Rowan, and Lee (1982) reviewed the research on effective schools and effective principals. Their review resulted in a specific framework of instructional leadership. The framework includes the context of the community (personal characteristics, district characteristics, and external characteristics), the principal's management behavior, the school climate and instructional organization, and student outcomes. This framework portrays linkages between principals' (leaders') behaviors and learning outcomes.

Using the Bossert et al. (1982) framework, Dwyer, Lee, Rowan, and Bossert (1983) conducted five pilot studies. These were followed by seven case studies by Dwyer et al. (1985). Several refinements were made in the initial framework. Five of the seven factors were renamed and specific elements associated with each factor were specified. The new factors are community, beliefs and experiences, institutional context, principal's routine behaviors, instructional climate, instructional organization, and student outcomes. Specific elements for each factor are sets of information or variables that contribute to the factor.

Burrello et al. (1989) adapted this refined framework (Dwyer et al., 1983, 1985) to include special education, based on the recognition that special education is a subset of regular education and that special education administration/leadership is a subset of regular education administration/leadership. The literature for the adaptation included critical success factors for special education leaders (Burrello & Zadnik, 1986; Johnson & Burrello, 1986). An external evaluation from a panel of experts in educational administration at the college/university and public school levels was used to confirm the validity of the adaptation.

Rationale for Use

The adapted framework for the principal as the instructional leader in special education was selected for application to the council coordinator for five reasons. First, the coordinator's goal is similar to the principal's goal—providing high-quality services to students. Second, the coordinator emphasizes instructional/service climate and instructional/service organization similar to the principal; however, the coordinator's definition of instruction is larger because it includes a variety of services in the community. Third, the coordinator focuses on student outcomes similar to the principal. Again, however, the focus is on the needs of preschool children with disabilities and those at risk and their families, rather than on the needs of the school-age group. Fourth, the council coordinator is a leader as well as an administrator—another similarity to the role of an effective principal. Fifth, because the public school is either the lead agency for the implementation of preschool programs or the eventual recipient of the graduates (in those states where another agency is the lead agency), the enhancement of a paradigm based on the schools is appropriate.

Description of the Paradigm

The Van Horn, Burrello, and DeClue (1992) framework has been enhanced to include elements from the literature on interagency collaboration and preschool programs. This enhanced paradigm is designed to be dynamic; to consider the diverse realities of our current society, as well as research issues in planning and implementing programs for preschool children with disabilities and those at risk and their families; and to focus on the unique roles of a local interagency council coordinator. As Burrello et al. (1989) suggested, the framework has been expanded to provide coordinators with specific, but flexible, information to incorporate diverse situations within a variety of local communities.

The enhanced paradigm (Figure 1) is organized into three columns—context, process, and results. Each of the factors (and elements within the factors) is described to provide a perspective of the leadership knowledge and skills that a coordinator needs to function effectively. The entries in standard print are from Van Horn et al. (1992), based on the work by Dwyer et al. (1983, 1985); the entries in bold are enhancements provided by the authors.

Context   The context dimension has three factors: 1) community, 2) beliefs and experiences, and 3) institutional context.

Community   The seven elements of locale, socioeconomic status (SES), ethnic composition, transiency, parent support, advocacy groups, and agency relationships constitute this factor. The coordinator must know the characteristics of the entire community, not just those of the coordinator's agency or program. Examples of these characteristics are:

Locale or community—transportation, housing, business development, and other features

Socioeconomic status—distributions across the community

Ethnic composition—racial and ethnic groups

Transiency of families within the community, exiting the community, and entering the community

Parent support—parental commitment to particular agencies or programs and willingness to participate

Advocacy groups—variety of coalitions in education by area of disability and in medical, social, and family services

Agency relationships (Morgan & Swan, 1988) include the historical and current formal alliances, as well as the informal relationships among the agencies and their staffs and boards. These relationships can provide either a springboard or a barrier to collaboration and growth. Without accurate knowledge of these relationships, the coor-

PROCESS

RESULTS

CONTEXT

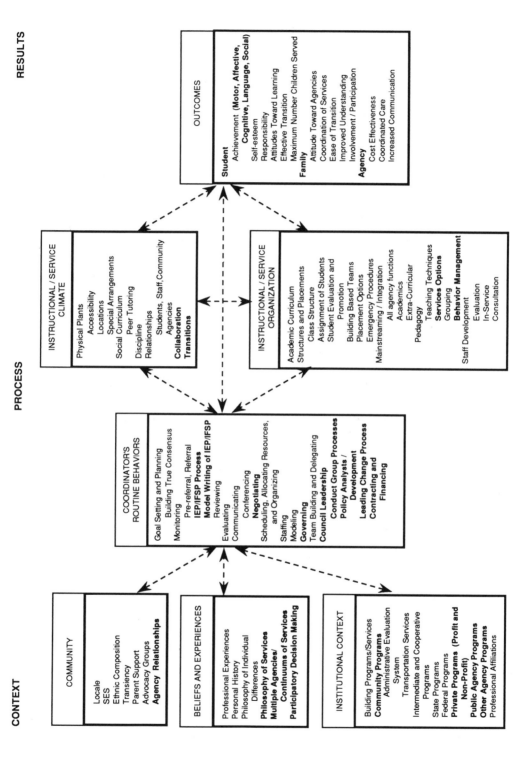

Figure 1. Framework for the coordinator of a preschool interagency council. (Adapted from Burrello, Schrup, & Barnett [1989], Dwyer, Lee, Barnett, Filby, Rowan, & Kojimoto [1985], and Van Horn, Burrello, & De Clue [1992].) (Entries in standard print are from Van Horn et al. [1992], based on the work by Dwyer et al. [1983, 1985]; the entries in bold are enhancements provided by the authors.)

dinator cannot lead effectively. Significant time and effort are needed to acquire information about these elements and insights into the dynamics of the community. For this reason, it is generally desirable for the coordinator to be selected from community personnel who have this knowledge.

Beliefs and Experiences This factor is composed of six elements. Professional experience and personal history are the foundations of the coordinator's ability to lead. If past experiences with interagency endeavors have been negative, compensating for the experiences may be a challenge for the coordinator. Positive experiences are assets on which the coordinator and council can build for the future. The philosophy of individual differences is consistent with PL 99-457 (as amended) regarding the diverse needs (educational, medical, social, and family) of preschool children with disabilities and those at risk and their families (Decker & Decker, 1984; Linder, 1983; Morgan & Swan, 1988; Peterson, 1991). This philosophy is central to all special education leaders and, increasingly, to regular education leaders, as well. It gives direction for viewing agency programs and personnel in terms of both strengths and needs. The philosophy of services is also consistent with PL 99-457 (as amended) regarding the diverse needs of preschool children with disabilities and those at risk and their families (Decker & Decker, 1984; Linder, 1983; Morgan & Swan, 1988; Peterson, 1991).

The multiple agencies/continuums of services element is an integral part of PL 99-457 and a requirement for local communities (Decker & Decker, 1984; Linder, 1983; Morgan & Swan, 1988; Shearer & Mori, 1987). No one agency has the resources to meet the array of needs required under the law. The lead agency approach confirms the letter and spirit of the law regarding the involvement and commitment of all local community child and family service agencies to work together toward the goal of serving each child. Multiple agencies can provide a continuum of services by avoiding unnec-

essary duplication. Participating and networking (McNulty, 1989; Morgan & Swan, 1988) are requirements for collaboration in a council. If the council members and coordinator do not know the requirements for participatory leadership and the need for sharing information on a formal basis, as well as informally (networking), they cannot work collaboratively toward achieving the goal for all children and for all agencies. The council coordinator cannot lead the council in problem solving and service improvement without these beliefs and experiences.

Institutional Context This third factor includes community programs and services, as well as school programs for preschool children and their families. The focus on building programs and services includes all facilities in the community. The local council coordinator must be knowledgeable about all community programs, services, and facilities for preschool children with disabilities and those at risk and their families.

One way for agency leaders to establish the priority of collaborative action is by inserting an item in their annual administrative evaluations. Agencies can review leader behavior to ensure that their personnel emphasize collaboration in providing services. Transportation services include both school bus systems and agency or private transportation under other programs. Intermediate and cooperative programs include those jointly sponsored by community child and family services agencies. State programs include educational, medical, social, and family services. Thiele and Hamilton (1991) list 16 federal programs that have an impact on services for preschool children with disabilities and those at risk and their families. Access to federal programs at the local level is complicated by interpretations of federal programs through federal, state, and local rules, regulations, and priorities. An effective coordinator must apply the federal, state, and local programs in creative ways in order to provide high-quality local programs.

Private nonprofit programs, private for-profit programs, and other agency programs (e.g., department of human resources) (Decker & Decker, 1984; Hanson, 1985; Linder, 1983; Morgan & Swan, 1988) are important components of community services. Prior to the enactment of PL 99-457, the emphasis for providing services to preschool children with disabilities and those at risk and their families was on educational and related services furnished primarily by the schools and sometimes through contracts with other agencies. The intent of PL 99-457 is for all agencies to work together in providing an array of services. The coordinator must be cognizant of the characteristics and resources of private nonprofit and private for-profit agencies, as well as state-funded and locally funded agencies. Varying eligibility requirements, focus for services, quality of services, array of expertise, rules and regulations, service priorities, and continuing development of these other agencies are critical in determining the institutional context for programs for preschool children with disabilities and those at risk and their families.

Professional affiliations include a variety of organizations that encompass the professions found in the various community child and family services agencies. The agencies represented on the council include medical, social, and family services, each of which has one or more professional organizations that may be assets in achieving the council's goal.

The context dimension for coordinator leadership suggests that the person occupying this position should have both experience with other programs and respect from leaders of these programs in order to be effective. The complexity of the coordinator's leadership role cannot be underestimated. The multiple foci require a person with a unique set of formidable knowledge and skills. The context provides the foundation from which the local council coordinator acts in assisting the council to reach its child- and family-centered goal.

Process   The process dimension is com-posed of three factors: 1) the coordinator's routine behaviors, 2) instructional/service climate, and 3) instructional/service organization.

Coordinator's Routine Behaviors   The context of the community characteristics, the beliefs and experiences of the coordinator, and the institutional context across agencies provide the foundation for the coordinator's routine behaviors. Building a true consensus as a part of goal setting and planning is a challenging endeavor. As the local council develops through the cooperative, coordinative, and collaborative stages, the coordinator must facilitate the building of this consensus, which is based on both actions and words of council members (*Building interagency teams,* 1990). Collaboration among members of the council may take significant time to achieve.

The monitoring activities include both pre-referral and referral procedures because duplication is common among community agencies. The coordinator's leadership can reduce unnecessary duplication in such areas as screening and diagnostic efforts. Both the individualized education program (IEP) for children 3 through 5 years of age and the individualized family service plan (IFSP) for infants and toddlers from birth to 3 years of age are included. The IEP focuses on special education and related services; the IFSP is expanded to include medical, social, family, and other early intervention services. The inclusion of other agencies on the IFSP team is quite different from most school system procedures. Procedures for development of the IFSP may contrast significantly with those of the IEP, as do the requirements of PL 99-457 from those of PL 94-142. The coordinator must be well versed in both programs to weave the processes together creatively for the service providers and to model the processes for others as required in meeting the council's goal.

The coordinator must be an effective communicator both in conferencing and in negotiating. He or she must be able to facilitate individuals or small group conferences to focus on problem resolution. Some topics require exchanges of information and clarification, whereas others involve negotiation among the parties to achieve problem resolution (Morgan & Swan, 1988). The coordinator must ensure that problems are identified and resolved (Decker & Decker, 1984; Linder, 1983; Peterson, 1991). For example, an unserved, multiply impaired child may be found to need a center-based educational setting, therapy that is both educationally and medically necessary, medical services, transportation, and specialized equipment. In addition, the family may require parent support services and respite care. The council coordinator, in facilitating provision of the complete array of services needed by the child and family in the most coordinated and effective manner, must be able to engage the interagency team in determining respective roles and responsibilities in the provision of these services. This function requires the coordinator to be skilled in group dynamics and group negotiation. Assisting the team to reach a decision also demands a knowledge of eligibility, potential combinations of services, possible funding sources, and alternatives involving trade-offs.

The day-to-day requirements of scheduling, allocating resources, and organizing activities across multiple agencies are challenges for a leader. The coordinator may be effective within his or her own agency, but working well with other agencies requires exceptional negotiation skills and flexibility that is built on trust and participatory problem solving. Staffing may call for suggestions from the coordinator as to the most qualified personnel, especially for program expansion. Modeling requires the coordinator to behave in a manner consistent with council philosophy and to demonstrate appropriate council actions and procedures (e.g., problem resolution skills, participatory leadership). Modeling is critical because the way that the coordinator implements change becomes the means by which the council works effectively with changing parameters.

The coordinator's leadership must be consistent with the principles governing the council. In conjunction with the PL 99-457 mandates concerning collaboration and councils, a participatory leadership approach is needed. Team building and task delegating must be consistent with these modeling and governing actions. The more team building that the leader encourages and the more responsibilities that he or she delegates, the more effective the council will become. All council members should feel they are part of the team and trust each other during discussion of sensitive issues.

Council leadership (*Building interagency teams*, 1990; McNulty, 1989; Morgan & Swan, 1988; Peterson, 1991) consists of four sub-elements. The coordinator must conduct group processes effectively (Elder, 1980; McNulty, 1989; Morgan & Swan, 1988). This includes ensuring that all persons necessary for a decision are present, managing the participation in and development of the group culture, encouraging a high relationship orientation among group members, and creating a spirit of understanding and collaboration. The coordinator must analyze and develop policy (McNulty, 1989; Sage & Burrello, 1986; Swan, 1985). The creation of new programs requires the development of new operating methods among agencies that are often foreign to veteran employees of those agencies. In leading the change process (McNulty, 1989; Morgan, 1989), the coordinator should provide a predictable pattern of group process and organize the meeting agenda to ensure focus on the task, task orientation and accomplishment, and effective mechanics of conduct. Perhaps the most threatening aspect of change is the unknown. By minimizing the unknown and maximizing trust and predictable procedures, the coordinator can manage the change process for the council.

Contracting and financial skills are required for effective council operation. Knowledge, skill, and behavior in these areas demonstrate commitment to member agencies, as well as commitment to the children and families that they will be appropriately served. Knowledge of fund generation under all federal, state, and local programs in the community is necessary to develop a community system to finance early intervention services. It is also necessary to facilitate the emergence of reasonable and fair contracts. The coordinator should recognize reasonable and customary payments and conditions under which services can be reimbursed. Contracting is the concrete expression of the joint commitment of the council members to provide needed services, and it represents the lead agency's commitment to ensure that one agency does not provide all of the services. The fiscal support procedures of the continuum of services represent a vital link in meeting the council's goal. Knowledge of financing procedures of the various agencies is required so that funding fluctuations during economic crises or change can be effectively managed.

Instructional/Service Climate The climate of the instructional/service setting is essential to desired student outcomes. It has been suggested (Schein, 1985, as quoted in Burrello et al., 1989) that the primary role of a leader is to establish a supportive and proactive instructional/service climate both for those providing the service and for those receiving the service.

The physical facilities used for services to young children and their families require equipment in appropriate sizes, adequate recreation and recess areas, accessibility, and other special arrangements (Decker & Decker, 1984; Linder, 1983). Special arrangements include relationships with day care programs that serve the children and train personnel to work with the increasing number of medically fragile children.

Emphasis on the social curriculum is a primary consideration in preschool programs (Decker & Decker, 1984; Linder, 1983; Wood, Combs, Gunn, & Weller, 1986). The socio-emotional growth of preschool children provides a critical foundation for their later development. Interaction with peers (e.g., placement in the mainstream, peer tutoring, establishment of peer relations) is a vital part of building positive expectations and role models for these children and their families.

Discipline stresses the positive aspect of teaching and encourages learning. It is an integral part of early learning experiences and central to later development of knowledge and skills in all areas. Discipline with preschool children does not include suspension and expulsion as used in the instructional climate for older students.

The relationships among students, staff, and the community focus on consistent learning experiences for the child and family in all settings (Decker & Decker, 1984; Linder, 1983; Shearer & Mori, 1987). This climate requires the establishment of trust among all those associated with the education of the child in order to maximize learning opportunities.

Transition services concern the movement from one service provider or program to another (Individuals with Disabilities Act, 1990; Shearer & Mori, 1987). Transition occurs from center-based to preschool programs, home-based to community settings, special education to integrated programs, preschool programs to kindergarten, and kindergarten to elementary school. Transition services between programs are a function of lead agency shifts (programs for children from birth through 2 years of age to preschool programs). The Individuals with Disabilities Education Act (1990) (as amended) requires that transition services be incorporated wherever appropriate. This critical activity of preschool programs minimizes interruption of services to children and assists families in understanding the changes.

The instructional/service climate is a significant factor in providing services to meet the council's goal. The climate established by the coordinator in all of these elements and across the agencies is a model to be followed by others. The child-centered focus and the continued reinforcement of that approach are vital in meeting the council's goal.

Instructional/Service Organization The curriculum for young children through 5 years of age focuses on cognitive, motor (gross and fine), language (receptive and expressive), and social/affective development (Decker & Decker, 1984; Linder, 1983; Shearer & Mori, 1987), rather than on academic skills found in programs for older students. The areas of medical, social, and family services have been added in line with the requirements of PL 99-457 (as amended), as well as the recognition that only through emphasis on all of these areas can children achieve their optimal growth.

Defining the structure of the service delivery and placing children across settings and services are primary objectives. The task of the coordinator is to facilitate a full continuum of community services, including a wide variety of service options.

Pedagogy focuses on teaching techniques. The knowledge and skills available for the education of these children and their families are significant. A broad scope of literature exists on the best practices for both early intervention programs and the education of students with specific disabilities. The role of the coordinator is to emphasize the minimally required features of programs and to enhance the quality of services, rather than to prescribe or encourage the use of a particular curriculum or series of teaching techniques across all agencies. The strength of the council is diversity through its focus on creating a full array of community services.

Results The results factor focuses on child outcomes, the logical result of the context, and the process of instruction/services. Although the coordinator may not measure the results directly, each agency is responsible for measuring impact under the IEP or IFSP. One valuable function of the council may be to assist all agencies in using an appropriate uniform measure to assess student outcomes across all agencies. Overall, council efforts should result in increasing numbers of children and families who receive services from community agency

programs consistent with the goal of the council.

Another outcome relates specifically to families. The council should encourage agencies to help parents achieve positive attitudes in relation to the agencies, the coordination of services, and effective transitions. Parents should be actively involved in their children's programs and participate with their children in accordance with the IEP or IFSP. Improved understanding on the part of parents is critical to the continued support required in developing an array of community-based services for all students and families who need them.

Agencies should realize cost benefits in working collaboratively with the council. Reducing duplication of services and redirecting efforts toward established goals can increase available services and maximize the value of community agencies. Each agency should realize a positive outcome of coordination of care consistent with its emphasis on quality services to children and their families. Collaboration should also increase the quality and quantity of communication among agencies, particularly in relation to problem solving, future planning, and vitality of agency efforts.

LEADERSHIP STYLES AND ROLES

Styles

A study by Morgan, Guetzloe, and Swan (1991) suggested that the council coordinator use a situational leadership style incorporating high-task orientation and high-relationship orientation simultaneously, regardless of the size of the community or the maturity of the council. This style requires the council coordinator to develop an individual relationship with every member of the council in order to identify their priorities, to identify strengths and needs, to assign tasks appropriately to achieve the goals of the council, and to share the success of the council. Consistent with the administrative and leadership aspects of the council, the coordinator should influence, rather than direct, many of the decisions.

Roles

The coordinator serves in multiple leadership roles, such as using group processes effectively to build a culture, conducting policy analysis and development, leading the change process, contracting, and financing. A forum for the exploration of diverse realities (McNulty, 1989) is essential to problem solving and program development and refinement. The council coordinator must provide a forum where members can share their views with trust among each other (*Building interagency teams,* 1990), without creating animosity, and achieve resolution with mutual respect. The coordinator must also facilitate future projections through the group process. This requires the integration of the varied agency and community service needs and perceptions into future actions that are feasible (McNulty, 1989). Considering problems without achieving their resolution can doom the council to inaction and disintegration. If the council does not have impact, the members will not spend their time in working with others.

As a leader of leaders, the coordinator must have a vision of what the council should be; a mission or strategy for achieving the vision; and passion, energy, and commitment to ensure attention and action in accomplishing the mission. The coordinator must be able to influence others effectively and also to listen so that he or she can be influenced by the perceptions of others. The coordinator can lead the council in developing a collaborative vision, mission, and passion that can be shared by all members.

REFERENCES

Barker, J.A., & Christensen, R.J. (1989). *The business of paradigms: Discovering the future.* Burnsville, MN: Charthouse Learning Corporation.

Bass, B.M. (1981). *Leadership, psychology, and organizational behavior* (2nd ed.). New York: Harper & Row.

Bossert, S.T., Dwyer, D.C., Rowan, B., & Lee, G.V. (1982). The instructional management role of the principal. *Educational Administration Quarterly, 18,* 34–64.

Building interagency teams. (1990). Tallahassee: Florida Department of Education, Bureau of Education for Exceptional Students.

Burrello, L.C., Schrup, M.G., & Barnett, B.G. (1989). *The principal as the special education instructional leader.* Bloomington: Indiana University, School of Education, Principal Training Simulator in Special Education Project.

Burrello, L.C., & Zadnik, D.J. (1986). Critical success factors of special education administrators. *The Journal of Special Education, 20,* 367–377.

Byrd, C. (1948). *Social psychology.* New York: Appleton-Century-Crofts.

Decker, C.A., & Decker, J.R. (1984). *Planning and administering early childhood programs* (3rd ed.). Columbus, OH: Charles E. Merrill.

Dokecki, P.R., & Heflinger, C.A. (1989). Strengthening families of young children with handicapping conditions: Mapping backward from the street level. In J.J. Gallagher, P.L. Trohanis, & R.M. Clifford (Eds.), *Policy implementation and PL 99-457: Planning for young children with special needs* (pp. 59–84). Baltimore: Paul H. Brookes Publishing Co.

Doyle, W.J. (1971). Effectiveness of achieved leader status of leader on productivity of groups. *Administrative Science Quarterly, 16,* 40–50.

Dwyer, D.C., Lee, G.V., Barnett, B.G., Filby, N.N., Rowan, B., & Kojimoto, C. (1985). *Understanding the principal's contribution to instruction: Seven principals, seven stories.* San Francisco: Far West Laboratory for Educational Research and Development.

Dwyer, D.C., Lee, G.V., Rowan, B., & Bossert, S.T. (1983). *Five principals in action: Perspectives in instructional management.* San Francisco: Far West Laboratory for Educational Research and Development.

Education of the Handicapped Act Amendments of 1986, PL 99-457 (October 8, 1986). 100 § 1145-1177.

Elder, J.O. (1980). Essential components in development of interagency collaboration. In J.O. Elder & P.R. Magrab (Eds.). *Coordinating services to handicapped children: A handbook for interagency collaboration* (pp. 181–201). Baltimore: Paul H. Brookes Publishing Co.

Fiedler, F.E. (1958). *Leader attitudes and group effectiveness.* Urbana: University of Illinois Press.

Fiedler, F.E., & Chemers, M.M. (1974). *Leadership and effective management.* Glenview, IL: Scott, Foresman.

Getzels, J.W., Lipham, J.M., & Campbell, R.F. (1968). *Educational administration as a social process: Theory, research, and practice.* New York: Harper & Row.

Glickman, C.D. (1990) *Supervision of instruction: A developmental approach* (2nd ed.). Newton, MA: Allyn & Bacon.

Hanson, M.J. (1985). Administration of private versus public early childhood special education programs.

Topics in Early Childhood Special Education, 5(1), 25–38.

Hersey, P., & Blanchard, K.H. (1988). *Management of organizational behavior* (5th ed.). Englewood Cliffs, NJ: Prentice Hall.

Hoy, W.K., & Miskel, C.G. (1991). *Educational administration: Theory, research, practice* (4th ed.). New York: McGraw-Hill.

Individuals with Disabilities Education Act of 1990, PL 101-476. (The 1990 Education of the Handicapped Act Amendments), 20 U.S.C. § 1400-1495 (1990).

Individuals with Disabilities Education Amendments of 1991, PL 102-119.

Interagency problem solving. (1989). Tallahassee: Florida Department of Education, Bureau of Education for Exceptional Students.

Jenkins, W.O. (1947). A review of leadership studies with particular reference to military problems. *Psychological Bulletin, 44,* 54–79.

Johnson, V.L., & Burrello, L.C. (1986). Critical success factors, rural and urban, special education administration. *Journal of Special Services in the Schools, 4*(1–2), 1–16.

Johnson, W., McLaughlin, J.A., & Christensen, M. (1982). Interagency collaboration: Driving and restraining forces. *Exceptional Children, 48*(5), 395–399.

Kazuk, E. (1980). Development of a community-based interagency model. In J.O. Elder & P.R. Magrab (Eds.), *Coordinating services to handicapped children: A handbook for interagency collaboration* (pp. 99–131). Baltimore: Paul H. Brooks Publishing Co.

Lamotey, K., & Swanson, A. (1989). Restructuring school governance: Learning from the experiences of urban and rural schools. In S.L. Jacobson & J.A. Conway (Eds.). *Educational leadership in the age of reform.* White Plains, NY: Longman.

Linder, T.W. (1983). *Early childhood special education: Program development and administration.* Baltimore: Paul H. Brookes Publishing Co.

McNulty, B.A. (1989). Leadership and policy strategies for interagency planning: Meeting the early childhood mandate. In J.J. Gallagher, P.L. Trohanis, & R.M. Clifford (Eds.), *Policy implementation and PL 99-457: Planning for young children with special needs* (pp. 147–167). Baltimore: Paul H. Brookes Publishing Co.

Morgan, J.L. (1989) *An investigation of the leadership styles of preschool interagency council coordinators in Florida.* Unpublished doctoral dissertation, University of South Florida, Tampa.

Morgan, J.L., Guetzloe, E.C., & Swan, W.W. (1991). Leadership for local interagency coordinating councils. *Journal of Early Intervention, 15*(3), 255–267.

Morgan, J.L., & Swan, W.W. (1988). *Local interagency councils for preschool handicapped programs: An effective strategy to implement the mandate.* Bloomington: Indiana University, Council for Administrators of Special Education, Inc. (CASE) (A Division of the Council for Exceptional Children).

Mulvenon, J. (1980). Development of preschool interagency teams. In J.O. Elder & P.R. Magrab (Eds.), *Coordinating services to handicapped children: A handbook for interagency collaboration* (pp. 133–162). Baltimore: Paul H. Brookes Publishing Co.

Peterson, N.L. (1991). Interagency collaboration under Part H: The key to comprehensive multidisciplinary, coordinated infant/toddler intervention services. *Journal of Early Intervention, 15*(1), 89–105.

Sage, D.D., & Burrello, L.C. (1986). *Policy and management in special education.* Englewood Cliffs, NJ: Prentice Hall.

Schein, E.H. (1985). *Organizational culture and leadership.* San Francisco: Jossey-Bass.

Shearer, M.S., & Mori, A.A. (1987). Administration of preschool special education programs: Strategies for effectiveness. *Journal of the Division for Early Childhood, 11*(2), 161–180.

Stogdill, R.M. (1948). Personal factors associated with leadership: A survey of the literature. *Journal of Psychology, 25,* 35–71.

Swan, W.W. (1985). Implications of current research for the administration and leadership of preschool programs. *Topics in Early Childhood Special Education, 5*(1), 83–96.

Tannenbaum, R., Weschler, I.R., & Massarik, F. (1961). *Leadership and organization: A behavioral science approach.* New York: McGraw-Hill.

Thiele, J.E., & Hamilton, J.L. (1991). Implementing the early childhood formula: Programs under PL 99–457. *Journal of Early Intervention, 15*(1), 5–12.

Van Horn, G.P., Burrello, L.C., & De Clue, L. (1992). An instructional leadership framework. The principal's leadership role in special education. (Submitted to *Special Education Leadership Review*).

Wood, M.M., Combs, C., Gunn, A., & Weller, D. (1986). *Developmental therapy in the classroom* (2nd ed.). Austin, TX: PRO-ED.

Chapter 7

Group Processes
and Council Meetings

Leading a council requires knowledge and skill in effective group processes. Implementation of the Education of the Handicapped Act Amendments of 1986 (PL 99-457) (as amended) will mean changes in the methods agencies use to plan and deliver services to preschool children with disabilities and those at risk, and to their families. The council coordinator must bring council members (other agency leaders) together to process information for planning, solving problems, and making decisions (Daniels, 1986).

Council meetings are the vehicle for establishing a collaborative vision of what local service delivery systems must do to implement PL 99-457, providing a forum for discussion of issues and procedures, identifying the objectives and goals to make the vision a reality, stimulating development of action plans, and evaluating progress toward the vision. The meetings should be designed to enhance trust and working relationships among council members. The group process is the foundation of all council activities.

GROUP DEVELOPMENT

The development of a group requires consideration of multiple variables. These include identifying the parameters for forming the group, such as voluntary versus required membership, group size, frequency and length of meetings, and meeting places; identifying and preparing the leader; announcing the group; and recruiting, screening, and selecting group members.

Corey (1990) cites three stages in the development of a group. The initial stage focuses on group orientation and explora-

tion. Primary tasks are identifying and orienting members, establishing and maintaining trust, identifying goals, dividing responsibilities, and structuring the group. Members determine their degree of commitment and participation in the group and build a trust relationship with other members.

The second or transition stage provides the opportunity to deal with resistance. Characteristics of this stage include anxiety, conflict, struggle for control, challenge of the group leader, and resistance. The leader and the group must cooperate to create a supportive, yet challenging, environment for all group members

The third or working stage focuses on cohesion and productivity. Group members recognize the group's attractiveness and develop a sense of belonging, inclusion, and solidarity. A here-and-now focus is characteristic of this stage. Members identify and take responsibility for goals and concerns, are willing to work outside the group for the group's efforts, feel included in the group, and initiate change for improvement. As Friend and Cook (1992) suggest, the team (group) becomes a set of interdependent individuals who work and interact directly in a coordinated manner to achieve a common purpose. The group may be characterized as an orchestra—individuals listen to one another and do productive work together.

GROUP PROCESS

The council's effectiveness in reaching the working stage is directly related to the group process skills and characteristics of the council coordinator and members (Corey, 1990). An effective council is a team of agency representatives, each with specific knowledge and skills, who share information and collaborate with each other to solve problems, implement solutions, and achieve common goals (Friend & Cook, 1992; Handley & Spencer, 1986). The diversity of the members is one of the council's primary strengths when there is acknowledgement that each member brings a different and necessary perspective to meeting the needs of preschool children with disabilities and those at risk and their families.

Group Participation

For the group to reach its goal, each member must accept the responsibility to participate by performing certain task-related and maintenance-related functions as shown in Table 1. Task-related functions allow the council members to process the information they receive to achieve identified goals. Maintenance-related functions facilitate the collaborative spirit of the council to maintain the perspective of equality in the council's normal state. The *norm state* of any group refers to the normal distribution of power among the members. The ideal norm state is equality of the members and of their influence (Daniels, 1986).

Group Skills and Qualities

Council members must demonstrate other skills and qualities that are essential to effective group functioning (Corey, 1990).

Communication Council members must attend, both verbally and with body language, to what each member says in order to respond and communicate effectively. Without effective communication, the council cannot conduct its work in a proper manner. Concrete, specific statements facilitate meaningful dialogue. Generalities and vague statements preclude this possibility.

Council members must understand and accept what another member is saying without judgment. Empathy is one of the most

Table 1. Required task-related and maintenance-related group member functions

Task-Related Group Member Functions:

1. *Initiating* Introducing new ideas for consideration
2. *Providing/seeking information and perceptions* Offering relevant information and perceptions based on a personal sense of obligation to share; seeking information and perceptions in areas in which one is ignorant
3. *Clarifying* Restating, questioning, or testing answers to questions or examples until the information is understood
4. *Elaborating* Providing implications of an idea or situation
5. *Summarizing* Stating the position of the council so that direction is not lost
6. *Compromising* Listening to the varied perspectives on a topic, recognizing conflict, and offering a suggestion that is both fair to the varied perspectives and unifies them in concept.

Maintenance-Related Group Member Functions:

1. *Gatekeeping* Inviting one another to speak or assisting others to share their perceptions; redirecting attention from one who is talking excessively to another who needs to share
2. *Testing the norm state* Re-establishing equal status or influence among members in a deliberate way by a focus of attention on a pattern working against an equal-influence structure
3. *Harmonizing* Calming those who engage in intensive emotionality in a discussion
4. *Encouraging* Recalling past successes to provide a solution-oriented perspective in frustrating situations

Source: Daniels (1986).

effective means of establishing rapport and support among group members.

Honesty, spontaneity, good will, and integrity are indicators of genuine behavior. Genuine communications among members are open, natural, and consistent.

Regard for Others Positive regard of council members for each other is necessary for constructive challenges. Members should demonstrate respect by attending to others, working with others, recognizing another's uniqueness, expressing warmth through support and encouragement, and being genuine.

Members must trust and accept each other. A member should feel free to express meaningful reactions and perceptions without fearing rejection. Each must be true to his or her own values and not feel pressured to please everyone.

Group Interaction Self-disclosure and sharing needs and feelings about strengths and weaknesses are important as council members obtain support and assistance from one another in resolving problems.

Confrontation is essential to growth. Although often feared and avoided by members, the quality of confrontation is an indicator of council development. When the council has established a firm foundation through trust and respect, members can deal effectively with criticism. The continued growth of the council demands sensitive challenges. A council ceases to be effective if its members are able to interact only on a supportive level by focusing on strengths alone. Unwillingness to examine agency programs critically may result in polite exchanges that will do nothing to improve the service delivery system for children and families.

Through the development of a shared vision in implementing PL 99-457, council members should recognize the need for commitment to change. This commitment by each agency is mandatory if services for preschool children with disabilities and those at risk and their families are to be improved.

The ability to experiment with innovative methods in identifying and solving problems is a necessary skill for council members. The freedom of members to explore new perceptions and strategies represents a dynamic aspect of a creative council.

Selection of Council Members

The success and productivity of the group process depends on the knowledge, group skills, and spirit of collaboration held by all council members. To improve the quality of services to preschool children with disabilities and those at risk and their families, council members must have expertise in early childhood special education. They must have a vision of how the service delivery system is to be created and what must be changed. Achieving this vision requires members to

work collaboratively with other agency leaders in innovative, not traditional, ways. Table 2 provides sample characteristics to be considered in selecting council members.

Agency leaders who demonstrate these behaviors are the appropriate candidates for council membership. The correct balance of knowledge, group skills, motivation, vision, ability to stimulate needed change, and willingness to participate must be achieved by each council member. In existing councils, resignations and reassignments will provide the coordinator an opportunity to apply these characteristics when selecting new council representatives.

Responsibilities of Council Members

Members must contribute to the successful operation of the council through effective group skills. The following behaviors help to guide the group process toward achievement of the council's goals (*Building interagency teams*, 1990):

Prepare adequately for each meeting. Identify the topics to be discussed and take needed materials to share.
Arrive on time for each meeting and attend regularly. Member continuity is necessary for meaningful, productive discussions.
Listen actively to all meeting discussions.

Table 2. Selection characteristics for council members

Demonstrates knowledge and skills in early childhood special education
Administers or leads a preschool program that provides direct services to children and/or families
Assigns priority to the child and family, rather than to the agency
Demonstrates effective group process skills
Communicates effectively both orally and in writing
Demonstrates task and relationship orientation skills
Confronts problems constructively and solves problems effectively
Demonstrates and is committed to collaboration
Authorized to commit agency resources
Attends meetings consistently
Takes risks and tries new approaches
Promotes equality among all members
Demonstrates empathy and genuine respect
Demonstrates trustworthiness and trusts others

Participate actively in discussions by contributing relevant information and perceptions.

Organize thoughts and contributions. Be thorough but brief and remain on task.

Communicate one idea at a time and support each idea with valid evidence.

Speak clearly and decisively. Speak loud enough to be heard and comprehended by others.

Share conflicting opinions in a fair and objective manner. Avoid sarcasm or hostile remarks.

Monitor nonverbal communication. Avoid negative facial expressions, yawning, absence of eye contact, and doodling.

Take accurate notes of the meeting.

Complete follow-up activities and assignments in a timely and quality manner.

Role of the Council Coordinator

Bates, Johnson, and Blaker (1982) state that a group mirrors its leader and "will only be as good as the leader, as good as his or her skills, and as good as the leader's own being" (p. 73). The most effective group direction is the leader's modeling of the desired behaviors for group members (Corey, 1990). The coordinator must demonstrate competence in group leadership techniques and be motivated by a genuine effort to guide the group in problem-solving tasks that result in an improved service delivery system.

Corey (1990) indicates several personal characteristics of effective group leaders. Presence suggests that the leader is organized for the meeting, has focused attention on the meeting, and is open to reactions of the group. Personal power characterizes the leader's self-confidence and awareness of his or her influence on others. Self-awareness and a willingness to confront oneself convey the leader's knowledge of his or her strengths and areas in which assistance is needed. Sincerity and authenticity suggest that the leader has a sincere interest in the well-being and growth of the council members. Furthermore, the leader is honest and straightforward with council members and has a clear sense of his or her own identity. The leader demonstrates enthusiasm and clear belief in the group process, as well as inventiveness and creativity in problem solving in a variety of areas. These personal characteristics provide a foundation for guiding the development of the council.

Critical Leader Techniques Although an individual may possess all of the personal characteristics noted above, an effective leader also needs significant expertise in working with the verbal dimensions of group interaction. Bates et al. (1982) identified six of the most critical dimensions: attending, feedback, questioning, confrontation, opening a meeting, and closing a meeting.

Attending The leader focuses on the council member who is speaking, as well as being aware of the others. Simultaneously attending to everyone is a skill that must be learned, and it requires the leader to be sensitive to environmental information. The leader must be attuned to the interactions among all council members to ensure that those who need to interact have the opportunity to do so. Eye contact is necessary to maintain the values of the council and confirm that every member is important and worthy of sharing information.

Feedback The coordinator must give and receive feedback to and from each member. Without feedback, people and agencies continue to repeat the same behavior day after day. One may have a vague awareness of a problem but not be able to identify what is causing unwanted reactions in others.

Giving feedback is difficult. Because it involves a risk that many people are reluctant to take, some rarely give or receive feedback. To assist council members in learning how to give and receive feedback, the coordinator must model effective forms. Helpful feedback uses behaviors that are current and can be changed (Bates et al., 1982). Feedback also must be clear and specific.

Group interaction requires feedback. The effectiveness of a council depends on the quality of the feedback contained in the interaction. The coordinator is responsible for controlling the quality of the feedback. Through honest, helpful feedback, members gain an increased awareness and understanding of the effects of procedures and agency behavior.

Questioning Questions should be facilitative and provide direction for the discussion. Excessive use of questions by the coordinator can appear to establish his or her authority as one who seeks information from others without revealing much of oneself. For example, "why" questions can make members feel as if they are being interrogated. The coordinator should encourage members to rephrase questions into statements that clarify their positions and discourage excessive questioning.

Confrontation Confrontation provides a different perspective from which to view a problem or reveals information of which another person is unaware. Confrontation is a form of feedback. To be effective, confrontation must be implemented with empathy, positive regard, authenticity, concreteness, self-disclosure, and sensitivity (Anderson, 1968; Bates et al., 1982; Blaker, 1973; Corey, 1990; Hill, 1965). Without these features, confrontation can become hostile and counterproductive for both the sender and the receiver.

Change requires confrontation. The purpose of confrontation is to share perceptions and communication, not to prove a point or to identify a "right" view. In confrontation, council members state their positions, feelings, and perceptions in a here-and-now perspective. They can determine how their perceptions are discrepant with those offered by another member.

Confrontation involves a risk. The confronter cannot be certain how others will respond or if he or she will be properly understood. The coordinator must encourage members to engage in confrontation in order to share important views and perceptions. Used properly, this technique results in greater understanding and respect. The presentation of different views and perspec-

tives is primary in achieving group consensus on possible solutions to problems.

Opening a Meeting A meeting can begin by such statements as "Let's get started," or "It's time to begin." A focused sharing activity in which each person participates can be used to begin a meeting. This procedure encourages discussion; places the responsibility for discussion on the council members, rather than on the coordinator; and avoids the attitude that the meeting belongs to the coordinator or that the coordinator has sole control and authority to share information with the members. An initial sharing activity provides a starting point for discussion of issues and concerns that should be addressed during the meeting. The coordinator can then facilitate the discussion through appropriate use of confrontation and feedback.

Closing a Meeting The meeting must end on time. The coordinator can slow down interaction near the end of the session so that discussion gradually tapers off. The coordinator should encourage a summary of the discussion and may want to allow the group to reiterate any assignments or follow-up to be completed by the next meeting. Council members may write their own logs or minutes of the meeting. This encourages the notion of group ownership of the meetings and facilitates follow-up.

Leading Difficult Council Members To maintain effective operation of the council, the coordinator must ensure that all members are included as contributors to the group process. Although most members respond positively to the group process, some may display resistive behavior that disrupts the problem-solving process and other council activities. A member's resistance may be directed toward a fellow group member, the council coordinator, the council as a whole, or taking responsibility for action. The coordinator must reduce resistive behaviors in the council to keep the focus on achieving goals.

Hendricks (1987) listed several causes of resistance, including resistance due to change, negativism, fear of the unknown, and perceived roles. Several factors may cause resistive behaviors in any one individual. The particular behaviors and their causes vary significantly among individuals.

Some resistance is an integral part of the group process and should be expected. However, when it exceeds reasonable bounds, the council may be less effective. If there is too much resistance, the members may decide that the council is not worth the effort to participate. The coordinator must use acceptable methods to maintain the openness of the group while simultaneously moving the council toward its goals.

Certain behaviors of leaders tend to reduce resistance. These include establishing eye contact to build respect; smiling; being genuine, likable, and trusting; being patient; listening proactively (engaging the mind); avoiding aggravation; avoiding fault-finding; asking questions to build rapport; using questions that seek a "yes" response; being empathetic and sympathetic appropriately; making others feel important; motivating and reinforcing others based on their needs; and practicing skills in reducing resistance of difficult people (Carnegie, 1981; Hendricks, 1987).

The council member who resists has a reason for this behavior. To redirect that member's behavior toward successful member and council outcomes, the coordinator must individualize his or her leadership approach to the member. This requires the coordinator to use an array of skills in various situations with different council members.

The following descriptions provide some examples of difficult members and strategies the coordinator might consider in leading these members and the council. The examples are based on syntheses of information from Bates et al. (1982), Hendricks (1987), and practical experience.

The Aggressor This council member displays behavior that is confrontative, challenging, varied, and complex. The member may be very direct with boisterous verbal behavior, aggressive or belligerent verbal statements, and argumentative behavior or may be more subtle with passive-aggressive behaviors such as constant, but apparently supportive, criticism of the coordinator's perceived ineffective leadership behaviors. This behavior may be brief and temporary, unrelenting, or sporadic. The reason for the resistive behavior may be the member's need to win every exchange, the member's wish to be the leader of the group without accepting responsibility for leadership, or the member's attempt to control the coordinator and the group.

To lead the aggressor effectively, the council coordinator might employ one or more of the following nine behaviors:

1. Remain calm and objective—behave differently than the aggressor to provide a contrast for the aggressor and other members.
2. Give the aggressor time to exhaust his or her comments on the issue.
3. Ask the aggressor to explain or clarify the statement or issue of concern for the council. This may generate feedback to the aggressor by other council members.
4. Speak only for yourself concerning the issue at hand or seek comments on the issue from other council members.
5. Redirect the conversation from an attack on a person to an analysis of the issue or concern.
6. Avoid a battle in which there must be a winner and a loser. The council must behave as a team and reach consensus on tough problems, rather than identify individual members as winners or losers. The children and families served by the council should always be the winners.
7. Step into the exchange between the aggressor and the member being attacked. Model behavior that permits and considers differences of perception and opinion in appropriate and constructive ways.

8. Use humor to reduce the tension and stress of the aggressor.
9. Be friendly and keep the meeting relaxed, which may reduce the impact of the aggressor.

The Isolate This member attends but does not participate actively in council meetings. He or she may be a new member who waits for others to speak or is gaining a sense of the group or one who is anxious about speaking, afraid to commit to change because of potential negative consequences, or insecure in working with other members.

To lead the isolate effectively, the council coordinator may use any of the following seven behaviors:

1. Create situations for interaction among the council members to build the isolate's confidence.
2. Reward the isolate's participation in any council activity.
3. Ask the isolate to work with other council members on specifically assigned tasks.
4. Seek comments from the isolate based on the coordinator's knowledge of that person's areas of expertise.
5. Work personally with the isolate to explore ideas, and assist the isolate to present ideas to the council.
6. Ask questions that require more than a "yes" or "no" answer.
7. Be persistent and supportive in expressing a positive expectation and value of the isolate's participation in the council.

The Negative This council member usually has limited success, little motivation, and negatively responds—with both verbal and body language—to any new idea. The negative is often described as dispirited and afraid to take any risk. This person has sufficient self-concept to comment negatively on new ideas but insufficient self-concept to attempt problem resolution. He or she is the eternal pessimist.

To lead the negative, the council coordinator may consider the following six behaviors:

1. Do not accept the negativism, but reflect on the negative's responsibility to carry the load.
2. State your perception of the situation in a positive, nonargumentative way and seek input from the council members.
3. Ask the negative, "What is the worst-case scenario for this action?" and encourage council members to respond with their perceptions.
4. Do not solve the problem for this person.
5. Redirect analysis of the negative's problem or issue by having the council brainstorm methods to resolve it, based on the positive perceptions of the other members.
6. Build experiences for all council members that demonstrate skills they can use to solve difficult problems creatively by using a team approach.

The Monopolizer This council member talks, has something to say about every issue or concern, and takes excessive time to provide information or perceptions. The monopolizer is uncomfortable in participating in the council and resists problem solving by diverging and presenting tangential information and points of view. He or she interrupts and often tries to speak first, rather than listen to others.

To lead the monopolizer, the council coordinator may consider the following seven behaviors:

1. Monitor council member participation and ensure that all members have the opportunity to speak.
2. Encourage council members to provide feedback to each other on the value of their comments in positive, professional ways.
3. Provide a time limit for comments on particular issues so that all who wish to comment may do so.
4. Use a planned rotation approach to ensure that every council member provides a perception.
5. Stress relevance of comments and focus

for council meetings as a wise use of time for all members. Encourage members to meet with each other before or after a meeting to share personal information.

6. Use a sense of humor in indicating that the monoplizer is taking everyone else's time and others might have valid points of view.

7. Be sincere but directive in allowing all members the opportunity to participate.

The Imposter Expert This member pretends to possess the expertise to achieve tasks; however the imposter expert has significant talk but no depth of expertise. This person is harmful only if he or she is perceived to be an expert. During the development of a new council, the imposter expert often volunteers to initiate new activities. His other ideas may be useful, and this member can often contribute effectively to brainstorming activities. The imposter expert generally seeks respect and admiration from colleagues. Although this person has strengths, he or she does not usually have the structure to complete the task.

To lead the imposter expert, the council coordinator might consider the following four behaviors:

1. Restate the facts of the situation and explore with the council the specific expertise required to complete the task.

2. Give the imposter expert the opportunity to save face by reflecting on his or her multiple commitments.

3. Seek the views of other members concerning the imposter expert's comments.

4. Redirect the imposter expert's efforts to other tasks to which this member can contribute effectively.

COUNCIL MEETINGS

Strategies for Effective Meetings

An effective meeting brings people together to utilize their knowledge and understand-ing in problem solving, planning, and decision making. A meeting is an intellectual task that engages members in the problem-solving process in order to achieve an improved level or quality of understanding. By bringing together different minds with varied perspectives in an active way, an effective meeting yields a product through analyses, solutions, decisions, and plans. The interagency council meeting organizes and mobilizes the unique strengths of its members in the best interests of preschool children with disabilities and those at risk and their families and formally guides the coordination and collaboration process (*Building interagency teams,* 1990).

Regularly scheduled council meetings (at least monthly) stimulate both formal activities and informal networking and constitute the most readily visible evidence of relationships among the agencies. The meetings are important, however, only to the extent that they produce a direct impact on the type and quality of the preschool services provided.

The first few meetings of a newly developed council provide a forum to permit members to become acquainted, determine the initial structure of the group, establish the philosophy and mission of the council, and identify tentative operating procedures. The focus of these early meetings is on formal operating structure (Foster, 1986), and members often carefully maintain a guarded, cautious approach. They establish their places in the group and identify the expectations that will guide their relationships with each other.

The council's intent and goals may be ambiguous at this early stage, and the coordinator's role is critical to the overall success of the meetings. Agency leaders form an impression of the worth and importance of the council during the first few meetings. When council leadership is strong and beneficial results are expected, the agency leaders will commit their time, energy, and efforts. If the first meetings appear disorganized, loosely structured, or primarily designed to meet the objectives of the organizing agency, they may be skeptical and unwilling to make commitments.

These initial organizational meetings set the tone for the perceived worth of the council itself. The council must receive substantial support in achieving its goal of building an array of comprehensive community services for children and their families. It serves as the visible representation of interagency collaboration and must be regarded as a valuable group. The perception of the council, as it matures, conveys its power and influence and highlights the need for dynamic, organized, and productive meetings. If meetings continue to appear disorganized, convey no specific agenda or sense of purpose, or fail to result in clearly definable consequences or positive outcomes, the council will simply fall into the category of "another unnecessary meeting." Fourteen strategies have been developed to ensure effective council meetings and productive outcomes (*Building interagency teams*, 1990).

Schedule Monthly Council Meetings Meetings should be scheduled regularly, on a specified date and time, and at least monthly. Meetings conducted less frequently do not allow sufficient time for group development, identification of problems, and generation of feasible solutions. Irregularly scheduled meetings convey disorganization and a lack of purpose. If the members perceive the council as important, their commitment to regularly scheduled meetings is more enthusiastic.

Council meetings are a key strategy in bringing together primary agency leaders who can impact the service delivery system. These leaders need an environment that guarantees sufficient time to know one another, develop understanding of the other agencies and programs, nurture and encourage working relationships, establish trust and mutual respect, and stimulate adoption of a common goal and vision for children within the community. With this foundation and commonality of purpose, successful coordination of services and solutions to identified problems can emerge. More frequent meetings may be desirable in the initial stages of council development and when critical issues are at hand.

Rotate Council Meeting Sites Meetings should be held at agency sites on a rotating basis when possible. Although the council must be perceived as a team in spirit, agency leaders should feel that their autonomy is secure. Meeting at member agency sites confirms the belief that each agency is an equal partner in the activities, contributions, and successes of the council.

Rotating meeting sites can increase each member's understanding of the services, programs, and personnel within each community agency. Visiting other facilities enhances each member's familiarity with the various programs. It also serves to create good will and increase mutual respect. A brief tour of an agency's facility, program, or classrooms may be scheduled immediately prior to or following a council meeting.

Restaurants and other nonrelated facilities are emotionally removed from the focus of the interagency council. They do not offer appropriate meeting locations or serve to reinforce the bonds needed for development of council programs.

Meet in Locations Conducive to Task Orientation The meeting room should be pleasant, comfortable, quiet, and well lighted and ventilated. The quality of council interactions are directly proportional to the comfort and friendly environment offered by the surroundings. The room should comfortably accommodate the members but be small enough to convey a warm and personal quality (Hazel et al., 1988). Avoid restaurant meals and brown-bag lunches; these settings give the impression of a social gathering rather than a serious meeting. The council should focus on interagency goals and not be disrupted by food.

Maintain a Positive Climate Council members should be seated around a table in a manner that reinforces a sense of equality of influence. The council consists of peers, not a superior and subordinates. In order to emphasize the equal relationship and responsibility of members, the coordinator should not sit at the head of the table or stand in front of the group. This sensitivity to body language regulates and distributes the responsibility within the group.

Seating arrangements may consist of a round table or rectangular tables pushed together to approximate a square shape. Avoid placing tables in a large U-shaped configuration that physically distances members. Seating members close together conveys a more personal and friendly situation. Physical proximity enhances discussion, particularly for reserved group members.

The coordinator should be sensitive to the members' attachment to the group and continually work to strengthen it. Each member must feel and receive feedback confirming that participation and involvement are crucial. As council members arrive for a meeting, they should be recognized and greeted in a friendly manner, even if they are late. Chairs should be moved, if necessary, to accommodate latecomers within the group. Members should not be permitted to sit in a corner or inconspicuous spot or allowed to feel they are on the fringe of the group. They should always feel that their presence is acknowledged, needed, and appreciated.

Formal, around-the-table introductions should not be made at each meeting. If this occurs on a regular basis, it may indicate that attendance or representation is not as consistent as desired. Inconsistency of attendance should be corrected. To make new members comfortable, personal or casual introductions as other members arrive are conducive to integrating them into the interagency team.

Establish the Norm State The coordinator must distribute talking time in an equitable manner to provide a balanced discussion and a high probability of council productivity. A method called an inclusion activity at the opening of each meeting can be used to establish the ideal norm state of equality of influence (Daniels, 1986). All council members take brief turns in talking

for equal periods of time. This uniformity of behavior in the first few minutes increases the probability that the group will resolve the influence and membership agendas in favor of a norm state of equality. The norm state provides every member equal potential to influence the group.

The coordinator should avoid dominating the discussion and assuming a disproportionate amount of talking time. Each member has expertise, knowledge, and skills to contribute important and possible solutions and should take an active role in the discussion.

Use Familiar Terms All council members should use terms that are consistent across agencies. Council discussions filled with unknown terms, acronyms, and other jargon can isolate and shut out members. The coordinator and members must be sensitive to the use of jargon, particularly as new members join the group. The members should explain jargon, use substitute terms, or ask for clarification without exposing members to embarrassment. Council members may wish to review and define terms at an early organizational meeting and emphasize terms with consistent communication value.

Limit Guests The council's problem-solving and decision-making activities require that the number of members should remain small enough to permit discussion and appropriate group dynamics. Agency personnel may indicate that they would like to attend council meetings. Although this desire is a testimony to the attractiveness of the council, their attendance could have a deleterious effect on group dynamics and organization, not to mention concern for confidentiality.

The coordinator may need to clarify for all members and agencies that one program leader is needed to represent each primary agency consistently at council meetings. A written list of the names, addresses, and telephone numbers of council members may also confirm this principle. If guests attend, the coordinator may wish to introduce them as guests at the beginning of the meeting and make a friendly but clear and nonoffensive statement that guests occasionally visit to get a firsthand idea of the role and activities of the council. The statement indicates that the council is not a large or open group and that its members represent their agencies and hold clear responsibilities.

Integrate New Council Members As new members join the council, whether they represent additional agencies or replace former members, the coordinator must quickly orient and integrate them into the group. Assuming a role in an existing group, in which there is significant cohesion among members, can be awkward and difficult for new members. The coordinator should seek their perceptions, involve them in discussions, encourage them to share specific information, and perhaps ask other members to act accordingly.

Similar strategies may be necessary for quiet, shy members of the group to ensure that they have the opportunity to speak and interact in discussions. Such techniques as brainstorming and regulated reporting can be useful.

Begin and End Meetings on Time Council members place a priority on the wise use of time. If the meeting content does not meet their immediate needs, solve problems, or provide important information, they will not allocate time to participate in meetings. Meeting time should be used productively.

Prepare a Meeting Agenda The coordinator should prepare an agenda for each council meeting. The agenda serves as a structured guide for achieving the council's objectives. A tentative agenda should be distributed in advance as a part of the meeting notice and revised as needed at the beginning of the meeting.

Agenda items for the following month can be identified at the end of each meeting. Having council members identify the issues to be discussed provides continuity across meetings and helps to ensure cooperation. Without this planning, the meeting is likely

to be rambling and unproductive. Members should verify that the agenda is followed and the meeting stays on task.

Focus on the Task The coordinator uses the agenda to focus the members' attention on the council's purposes and tasks. The most commonly reported problem with meetings is going off task (Mosvick & Nelson, 1987); this occurs when a meeting lacks structure, contains extensive topic jumping, or includes irrelevant discussion. Changing topics is a natural occurrence in the dynamics of a typical discussion, however, and may be tolerated if it does not divert attention for a prolonged time. It should be monitored carefully so that it does not become excessive and interfere with decision making. The coordinator or a council member should be able to say: "Wait a minute. Can we take a moment to complete or summarize this issue before we go on to the next one?"

Preplan and Distribute Written Materials The coordinator should take time to plan, create a specific agenda to guide the meeting, prepare a sufficient number of handouts for distribution, and identify potential outcomes. A poorly planned meeting can create confusion about its purpose. Members may be poorly prepared and spend excessive time in irrelevant talk. A checklist as shown in Figure 1 is helpful in remembering important planning details.

Written material related to the discussion topics should be distributed at the meeting. Receiving important, current information at each meeting, particularly in written form, reinforces member participation. The coordinator should ensure that members are kept informed of all local, state, and federal issues and developments regarding preschool programs and provide written documents and data as needed.

Prepare and Disseminate Meeting Minutes Minutes of council meetings should be written and distributed. If time prevents this, members may be provided with notebooks to keep their own minutes and notes. A standard format can be developed. The

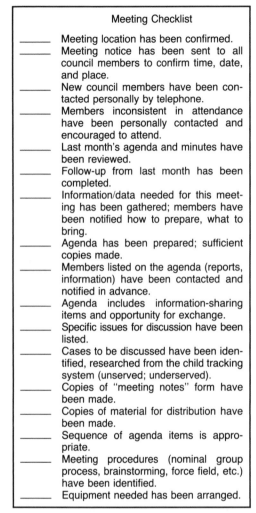

Meeting Checklist

_____ Meeting location has been confirmed.
_____ Meeting notice has been sent to all council members to confirm time, date, and place.
_____ New council members have been contacted personally by telephone.
_____ Members inconsistent in attendance have been personally contacted and encouraged to attend.
_____ Last month's agenda and minutes have been reviewed.
_____ Follow-up from last month has been completed.
_____ Information/data needed for this meeting has been gathered; members have been notified how to prepare, what to bring.
_____ Agenda has been prepared; sufficient copies made.
_____ Members listed on the agenda (reports, information) have been contacted and notified in advance.
_____ Agenda includes information-sharing items and opportunity for exchange.
_____ Specific issues for discussion have been listed.
_____ Cases to be discussed have been identified, researched from the child tracking system (unserved; underserved).
_____ Copies of "meeting notes" form have been made.
_____ Copies of material for distribution have been made.
_____ Sequence of agenda items is appropriate.
_____ Meeting procedures (nominal group process, brainstorming, force field, etc.) have been identified.
_____ Equipment needed has been arranged.

Figure 1. Checklist for planning an effective council meeting. (Used with Permission of the Florida Department of Education, Bureau of Education for Exceptional Students, from *Building interagency teams*, [1990], p. 81)

council should decide on the procedure it prefers.

Summarize Effectively Effective information processing requires discipline and a systematic procedure throughout the meeting. Subpoints must be clarified and summarized during the meeting as well as at the end. The coordinator checks the consensus of the council and allows for additional discussion before summarizing and moving the council to the next issue. Council members should always leave the meeting with a clear understanding of what was recommended, decided, or continued for discussion at the next meeting.

Development of the Meeting Agenda

The agenda for each council meeting should reflect both routine functions and the special projects under way. The agenda, based on the activities of the previous month's meeting and the goals set by the council, should be prepared by the coordinator and sent to members in advance of the meeting. This procedure can assist members in effective preparation and participation.

Each council meeting agenda should reflect four basic components: 1) information sharing, 2) ongoing council projects and activities, 3) case discussions to resolve service delivery problems, and 4) confirmation of the next meeting and determination of key parts of the agenda.

Information Sharing The opening action of the agenda serves a routine information-sharing function. During this time, members may announce important events, such as training opportunities open to everyone, and share important information, such as changes in staff, funding, programs, or services. Agency programs and services are always in a state of flux and change. Information about these changes is necessary to keep members current. Understanding the shifts in program capabilities is related to the manner in which referrals are handled, transition is effected, and children are served. Shared information may result in a situation that requires immediate discussion or determination of a specific course of action by the council.

This information-sharing time may be used periodically to include a guest from a related program, such as March of Dimes, division of blind services, Medicaid, or a new health clinic, for the purpose of explaining its resources and services. This portion of the agenda allows council members to stay up to date and to be aware of all available resources.

Council Projects The second section of the agenda is reserved for special projects of the council. Initially, these activities involve development of a written philosophy statement, creation of council letterhead and stationery, explanation of agency programs, identification of existing services, development of a standard release of information form, and similar items. Later, the projects are focused on such issues as development of a child tracking system, identification of gaps in services, public awareness activities, coordination of case finding activities, standardization of forms for the individualized education program (IEP) and the individualized family service plan (IFSP), transition activities, and coordination of screening and evaluation procedures. This section of the agenda relates to the council's established goals that serve to improve the quality of coordination and services to children and families.

Case Discussions This section of the agenda, reserved for discussion of direct services to specific children, is often referred to as case coordination. The discussion centers on children for whom services are difficult to arrange or coordinate. The council does not need to discuss the majority of children served in the agency programs. They are identified, referred to programs, and served without great difficulty. Ongoing case management for most children remains with the primary service coordinator and is completed routinely on a day-to-day basis.

Some children, however, require the attention and problem-solving capability of the entire council because of complicated cases involving multiple agencies. The respective role and responsibility of each agency must be determined by all of the council members in order to minimize confusion and duplication of effort in serving these children. The council may also discuss specific children who are unserved, underserved, or who pose difficult service delivery problems. Council discussion can resolve these problems by defining roles, generating and creating solutions, and suggesting collaborative efforts.

Planning the Next Meeting The final item on the monthly agenda should be a confirmation of the next meeting date and a decision on the location. The meeting date should be consistent, such as the second

Monday of every month at the same time of the day. The location should be rotated, with selection determined by special events or need. For example, with the opening of a new health department building, the council may choose to schedule the next meeting at that facility. Council members can visit the building, learn about its new location and hours of operation, and become aware of any expansion in services that have resulted from the move. Opportunities for council members to visit agency facilities serve to strengthen not only understanding but also a sense of familiarity and emotional bonds.

The main items and issues to be placed on the agenda also can be discussed. Council projects continue over a period of many meetings. As new situations and concerns are identified, they are placed on the agenda for council attention. Spending a few moments to identify the topics for the next meeting provides closure for the members on the current meeting and assists them in preparing for the next meeting.

Meeting Minutes and Follow-Up

A procedural item that requires discussion is maintaining council minutes. Keeping detailed written minutes, typing, and forwarding them to council members require concentration, time, secretarial assistance, copying, and mailing. If these resources are not readily available, the members may wish to require each member to maintain his or her own written notes and minutes. Although informal, this means of keeping a record of meetings can be effective. A sample form for members to use in recording minutes and recommended follow-up is shown in Figure 6 of Chapter 9.

If printed minutes are desired, the coordinator may identify a member of the group who is adept at keeping notes and request a copy after the meeting. The coordinator can synthesize the information into summary form, have it typed, and forward a copy to each member. Printed minutes should contain specific information discussed and used in a functional manner as shown in Table 3. Meeting minutes should be re-

Table 3. Sample council meeting minutes

PRESCHOOL COUNCIL

February 20, 1992

ATTENDING: Jan Moore, Coordinator, School System
Alice Wade, Children's Medical Services
Eddie James, Parent Training
Sally Blank, Project Child
John Mitchell, Easter Seal Society
Kathy Smith, Child Find
Sue McAllister, Memorial Hospital
Colleen Williams, The Arc
Jean Mason, Child and Family Center
Ruby Poole, Head Start
Jane Walton, Parent-to-Parent

I. AGENCY INFORMATION

Kathy Smith, the new Child Find Specialist, was introduced to council members. Many of the members have already had a chance to speak with Kathy on the telephone. In order to orient her quickly to her new position and responsibilities, visitations were scheduled with those programs with which she is not yet familiar.

Council members were reminded of the workshop on Room Arrangements scheduled for Friday, February 28, at the Preschool Center. Teachers and supervisors from all community programs are scheduled to attend.

Information was provided on the new audiologist, May Simpkins. She is located in Palm View and is a Medicaid provider.

Alice Wade, Children's Medical Services, announced that their budget will soon be depleted and other arrangements will need to be made to provide occupational and physical therapy currently sponsored by CMS. Council discussed five children under the age of 3. UCP will provide services to two of the children at their current day school site. Developmental Disabilities will request funding for the remaining three children who are clients.

Colleen Williams, The Arc, reported that they no longer have openings in their Early Development (0–3 years) class. Agency personnel should refer children needing full-day, center-based services to the Easter Seal Society.

John Mitchell, Easter Seal Society, reported changes in the Children's Resource Program. They have recently hired a certified teacher who has 7 years of Head Start experience. They currently have 13 children under 3 years of age enrolled in their program and have openings for three additional full-time placements. They have recently been approved for three Title XX slots for children which will take effect on February 24. Occupational and physical therapy services are now also being extended out of the center where children may be served in the home or in daycare settings.

The Speech Pathology Department at Memorial Hospital is able to take more preschool children with the additional staff member hired. They will continue to have difficulty providing OT because of a change in staff positions. If OT is required, the Easter Seal Society may be a better option at this time.

II. PARENT EDUCATION

The February parent education newsletter was distributed to all council members for their use. Planning for the February and March workshops was done.

The final draft copy of the Directory of Parent Lending Libraries was reviewed. Distribution was discussed; each member indicated the number of copies needed. The directory will be provided to all teachers, parent trainers, and parents. As new children are enrolled, a copy of the directory will be placed in the parent's information packet.

III. TRANSITION PLANNING

Council discussed the successes and weaknesses of last year's transition activities. Improvements and refinements of procedure were identified along with timelines for evaluations, forwarding of records, parent orientation meetings, and student visits.

Jan distributed a list generated from the tracking system indicating the children age-eligible for school district services in the fall. Children were discussed relative to evaluation needs, parent concerns, placement/service delivery options, etc.

Council discussed infants and toddlers currently in home-based settings and parent training models who should be considered for more intensive classroom and/or therapeutic settings next year. Council members were designated for follow-up in these cases. Continue at next month's meeting.

(continued)

Table 3. (continued)

IV. CASE CONFERENCES/UNSERVED CHILDREN

Case 1
Type: Transition
M.G. (BD: 9-26-89)

Discussed this 2½-year-old profoundly hearing impaired youngster who has just moved to the area. As an infant, she lived in Scott County and was known to both Easter Seal and Parent Training. Both agencies were requested to forward their records to the Council Coordinator. The family contacted our office during the summer, wanting a private therapist to work with her in the home. Debbie Smith, teacher of the hearing impaired, has been working with them. Referred back to Easter Seal for audiological care/hearing aid evaluation. The child has not been aided due to mother's objections; the parent may not be open to other services at this time.

   Recommendations: Schools to schedule any needed evaluations when all the records are compiled and reviewed. Staffing will be scheduled. Follow up at the next council meeting.

Case 2
Type: Unserved
T.T. (BD: 2-6-88)

Discussed this 4-year-old Down syndrome child who formerly resided in the county and moved last year. He was scheduled in May 1991 for evaluation by the schools but the appointment was canceled due to illness. The family has just returned to this county and lives in Palmetto. Colleen Williams, The Arc, brought his case file to today's meeting. Eddie James, Parent Training, will request the HRS records to determine whether a current psychological evaluation report is available. This youngster appears to need a speech-language evaluation, social-developmental case history, OT/PT evaluations, and possibly a psychological evaluation. The HRS case should be reactivated; staffing will be scheduled for placement in the school's Preschool Program. Determination needs to be made whether he is most appropriately placed in the Bronton Elementary Program or the The Arc program. Because he lives in Palmetto, placement in the ARC Program would result in an extremely long bus ride each day so the Bronton placement may be preferable. A meeting will be scheduled with the parent and with those agency representatives involved to discuss necessary evaluation and case management. Parent training will be requested by the parent. There do not appear to be any significant medical problems. No cardiac problems are reported and the youngster is not a client of CMS.

   Recommendations: Secure records, complete evaluations, reopen HRS case, schedule staffing to determine placement and services.

Case 3
Type: Unserved
M.L. (BD: 4-17-88)

Discussed this 4-year-old youngster in need of speech-language therapy. The family has been assigned a caseworker from Voluntary Family Services to assist with the many social service needs. This child was referred for Head Start placement this past fall but unable to attend due to transportation problems. Mother is bedridden and has been very ill. Discussed initiating services at Memorial Hospital in their language class, with funding and transportation to be arranged by the schools. Mother prefers this setting.

   Recommendations: The speech-language report done through the schools will be immediately sent to Memorial. The HRS case worker will discuss this option with the parent and facilitate scheduling of a placement/IEP staffing.

V. MARCH MEETING

The March meeting of the Council will be held on the second Thursday at Children's Medical Services. Be prepared to discuss: Transition, parent workshops, planning for the Early Intervention Grant application, and the Preschool Entitlement Grant application for next year's programs.

(Adapted with Permission of the Florida Department of Education, Bureau of Education for Exceptional Students, from *Building interagency teams*, [1990], pp. 85–88)

garded as a communication and coordination strategy and not viewed simply as an independent or fragmented activity.

Most importantly, the minutes should list the recommendations and specific assignments relative to any children discussed. The names of the children are not included in the written minutes in any manner in order to maintain confidentiality. Code numbers, initials, birth dates, or combinations of these can be substituted for names.

Inclusion Activities

Inclusion activities are structured to provide for participation of all council members. These activities seek to establish equality of

influence among members, maximize participation, and minimize the probability that
one or two members will dominate the discussion and exchange of ideas. Two examples of inclusion activities are shown in
Figure 2.

Activities Relating to Problems and Solutions

Interagency council meetings should focus
on identification of problems within the
service delivery system and identification of

Getting To Know You

When To Use:
1. As an inclusion device when the group members do not know one another well or do not work together on a continual basis
2. At the beginning of a meeting

Materials Needed:
1. Pencils for all group members
2. Paper or note pads for each group member
3. A flip chart and a prepared list of questions

How To Use:
1. The group leader says, "I think it would be a good idea for us to take a few minutes to meet one another before we begin today's agenda. Team up with one person in the room that you are least familiar with, and interview each other during the next 5 minutes. The interview questions are on the flip chart. At the end of the 5 mintues, you will be asked to introduce the other person by sharing this information."
2. Members of the group pair up and spend 5 minutes interviewing each other. The questions provided should be relevant to the people in the group, agencies, and issues involved. The questions should be simple, positive in their focus, and low risk in terms of how much they require people to disclose. Questions may include:
   Name and current position/title?
   Length of time in current position?
   Job responsibilities?
   Previous positions or experience?
   Primary concerns or initiatives?
3. When the interviews are completed, the leader asks each to introduce his or her partner to the group.

Expression of Ideas or Information

When To Use:
1. As an inclusion technique when working with a group in which the members are familiar with one another and with working together
2. At the beginning of a meeting or with the initiation of a new agenda item

Materials Needed:
   None

How To Use:
1. The leader asks each member of the group to express his or her feelings or provide input on the first agenda item. Time for the response is specified—1–2 minutes—without interruption. Communication is structured, formal, and controlled by the leader. Questions may be addressed to the group member when he or she is finished.
2. Each group member takes a turn, in round-robin fashion, taking 1–2 minutes.
3. When all the group members have spoken, the leader briefly summarizes the basic positions that have been stated. This summary becomes the starting point for work on the agenda item.
4. If this activity has been used for general information sharing and agency updates on the agenda, the key issues or problems reported should then be placed on the agenda for discussion or resolution.

Figure 2. Inclusion activities for council meetings. (Reprinted from Solley, E. L. [1973]. Peter-Paul: Getting acquainted [pp. 7–8]. In *The 1973 annual handbook for group facilitators*. San Diego, CA: Pfeiffer & Company, 1973. Used with permission.)

potential solutions. Brainstorming is effective in generating a large number of factors associated with a problem and potential solutions (see chap. 9, this volume, for more detailed information). Other procedures include the nominal group process, reflective thinking format, Ross four-step Agenda, the single question format, and the Delphi method (Daniels, 1986; Mosvick & Nelson, 1987). These procedures are better oriented to the whole decision process than others.

Action Planning

The council products are achieved through action planning. All of the council coordinator's group leadership skills are focused on action planning to achieve the council's goals. The interagency council must proceed through three stages in order to engage in decision making and problem solving in an orderly fashion (Daniels, 1986):

1. Build an information base.
2. Analyze the information base.
3. Resolve the problem by arriving at a group decision or common agreement about the meaning of the information.

Unskilled and poorly led groups attempt to do all of these stages simultaneously. The stages then become mixed; confusion and ineffective group work predominate. If decisions are made before all of the information is collected, the result will be incorrect or faulty resolution. A skilled, well-led group approaches its task by first determining that all of the available and pertinent facts have been collected. The council makes certain that information is collected from all member and agency sources, but analysis of the information is not conducted at this point.

When the collected information is understood by the members, the council progresses to the second stage of analysis. Members discuss the facts and express their opinions. Discussion may include healthy conflict, differences of opinion, and con-

frontation. The resolution stage is reached only when the council is satisfied that the information has been thoroughly analyzed and all of the relevant alternatives have been identified. The council then seeks to reach the third stage of consensus, or agreement of the members, which often results in a heightened conflict. The final resolution may be reached by discovery of the cause of a problem, a decision to move in a particular direction, or a complete action plan. Resolutions reached by an orderly progression through the stages are usually superior in quality to the thinking of any individual member and are generally implemented with greater commitment and efficiency.

Building and Analyzing an Information Base Prior to developing specific goals and objectives that will comprise the action plan, the council must assess the current conditions, practices, and problems related to the particular concern. For example, if council members believe there is potential need for a more comprehensive case-finding system, they must begin with a careful study of existing practices. The council may choose to create a formal task force charged with the responsibility of studying current practices or conduct a form of self-study of agency policy and activities for case finding in the form of a needs assessment. When the information has been gathered, it is carefully analyzed so that relevant and specified goals, objectives, timelines, and responsibilities can be identified.

Developing a Plan A concrete action plan is the result of a thorough assessment of needs and status. In developing the plan, the council must determine the tasks necessary to accomplish each objective. An example of such a plan is shown in Figure 3. The council decides on the order for performing tasks and develops a timetable for each task. The council members then volunteer to perform each of the tasks as appropriate.

Development of the action plan requires the following six steps:

PROBLEM:		
OBJECTIVE:		
Task	Whose Responsibility	Completed By
1.		
2.		
3.		
4.		
5.		
6.		
7.		
8.		
9.		
10.		

Figure 3.   Format for council action plan.

1. Identify the problem, the degree of impact that change will create, and the priority of the problem.
2. Identify the source or level of the problem.
3. Identify the personnel who can implement the change and take the course of least resistance.
4. Identify the actions or tasks that are required to make the change by taking the course of least resistance.
5. Identify the forces and the strength of the forces both in favor of and in opposition to the change.
6. Identify the timeliness of the change and the probability that it can occur.

Leadership of the interagency council, from the recognition of the need for a council through selection of the members, organizational activities, and group processes to maturity, culminates in the development of action plans. These plans enable the council to achieve its goal of providing a comprehensive array of services to meet the needs of preschool children with disabilities and those at risk, and their families.

REFERENCES

Anderson, S. (1968). Effects of confrontation by high- and low-functioning therapists. *Journal of Counseling Psychology, 15*(5), 411–416.

Bates, M., Johnson, C.D., & Blaker, K.E. (1982). *Group leadership: A manual for group counseling leaders*. Denver, CO: Love Publishing Company.

Blaker, K.E. (1973). Confrontation. In A.M. Mitchell & C.D. Johnson (Eds.), *Therapeutic techniques: Working models for the helping profession*. Fullerton: California Personnel and Guidance Association.

Building interagency teams. (1990). Tallahassee: Florida Department of Education, Bureau of Education for Exceptional Students.

Carnegie, D. (1981). *How to win friends and influence people*. New York: Pocket Books.

Corey, G. (1990). *Theory and practice of group counseling* (3rd ed.). Pacific Grove, CA: Brooks/Cole Publishing Company.

Daniels, W.R. (1986). *Group power: A manager's guide to using meetings*. San Diego: University Associates.

Developing interagency councils. (1989), Tallahassee: Florida Department of Education, Bureau of Education for Exceptional Students.

Ford, D.L. (1975). Nominal group technique: An applied group problem-solving activity. *The 1975 annual handbook for group facilitators*. San Diego University Associates.

Foster, R.E. (1986). *An evaluation report on the state plan grant project to improve pre-kindergarten services to handicapped children in Florida*. Tallahassee: Florida Department of Education, Bureau of Education for Exceptional Students.

Friend, M., & Cook, L. (1992). *Interactions: Collaboration skills for school professionals.* New York, Longman.

Handley, E.E., & Spencer, P.E. (1986). *Decision-making for early services: A team approach.* Elk Grove Village, IL: American Academy of Pediatrics.

Hazel, R., Barber, P.A., Roberts, S., Behr, S.K., Helmstetter, E., & Guess, D. (1988). *A community approach to an integrated service system for children with special needs.* Baltimore: Paul H. Brookes Publishing Co.

Hendricks, W. (1987). *How to handle difficult people.* Workshop materials. Overland Park, KS: National Career Workshop.

Hill, W.F. (1965). *Hill interaction matrix.* Los Angeles: University of Southern California Press.

Mosvick, R.K., & Nelson, R.B. (1987). *We've got to start meeting like this!* Glenview, IL: Scott, Foresman.

Solley, E. L. (1973). Peter-Paul: Getting acquainted. In *The 1973 annual handbook for group facilitators* (pp. 7–8). San Diego, CA: Pfeiffer & Company.

Chapter 8

Initiating a Local Interagency Council

A key advantage of the local interagency coordinating council is a team of agency personnel that addresses the unique characteristics and needs of the immediate community. Such local factors as cultural diversity, family values, languages, community type and size, geography, population and economic demographics, and wealth of resources must be considered in developing the continuum of services.

PRELIMINARY PLANNING

This chapter outlines steps for creating a local interagency coordinating council. Initial steps require precise preliminary planning, knowledge of community resources, and understanding of the impending process. Preliminary planning demands an extensive time commitment, knowledge of the council's mission, and familiarity with community agencies and programs that will have primary roles. An understanding of the existing service delivery system is needed in order to identify and mobilize the agency personnel who can create a more responsive system. If the purposes of the council are clear, the appropriate people to involve and the initial agenda become readily apparent.

The first planning activity occurs when the need for formal interagency collaboration becomes apparent. Preliminary planning for a coordinating council is time-consuming and arduous. Often, preconceived notions, prejudices, and long-standing differences must be overcome before independent agencies can work together. Preliminary planning or preformation activ-

ities are crucial in charting the council's course and in strengthening the relationships among the members (Kagan, Rivera, & Parker, 1991).

The leadership personnel who assume responsibility for the initial planning and creation of a local interagency council must engage in a series of organizational steps. This planning culminates in the organizational meeting and provides a foundation for eventual development of a cohesive working team.

Ten preliminary planning steps are required to organize a local interagency council (*Developing interagency councils,* 1989):

1. Clarify the council's purpose.
2. Identify previous or existing councils.
3. Define the service or local catchment area.
4. Define the target population.
5. Identify the primary providers.
6. Identify potential agency representatives.
7. Select the appropriate invitational method.
8. Plan the organizational meeting.
9. Develop the meeting agenda.
10. Conduct the organizational meeting.

Clarify the Council's Purpose

The reason for the local interagency council must be clear or the organization and agency representation will be muddled from the outset. The council should be envisioned as a working interagency team that is capable of coordinating the respective roles of the community agencies required under the Education of the Handicapped Act Amendments of 1986 (PL 99-457). Many decisions are needed to implement the 14 minimum components of Part H. Interdisciplinary efforts are intended at the point of service delivery; interagency decision making is a special administrative feature of this legislation. One of the most difficult aspects of implementing PL 99-457 is deciding on the responsibilities of the agencies in relation to each aspect of the program. The local interagency council provides a vehicle for making these determinations, coordinating available funding sources, identifying and implementing interagency agreements, enacting contracts and collaborative programs, and determining procedures for resolution of interagency disputes.

The basic function of the local council is to provide an administrative framework for interagency program planning. The council can review existing policy, clarify agency responsibilities, and coordinate direct services to children and families. A primary focus should relate to eliminating duplication of services and resolving existing service gaps.

The council must not become a learning group, awareness group, advisory committee, or task force. These types of groups do not hold direct responsibility for programs but are limited to informational, fact-finding, advisory, and time-limited functions. The design of an interagency council should allow for membership with authority to remedy identified problems on an ongoing basis.

Identify Previous or Existing Councils

It is important to learn if any similar collaborative ventures have been previously attempted in the community. Information about their participants, progress, and outcomes and whether they continue to operate successfully or the reasons for their failure is necessary in planning a new council. Negative past experiences of community agencies may limit the outcome of a new effort at collaboration.

When an existing preschool interagency council is identified, it should be analyzed to determine if it might be expanded, modified, or adapted to meet present purposes. In exploring this possibility, local politics, history of the existing group, and implications for change should be carefully considered.

Before beginning a new interagency council, the leadership must verify that a similar council does not currently exist. The increasing popularity of interagency councils makes them a fashionable goal of every agency. Requirements for participation in interagency councils or for interagency planning often result in an erroneous perception that a categorical program must develop its own council. Such councils usually function merely as advisory committees. The creation of multiple interagency councils can defeat their original purposes if caution is not applied. The interagency council is a strategy to bring a variety of independent categorical programs together. It increases awareness of roles, capabilities, and constraints and creates an effective communication flow to coordinate activities.

The council composition must not be so narrowly focused that it precludes the type of collaboration desired. Councils serving specific age groups, such as birth through 2 years or 3 through 5 years, or those that focus on only one type of service, such as health and medical or drug exposure, reinforce turf guarding among activities and populations and isolate themselves from the remainder of the continuum. For example, an interagency council composed of agencies serving both children with disabilities and high-risk children, birth through 5, under different initiatives and funding sources can coordinate agency roles and avoid needless duplication. Identification of children, evaluation, service delivery, and transition among programs will be enhanced. On the other hand, a council that includes only programs serving medically complex infants and toddlers will be unable to develop workable strategies for serving children outside the scope of the narrowly defined population. It also will be unable to develop referral and placement procedures with other community programs and devise acceptable transition activities. Likewise, a council designed to focus on only high-risk 3- and 4-year-old children is ignoring overlaps among high-risk children and children with disabilities, and fails to realize that these populations are not separate and distinct. High-risk children, by any definition (premature, with a teenage parent, exposed to cocaine, chronically ill, developmentally delayed, with limited English proficiency, in foster care, abused, immature, or at the poverty level), also may have disabilities, and coordination with appropriate service providers is necessary. These examples of narrowly defined councils demonstrate another type of turf guarding by agencies and their intent to remain separate from planning activities with other community programs. Thus, they maintain their isolation and fragmentation that are problematic within the current service delivery system.

Define the Service or Local Catchment Area

The interagency council must coincide with the immediate service or local catchment area, including the primary community programs and services for children and families. The definition of the community and its boundaries determines the agency and program representatives who should participate in the organizational meeting. A final decision about what constitutes the community may be deferred for later consensus of the council.

Catchment areas of the various agencies can be expected to overlap. The school district may serve a single county, city, or township; other agencies, such as children's medical services or human resources, may serve a cluster of counties and result in agency boundaries that do not coincide. For the purposes of the interagency council, the primary or immediate service area must be defined. The council should coordinate ser-

vices that correspond directly to the area in which services are provided. Defining the areas as the immediate service area ensures that the council agenda and discussion topics meet the immediate needs of the council members. This area might correspond to an autonomous administrative unit used by the school district that may be a multicounty educational cooperative, a single city system, a single county system, or a subsection of a large county. However, the immediate service area might correspond to a remote, rural subsection of a large county that differs in population, services, and needs from the county's urban center.

Define the Target Population

To solve the problem of children who have "fallen between the cracks" and to facilitate effective transition between programs, the council should select a broad, rather than a narrowly defined, target population. The population should be sufficiently broad and flexibly defined so that it includes marginal children who otherwise may continue to be overlooked and unserved. If the council is designed as a strategy to achieve interagency coordination and collaboration consistent with the requirements of PL 99-457, the target population must include children from birth through 5 years of age. Particularly in areas where the lead agencies differ for the Part H program and for the preschool program for children 3 through 5 years of age, the council must include the entire age range for effective coordination of services and transition.

The council should also consider the needs of the broad range of children who are disabled, display established conditions, and are at high risk for later disabilities. The presence of overlapping populations within these groups of children served by community agencies is a definite fact. As shown in Figure 1 (Foster, 1987), an overlap in current initiatives exists because apparently discrete categories of children (i.e., with disabilities, disadvantaged, at risk, abused and neglected, developmentally delayed) do

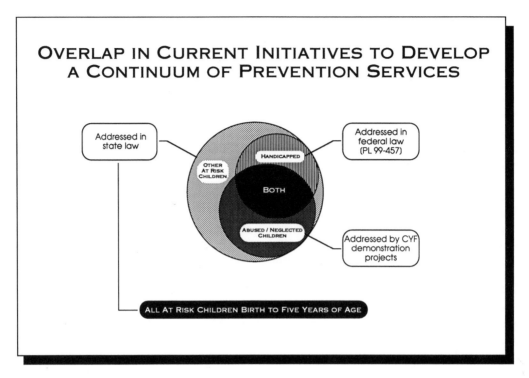

Figure 1. Overlapping populations of children within categorical groups. CYF: Children, Youth, and Families. (From Foster, R. E. [1986]; reprinted by permission.)

not exist in isolation but represent overlapping populations (Foster, 1986). Although the programs and services may change for a child, the need for continuity and appropriate services remains constant.

The target population addressed by the interagency council may be defined as children, birth through 5 years of age, who require early intervention services as a result of the presence of a disability, developmental delay, or a diagnosed physical or mental condition with a high probability of developmental delay. This target population includes children served by the various early intervention programs and is not so excessively narrow as to exclude children who do not meet precise categorical definitions.

Identify the Primary Providers

Council membership must include the primary providers of services to the target population so that the council can achieve its mission. It must include the scope of agency

programs providing primary education and therapeutic medical, social, and parent support services. The primary agencies and programs vary according to the type of community, its size and location, and other demographic characteristics, but they generally include the local school district, human resources department or health and rehabilitative services, Easter Seal Society, The Arc, United Cerebral Palsy, Head Start, Migrant Head Start, mental health services, children's medical services or crippled children's bureau, public health department, rural health clinics, neonatal intensive care centers, hospitals, speech and hearing clinics, university clinics, subsidized child care, and department of children, youth, and families.

The local interagency council should comprise agencies that represent various points the service continuum, such as full- and part-time special education programs, integrated settings, therapy, home-based programs, mainstreaming opportunities, consultative services, and parent training or support services. Agencies should be included that provide medical services, social and economic services, and such related services as transportation and specialized equipment. Other services, including respite care and home nursing services, are required for the families of children who are medically complex or fragile. These services are often some of the most difficult to access and should not be overlooked in creating the interagency team.

The agency programs selected to participate on the council should:

Hold primary responsibility for serving preschool children with disabilities and those at risk in the community.
Provide direct services (educational, therapeutic, medical, social, and parent support) to children and families.
Provide necessary related services.
Have the potential to provide problem-solving or service coordination strategies in the development of a complete continuum of community services.

The group should be relatively small and manageable because productivity and success are directly proportional to the working relationships and trust that develop among members. The primary programs and providers responsible for serving the preschool population must form the local council as they have the most to contribute to the effort (Ferrini, Matthews, Foster, & Workman, 1980) and the greatest motivation to participate.

An attempt to include all community agency programs serving preschool children and families will make the council unwieldy and counterproductive. A council consisting of 10–12 members facilitates open discussion, group cohesion, and effective problem solving. A total of eight members plus the coordinator is considered ideal (Ferrini et al., 1980). In groups larger than 12 members, it is difficult to encourage the interaction, consensus building, and change process required by an effective interagency council. Community agencies and foundations, such as the March of Dimes, Epilepsy Foundation, Multiple Sclerosis Association, American Red Cross, and League of Women Voters, that do not provide direct services, are not appropriate for membership. These organizations do not have the responsibility of providing direct services to children with disabilities and those at high risk, but informal networking with them can provide information and financial support for later council activities and for individual children and families.

It is easier to add agencies later than to exclude agencies after initial council development. Member turnover and replacement occurs naturally as the council matures. This refinement of the group's membership creates a smaller, more stable team as the interagency council matures (Foster, 1986).

Identify Potential Agency Representatives

After key agencies have been identified, the personnel who can best represent those agencies on the council must be selected. This step deserves careful planning. Membership alone can determine a council's success. A checklist to identify potential interagency council members is shown in Figure 2.

Agency representatives must possess: 1) decision-making authority and skill, 2) authority to commit resources, 3) understanding of preschool services and programs, 4) belief in shared decision making, and 5) willingness to commit the time required for the collaborative process (*Developing interagency councils,* 1989; Ferrini et al., 1980; Magrab, Elder, Kazuk, Pelosi, & Wiegerink, 1982; Olsen, 1983).

The nature of the collaborative effort depends on the trust and positive working relationships developed within the interagency team. These attributes result in a supportive network that influences the productivity of the group. The magical mix of the right personnel and personalities cannot

Selection of Council Members	Yes	No
Does the individual represent an agency that holds a primary responsibility for disabled or at-risk children under 5 and their families?	____	____
Does the individual have authority to speak on behalf of the agency, explain its criteria and policies, and clarify its contributions?	____	____
Does the individual have the authority to create changes in his program?	____	____
Does the individual have sufficiently close proximity to children and families to be aware of direct service issues? Problems? Potential solutions?	____	____
Will the individual be willing and able to commit the time required to attend monthly council meetings?	____	____
Does the individual have expertise in administration of services or programs to children under 5?	____	____
Does the individual have an understanding of the problems and gaps in the service system?	____	____
Will the individual be able to acknowledge problems in his or her own agency services so that changes can be proposed, discussed, and implemented?	____	____
Will the individual be open to compromise, negotiation, and changes in current procedures?	____	____
Does the individual believe in interagency collaboration?	____	____
Does the individual enjoy working with other agency personnel in problem-solving activities?	____	____
Is the individual capable of developing the trust and working relationships necessary for genuine collaboration?	____	____
Is the individual a risk taker, enthusiastic about new ideas, and open to change and innovation?	____	____
Does the individual have formal agency authority to engage in information exchange without violating confidentiality?	____	____
Is the individual capable of developing effective team skills?	____	____
Will the individual abide and promote the decisions made by group consensus even though they may not be his or her own?	____	____

Figure 2.   Checklist to identify potential interagency council members.

be underestimated. The ability of the team to engage in the necessary disclosure, negotiation, discussion, problem solving, and consensus building depends largely on these factors.

Interagency council members must believe in the mutual support of agencies; be flexible, open to change, task oriented, and sensitive to the needs and limitations of other agencies; and demonstrate effective group process and problem-solving skills. They must be able to work and interact as team players who provide an informal network to combine resources creatively and neutralize the constraints that often restrict the flow of services to children and families.

A council environment characterized by positive, cooperative attitudes enhances collaborative efforts. The effective local interagency council member is an exceptional person. Unfortunately, not every agency staff member displays the enthusiasm, the belief system, and team skills required for this interagency effort. Council members should never be selected at random.

Personnel who are negative, pessimistic, resistant to change, or unable to work in shared decision-making situations should be avoided. They represent significant barriers to a healthy collaborative process. Agency personnel with no administrative or policy-making authority also should be avoided. A council's ability to engage in necessary problem solving or policy revision is impaired with nonauthority figures. Representatives should not be selected solely on their willingness to participate because they may not have the necessary skills or authority. Furthermore, an appointed representative who is unwilling to serve does not demonstrate the same commitment as members who are enthusiastic about participation. The unwilling representative often shows poor meeting attendance and failure to engage in collaborative group undertakings.

Select the Appropriate Invitational Method

The manner of invitation to an organizational meeting can significantly influence the turnout, attitude of the participants, and expectations for the meeting. Politics, personalities, social dynamics, rules of formality, and chain of command differ widely across communities and agencies. The person who presents the invitation, as well as the manner in which it is done, may be critical to the outcome (Magrab et al., 1982). A history of agency feuds, mistrust, or past deceptions may have negative implications. The organizing agency and personnel will receive the most favorable response if they are perceived as sincere, credible, and operating in the best interests of children and families. The purpose of the meeting must be communicated clearly and with the understanding that no individual agency will receive advantages at the expense of others.

A personal invitation, made by telephone or visit, is always preferable when arranging a strategic event. Personal contact reinforces a spirit of shared decision making and trust that must develop within an interagency council. It allows the organizer to communicate the purpose of the meeting, discuss implications, secure input in planning, and generate enthusiasm for the group's poten-

tial. Personal contact is a critical part of preliminary planning and the beginning of trust and mutual commitment.

The agency chain of command must not be overlooked in the invitational process. Any offense may be counterproductive to emerging relationships. Some agencies require an agency head to request attendance of an employee through a formal letter of invitation. Other agencies are more informal. Council organizers must be sensitive to the issue of protocol. In contacting agencies that depend heavily on structure, formality, and protocol, the council organizers must be particularly adept and savvy. A danger might exist if the agency head is intent on appointing an undesirable staff member to the proposed council. Such situations demand creative strategies and careful planning to ensure that the most appropriate member is ultimately selected.

A letter should follow the personal invitation to confirm the date, time, and location of the organizational meeting. A sample letter of invitation is shown in Figure 3.

Plan the Organizational Meeting

The organizational meeting of the council sets the tone for establishing cooperative working relationships among agency personnel. A low-key, nonthreatening approach should be taken, particularly if there is a history of interagency competition or disputes. At the same time, an enthusiastic and positive tone should be conveyed, along with a sense of the meeting's importance.

A convenient day and time, scheduled mutually with the participants, should be established. The representatives can be asked to suggest times and dates when they are initially contacted. The meeting is confirmed by a written notice. It may be advisable to schedule the meeting at an early morning hour. This permits busy administrators to go directly to the council meeting and can prevent situations involving unexpected office activities or extended meetings that prevent them from getting to the meeting. The time of day should ensure maxi-

Delores Foster
Early Intervention Center
112 Pine Street
First City, Florida   34210

Betty Day, Nursing Supervisor
Health Department
555 Elm Street
First City, Florida   34219

Dear Betty:

I enjoyed our conversation this past week relative to initiation of a preschool interagency council in our county. We have all realized long ago that a systematic and continuous means of coordinating our agency programs and services has been needed. The "interagency council model" would appear to be the best way for us to improve our understanding of the agency services, identify existing capabilities, improve communication and information exchange, eliminate duplication of effort, fill our service gaps, and streamline our procedures for the benefit of the children and families we serve.

I have spoken to representatives from the main agencies serving children with disabilities birth to 5 years old and they are also excited about this organizational meeting. We have confirmed Tuesday September 8 at 8:15 A.M. for the meeting. We will be meeting in the second floor conference room at Children's Medical Services, County Memorial Hospital, 112 Oak Street.

I have attached a list of the agency representatives who will attend. Our agenda will include introductions and brief statements about the main focus of the various agencies. Don't worry about bringing brochures or handouts to this meeting—we will discuss agency services in detail after this first meeting. Our purpose will be to secure the commitment of the agencies to participate and to discuss organizational matters such as a regular meeting time and day. Stephanie Jones, Coordinator of the Cork County Interagency Council, will be the focus of the agenda. She will describe their experiences and accomplishments in the area of interagency collaboration and give us information to guide us in our efforts.

I'm excited about this new venture and looking forward to working with you. See you on September 8!

Most sincerely,

Delores Foster

Figure 3.   Sample letter of invitation to an organizational meeting. (Used with Permission of the Florida Department of Education, Bureau of Education for Exceptional Students, from *Developing interagency councils*, [1989], pp. 49–50)

mum attention, alertness, and lack of conflict with other obligations (Magrab et al., 1982).

The tone of the organizational meeting indicates that the interagency team is an important task-oriented planning group, rather than a social group. Luncheon or dinner meetings should be avoided. Handling food can be distracting and is incompatible with the demands of a work session. Serving coffee or cold drinks creates a relaxing and friendly environment but does not interfere with the task. Evening and weekend meetings also should be avoided. Interagency activities must be regarded as administrative/leadership functions, not extracurricular in nature.

The site for the organizational meeting should be convenient, centrally located, and easy to find. A restaurant should not be used. Neutral nonthreatening territory may be advisable for the organizational meeting.

The meeting site should contain a suitable conference room that comfortably seats the participants. The room should be pleasant, well lighted, and properly ventilated. Representatives should be seated so that they face one another in fairly close proximity, such as at a large conference table or two rectangular tables pushed together to create a larger table. Excessive distance between people and awkward seating arrangements (e.g., chairs placed in a circle or child-sized chairs) should be avoided. A comfortable, dignified, and friendly environment is necessary for a successful meeting.

Develop the Meeting Agenda

The agenda and a list of participants should be sent to all participants one week prior to the scheduled meeting. Providing early confirmation of the meeting is an important courtesy to the participants and maximizes attendance. Providing an agenda, as shown in Figure 4, reassures them of the meeting's purpose and content so they may prepare accordingly.

The organizational meeting provides the important first impression of the proposed interagency council. The group process that occurs during this first meeting is critical. This meeting should permit the agency representatives to become acquainted, gain an understanding of their roles and the advantages of interagency collaboration, and determine the level of commitment to the new council.

An external consultant or speaker knowledgeable about local interagency councils is a wise program strategy for this meeting. An impartial, neutral, and objective speaker does not pose a threat to any local agencies. Materials and examples provided by the outside party can assist the participants in understanding the role of the council and the potential outcomes to agencies, children, and families.

Conduct the Organizational Meeting

Careful preliminary planning for this first meeting establishes the foundation for uniting agency representatives into a cohesive team to coordinate existing services and eliminate service gaps. The meeting agenda may vary

---

MEETING AGENDA
3/15/91

8:15 A.M.   1.   Welcome and Introductions

      1.1 Opening comments and introduction of speaker: Shirley Roberts, Coordinator, Stranton County Interagency Council

      1.2 Purpose of meeting

8:30 A.M.   2.   Introduction of Meeting Participants

      2.1 Self-introduction by name, title, agency, or program

      2.2 Brief (1–2 minutes) summary of agency program, target population, criteria, and purpose

8:45 A.M.   3.   Presentation on Local Interagency Councils

      3.1 "Do you need to collaborate?" activity

      3.2 Background on interagency councils

      3.3 Purpose and organization of councils

9:15 A.M.   4.   Where Do We Go From Here?

      4.1 Agency interest and commitment

      4.2 Next meeting? Day? Time? Place?

9:45 A.M.   5.   Summary and Thanks

Figure 4. Sample organizational meeting agenda.

depending on the existing familiarity of personnel. In some areas, it is possible that agency personnel have never met; in others, informal networks and cooperative working relationships may have been long established. Distribution of the agenda prior to the meeting reduces anxieties about participation.

A 10-minute period for representatives to get coffee, circulate, and exchange conversation should be planned prior to the meeting. Name badges facilitate introductions between agency personnel who have spoken to each other by telephone but have never actually met. This initial "mixer" time should not be lengthy or the meeting may appear disorganized. The organizer should be sensitive to structured, task-oriented, and time-conscious representatives who believe that meetings should begin promptly as scheduled and who are offended by apparently wasted time.

The first agenda item should be a brief welcome by the organizer or facilitator and an expression of appreciation for the interest and time of those who have attended. The organizer should clearly state the purpose of the meeting and explain the role of the agency or personnel who assumed responsibility for the meeting. The facilitative role of the organizing group should be defined as a means of bringing together interested agency personnel for the mutual concern of developing strategies to improve and coordinate services for preschool children with disabilities (Magrab et al., 1982). It must not appear that the organizing agency has more to gain from collaboration than the other agencies.

The second agenda item is the introduction of agency personnel. Participants can be asked to introduce themselves and briefly state their positions and the functions of their agencies.

The third agenda item should include an explanation of interagency collaboration, its benefits, and the concept of an interagency council. The policy and legislative basis for interagency collaboration should be described with the aid of handouts. It is often advisable to ask a member of an existing interagency council in another district to give this talk. The speaker can explain the need for collaboration between and among agencies, the goals and functions of an interagency council, and the beneficial results. A speaker from outside the area offers several advantages. He or she can provide evidence of the value of the endeavor, remove suspicion that the organizing agency has more to gain than other agencies, and make impartial responses to objections and questions that might put local personnel in a difficult situation.

Following the presentation, the agency representatives must decide how to proceed. The group should elect the most convenient time and day for the next meeting and indicate commitment to the task of establishing an interagency council. The group should also determine the meeting site. If sites are rotated during the first year, a brief tour immediately before or after the meeting will acquaint everyone with the staff, facilities, and programs of each host agency.

Before adjournment, the organizer should describe how the group has already begun to work together at its first meeting, restate the council's mission, and confirm that a better understanding of each agency's potential contributions has been established. The participants can leave with a new sense of perspective and a vision of the problem-solving process to come.

REFERENCES

Developing interagency councils. (1989). Tallahassee: Florida Department of Education, Bureau of Education for Exceptional Students.

Ferrini, P., Matthews, B.L., Foster, J., & Workman, J. (1980). *The interdependent community: Collabora-* tive planning for handicapped youth. Cambridge, MA: Technical Education Research Centers.

Foster, R.E. (1986). *An evaluation report on the state plan grant project to improve pre-kindergarten services to handicapped children in Florida.* Tallahassee: Florida Department of Education, Bureau of Education for Exceptional Students.

Foster, R.E. (1987). *A pre-planning guide for implementing PL 99-457*. Tallahassee: O'Neall & Associates (A workbook prepared for the Bureau of Education for Exceptional Students, Florida Department of Education).

Kagan, S.L., Rivera, A.M., & Parker, F.L. (1991). *Collaborations in action: Reshaping services to young children and their families* (Executive Summary). Yale University: The Bush Center in Child Development and Social Policy.

Magrab, P., Elder, J., Kazuk, E., Pelosi, J., & Wiegerink, P. (1982). *Developing the community team*. American Association of University Affiliated Programs. (Prepared for Department of Health, Education, and Welfare, Interagency Task Force, under Grant #54-P-71476/3-02).

Olsen, K.R. (1983). *Obtaining related services through local interagency collaboration*. Lexington, Kentucky: Mid-South Regional Resource Center. Report funded by the Office of Special Education and Rehabilitative Services, Washington, DC (Report #300-80-0722) (ED 239-439).

Section III

Council Activities and Outcomes

Local interagency councils may choose from a varied array of potential activities. These activities may be determined by: 1) the stage of development of the interagency council, 2) program activities specific to the time of the year (e.g., transition activities), and 3) periodic fluctuations and changes in agencies, programs, and resources. There is no mix of activities that guarantees success. Rather, the council will be engaged on a continuing basis in determining priorities, building consensus, and selecting activities.

The earliest activities will be organizational and informational, characterized by cooperation (see Chapter 3). Efforts become increasingly sophisticated as the council matures into a cohesive team. Cooperation gives way to eventual adjustments in agency services and procedures and the next stage of services, coordination, begins to emerge. The emphasis then switches from an informational and agency focus to a child and family focus, and the group coordinates roles for the well-being of the child. As complex collaborative activities eventually emerge, they are based on trust and cohesive working relationships. Activities and objectives change with time and the increased problem-solving capability of the council.

Some activities are sequential; others occur simultaneously. The local interagency council, however, must identify short-term objectives that will lead to the overall goal of the council: serving all identified children by having a full continuum of community services. Table 1 provides an overview of the types of activities that councils may consider.

Achieving desired outcomes depends on the appropriate composition of the council and the skill of the council coordinator in motivating and guiding the group (see chap. 6, this volume). The coordinator must be knowledgeable about administration and leadership of preschool programs through direct involvement with service provision. Without an intimate understanding of the problems and constraints that must be overcome and the problem-solving process, the coordinator can be faced with substantial limitations in guiding the group. The role of the coordinator, particularly in the initial stages of council development, is critical to a task-oriented approach. Lacking a task-oriented direction, the council may falter as members are required to redirect their time, energy, and attention to more immediate problems in their daily schedules. Management-level personnel do not have time to waste on unproductive meetings.

The interagency team must define clear, appropriate, and obtainable goals. If the council composition includes administrators and program coordinators, policy and service delivery issues can be enhanced and council activities can be focused on the needs of both the children and the agencies.

Table 1. A menu of sample interagency activities and outcomes

Area	Activities and outcomes
Information Exchange	Improve awareness and understanding of agencies.
	Improve understanding of eligibility and procedures.
	Facilitate communication exchange.
	Clarify definitions and terminology.
	Share information about funding sources.
	Eliminate unnecessary duplication of services.
	Facilitate exchange of records/reports.
	Develop a standardized release of information form.
	Develop uniform IEP/IFSP forms across agencies.
	Disseminate computerized mailing labels for agencies.
	Coordinate IEP/IFSP planning.
	Provide for exchange and updates of information at council meetings.
	Identify primary contact people within agency programs.
Public Awareness	Educate parents and medical community about early identification.
	Increase public awareness of availability of services.
	Develop brochures explaining community early intervention services.
	Conduct mailing campaigns to physicians, preschools, hospitals, and parent groups.
	Compile a directory of services to provide to parents, physicians, and agencies.
	Speak to parent groups about child development.
	Promote parent awareness of the need for early intervention services.
Screening and Identification	Identify existing sources of screening and evaluation.
	Develop coordinated community-wide system for identification.
	Develop a collaborative program for screening children in conjunction with local health providers.
	Promote parent awareness of the need for early identification services.
	Educate private physicians about the availability of services.
	Coordinate screening programs and ensure referral of children to appropriate agency programs.
	Develop standards for assessment.
	Promote understanding of agency evaluation criteria and standards.
	Develop reciprocity regarding evaluation reports across agencies to avoid duplication.
	Establish qualification for evaluation of personnel.
	Develop a multidisciplinary team composed of personnel from various agencies.
Case Management	Develop a standard release of information form to facilitate exchange of information.
	Define the roles and responsibilities of the community programs.
	Develop an effective child-tracking system.
	Develop community-wide IEP/IFSP procedures.
	Develop coordinated case management procedures.

(continued)

Table 1. (*continued*)

Area	Activities and outcomes
Case Management (*continued*)	Develop a case conference procedure for monthly council meetings to discuss problem cases.
Child Find and Referral	Identify a single point of entry into the system.
	Develop effective referral procedures.
	Develop standard referral procedures among agencies.
	Coordinate mailing and public awareness campaigns for child-find efforts.
	Expand and coordinate child find activities.
	Develop a systematic procedure for referring children to programs.
	Share agency forms (referral, consent, release) to facilitate referrals.
	Identify contact people in various agency programs.
	Share agency brochures and written information.
	Update program information regarding program slots, waiting lists, program expansion, or cutbacks that require adjustments to referral or transition activities.
Transition	Develop transition activities for both children and parents.
	Develop county-wide timelines, guidelines, and procedures to transition children smoothly across programs.
	Use child tracking system to project transition needs.
Service Delivery	Complete a matrix of existing services and programs to identify available services.
	Define the roles and responsibilities of the community agencies with respect to educational, therapeutic, medical, parent, and social services, by age, exceptionality, or geographical area.
	Identify gaps in service delivery systems.
	Identify and eliminate sources of unnecessary duplication of efforts by rechanneling resources.
	Fill service gaps through program expansions, contracting, or collaborative programs.
	Coordinate scheduling of IEP, IFSP, and Service Plans across agencies.
	Use contracts and agreements to upgrade programs, create modification, or facilitate expansion.
	Influence policy makers for program improvements, modification, and/or expansion.
	Coordinate program standards and case management procedures.
	Formulate contracts and written agreements.
	Develop interagency transportation services.
	Share resources (staff, expertise, facilities).
	Explore sharing of physical space and facilities.
	Co-locate programs.
Parent Involvement	Identify existing parent training, education, and support services.
	Develop and expand parent support services.
	Compile parent guides and brochures.
	Coordinate parent education activities across agencies.
	Develop a continuum of parent services.
	Eliminate unnecessary duplication of effort.

(*continued*)

Table 1.   (*continued*)

Area	Activities and outcomes
Parent Involvement (*continued*)	Develop a directory or listing of available parent groups, target populations, meeting times and places, and activities.
	Identify a lead agency for parent services.
	Develop a compilation of parent-lending libraries for maximum utilization.
Staff Development	Establish a network to share staff expertise.
	Coordinate training and inservice opportunities.
	Identify available consultants and professional expertise.
	Share training materials.
	Conduct an interagency needs assessment.
	Designate a lead agency for inservice and personnel development.
	Coordinate inservice/personnel development activities across agencies.
	Assist nonpublic agencies in meeting certification standards.
Program Evaluation	Develop a child tracking and data collection system to document expansion of services through interagency council efforts.
	Develop procedures (e.g., surveys or questionnaires) to evaluate interagency efforts.
	Document the effectiveness of case management strategies.
	Continue operation in an effective manner as judged by other agencies and those being served.
	Document increased numbers of students with disabilities and those at risk, and their families being served.
	Survey parents and families.
	Complete the continuum of services.
	Establish standards to measure interagency outcomes and to report to relevant audiences.

Chapter 9

Organizational and Procedural Activities

Local council activities are related to the council's stage of development (see chap. 5, this volume). Stage 1 is the cooperation stage; early activities relate to council formation and organization, procedures, general information sharing, confidentiality, agency awareness, and an increased understanding of the community system of services. At stage 1 a council functions as a learning or awareness group while it establishes a base for later problem resolution.

Stage 1 activities also include analysis of the existing service delivery system, development of a thorough understanding of existing services and programs, and identification of the gaps and problems in the service delivery system. When the local council has a thorough knowledge of the capabilities of the individual agencies, the available funding sources, and the existing gaps and problems, it can move toward coordination and collaboration strategies to solve identified problems.

ORGANIZATION

The first three to five meetings of a local interagency council focus on orientation of members and development of a formal operating style. Members become acquainted, determine the initial structure of the group, arrive at a consensus on the purpose of the council, establish a guiding philosophy, and develop tentative operating procedures. Table 1 contains the organizational activities in stage 1. The focus of the group in these early meetings is on the formal operating

structure (Foster, 1986), and members often maintain a guarded, cautious approach. As members establish their places in the group, identify the expectations guiding their relationships with others, and examine the existing continuum of services, they may gain their first insight into the capabilities and roles of the community agencies.

Because the council's purpose may be ambiguous at this early stage, the leadership role of the organizer is critical to success. Agency representatives form an impression of the group's potential value during organizational meetings. When strong leadership suggests the likelihood of effective results, agency representatives are more willing to commit their time, energy, and effort. If initial meetings are disorganized, loosely structured, or favor one agency at the expense of others, representatives may be skeptical and unwilling to participate.

Table 1. Organizational activities in stage 1

Clarify the need for collaboration.

Establish consensus on basic premises for collaboration.

Develop a mission statement and purpose.

Develop a written philosophy and statement of beliefs.

Establish organizational procedures, including:
1. Specified meeting day and time
2. Frequency and length of meetings
3. Meeting locations
4. Council composition
5. Meeting notice and agenda
6. Minutes and written records
7. Role and responsibilities of the coordinator
8. Selection of the council coordinator

ANALYSIS OF
EXISTING SERVICES

After the organizational and housekeeping issues have been tentatively resolved, the focus of the emerging interagency team switches to analysis of available community services.

Need for Local Collaboration

Figure 1 in Chapter 2 called "Do You Need To Collaborate?" is useful as a handout during the organizational meeting of a new council. Participant responses on the handout can identify the presence of a positive climate for collaboration as well as review examples of the purposes of a local interagency council. The handout, also a helpful motivational tool, is designed to spark participant enthusiasm for interagency capabilities.

Specific Barriers Within
the Service Delivery System

Using a systematic group process technique, such as a brainstorming activity (Daniels,

1986) shown in Figure 1 or the nominal group process (Ford, 1975) shown in Figure 2, council members can identify the conditions, problems, and constraints existing in the local service delivery system that currently prevent the provision of a comprehensive array of needed services. When the problems and constraints are identified, the group should rank them in priority order. This ranking can be used to develop activities and outcomes for the council's efforts.

Basic Premises
of Interagency Collaboration

Interagency collaboration requires a dramatic change in the manner in which agencies plan, function, and work with one another. Council members may agree with the basic concepts of collaboration, but discussion of the basic premises as in Chapter 2 of this volume, including specific examples, is needed to clarify how agency perceptions and roles change as collaborative efforts are attempted. For example, agency personnel

---

When To Use:

1. When a large quantity of information and ideas are needed prior to problem solving, decision making, or planning
2. When there is a need to inspire creativity in the group thought process
3. When there is a need to stimulate participation by some shy or quiet members
4. With practical, solution-oriented problems rather than complex, value-laden questions

Materials Needed:

1. Flip chart
2. Markers

How To Use:

1. The group leader states the question or the subject about which a variety of alternatives or ideas are desired. For example: What are the local factors or barriers that interfere with provision of comprehensive services to infants, toddlers, and preschool children with disabilities? A time span, such as 5 minutes, is allotted.
2. Members of the group generate as many ideas as possible, placing emphasis on quantity—getting everyone talking as rapidly as possible to generate a large volume. As rapidly as the ideas are stated, the leader or recorder writes them on the chart. More than one recorder working simultaneously may be needed. All ideas are accepted. There is no discussion, critique, evaluation, judgment, or criticism of ideas in any way. Creativity is impaired with criticism.
3. When the period of brainstorming has ended, the group evaluates the volume of ideas generated. The members clarify, order, evaluate, and identify the ideas they think are more worthy of further elaboration and exploration.

Figure 1.   Directions for a brainstorming activity. (Reprinted from William R. Daniels, *Group power: A manager's guide to using meetings,* San Diego, CA: Pfeiffer & Company, 1986. Used with permission. Brainstorming was introduced in *Applied imagination: Principles and procedures of creative problem solving* [3rd Rev. Ed.] [p. 417] by A.F. Osborn, 1963, New York: Scribner.)

When To Use:

1. To ensure that group members thoroughly understand a problem before working on it
2. When group members are failing to engage in independent thinking and are simply reacting to one or two members' ideas
3. When participation in the group's task has become unbalanced or has been reduced into an argument among two or three members. This process can be used to restore the group's norm state of equal participation and can broaden the information base
4. When there is sufficient time to utilize this time-consuming process and the leader is skilled in its use
5. When it is important to bring the group to consensus about the relative importance of several aspects of the problem or solution in a rapid manner

Materials Needed:

1. Pencils for all group members
2. Paper or notepads for all group members
3. Flip chart
4. Markers

How To Use:

1. The group leader provides one question or the statement of the problem. Members individually write their perceptions of the problem within a designated time frame. Specific questions such as the following may be used but only one question can be presented at a time. Examples are:
    What are the obstacles to providing a full continuum of services for children with disabilities, birth through 5, in our community?
    What are the obstacles to implementing a child tracking program, birth through 5 years of age?
    What must our agencies do to eliminate the duplication of assessment that exists?
2. Members silently generate ideas during a specified time frame (usually 5 minutes) and write them on paper or a note card.
3. Members then verbally state one idea at a time, going in round-robin fashion around the table. The process must be carefully paced. A recorder writes the ideas, in the participant's own words, on the flip chart. Or, the note cards can be taped on the wall. While each member reports, no evaluation or elaboration is permitted.
4. The coordinator reads each item from the list and asks for clarification or questions from the group. The intent is to clarify ideas. Duplicate items may be eliminated at this point.
5. Each group member is asked to list a specified number of top priority items and rank them in order of importance. For example, the group may be asked to identify the eight most important items, placing them in rank order. It is best to identify between five and nine items in ranked order as research on human information processing indicates that sorting and ranking becomes more difficult among the nine-item limit (Mosvick & Nelson, 1987).
6. Members anonymously vote on preferred choices, by indicating their ranking. The ballots are then collected and tabulated.
7. The group discusses the preliminary vote. Patterns are discussed along with points of disagreement. If there are extreme discrepancies, the group should discuss the variance to determine if it has been caused by misinformation or lack of clarification.
8. A final vote is taken using the rankings.
9. The group states the final result by providing a summary of the problem. Next, the group will be ready to proceed to use one of a number of problem-solving procedures.

Figure 2. Directions for use of the nominal group process. (Based on "A Group Process Model for Problem Identification and Program Planning," by A.L. Debecq and A.H. Van de Ven, 1971, *Journal of Applied Behavioral Science, 7*, pp. 466–492, and on "Nominal Group Technique: An Applied Group Problem-Solving Activity," by D.L. Ford, Jr., in *The 1975 annual handbook for group facilitators* [pp. 35–36] by J.E. Jones and J.W. Pfeiffer [Eds.], 1975, San Diego, CA: Pfeiffer & Company. Reprinted from William R. Daniels, *Group power: A manager's guide to using meetings,* San Diego, CA: Pfeiffer & Company, 1986. Used with permission.)

should understand the procedures and strategies for eliminating agency competition and turf guarding. Implications exist for referral of children to other agencies, elimination of waiting lists, and mutual planning of programs. Simply attending meetings of the local interagency council does not constitute collaboration. True collaboration results in such outcomes as realignment of roles and responsibilities and shared decision making.

DEFINITION OF COUNCIL PHILOSOPHY

Mission and Purpose

Every organization needs a mission. The absence of an organizational mission or vision means there is no sense of direction or unity. An interagency council without a mission is a council without a plan.

A mission is the first step in strategic

planning by an organization, regardless of its type, size, and structure. Externally, the mission communicates the goal of the group to the community, the agencies, and the families who are served. It should be a clear, precise, dynamic statement that enables council members to focus their efforts. The mission is a logical starting point for determining short-term objectives, and it becomes the foundation on which to base the council's priorities, strategies, plans, and activities.

Council members must agree on a long-range, general goal, or mission, to guide their efforts and to maintain an emphasis on direct services to children and families. A clear "sense of mission" is an important, cohesive, and motivating factor. An example of a mission statement is:

To develop a complete continuum of services (medical, therapeutic, social, educational, and family) within the community to ensure that ap-propriate services are available to every pre-school child with disabilities or at high risk and his or her family.

The first component in a mission statement is the purpose of the organization. It describes the direction in which the group plans to go. To assist in clarifying and reinforcing the reason for the local interagency council and to begin the task of developing a cohesive interagency team, the purpose and long-term outcomes can be discussed and stated in written form. Figure 3 contains a sample of an interagency statement of purpose.

Philosophy and Beliefs

The second component consists of the organization's purpose and guiding principles. The purpose states the goal or direction of the group. The guiding principles state the philosophy, values, beliefs, best practices, convictions, and ethics held by the group.

Preschool Interagency Council
Statement of Purpose

To create a working interagency team of administrative personnel dedicated to the coordination, improvement, and expansion of needed services across the various categorical programs

To develop a comprehensive, coordinated system of services for all children with disabilities and those at risk, birth through 5 years, and their families

To align and define the respective roles and responsibilities of each agency with regard to the provision of services to children with disabilities and those at risk birth through 5 years, and their families

To promote effective interagency program planning and problem solving among all agencies within the community in the development of a complete continuum of services

To create a "community service delivery system" designed to facilitate easy access to services by families as opposed to an assortment of independent, isolated, and parallel programs

To promote mutual understanding of all agencies, including purpose, organization, services, eligibility criteria, policy and procedures, funding mechanism, and constraints

To eliminate unnecessary duplication of services among agency programs to maximize efficient expenditure of available funds

To synchronize federal, state, and local budgets and grant funds in order to maximize revenue, increase services, and eliminate gaps in the service delivery system

To create collaborative efforts in the identification, evaluation, referral, and initiation of services of children

To develop a formal, interagency child tracking system designed to ensure the delivery of services and avoid children becoming "lost" in the system

To create collaborative efforts and sharing of resources for program, staff development, and parent support activities

To increase awareness in the community of the importance of early intervention and the availability of existing programs and services

---

Figure 3.   Sample statement of purpose for an interagency council.

To reinforce the purpose of the group, council members should develop a philosophy statement—shown in Figure 4, a set of beliefs and values—shown in Figure 5, a council brochure, or some other form of written statement. The discussion and consensus building required to adopt such a written statement enhance the group process, create a cohesive effect, and mobilize efforts around a specified focus.

Beliefs of interagency group members usually differ to the degree that they need to discuss openly and achieve consensus on values and philosophy. Some councils composed of agency personnel with similar histories and values may achieve consensus immediately and painlessly. Other councils may have representatives with vastly different backgrounds and beliefs. Considerable discussion and compromise may be needed in order to agree on expectations, purpose of the group, members' respective roles in the process, direction, and procedures.

OPERATING PROCEDURES

As the interagency team forms, members must identify the council's operating procedures. Discussion during the council's organizational meeting generates some pref-

---

Preschool Interagency Council
Philosophy and Mission Statement

The purpose of the Council is development of a comprehensive, coordinated system of services for children with disabilities and those at high risk, birth through 5 years, and their families. Efforts will include ongoing planning, problem solving, and collaboration designed to improve and expand services, ensuring that all children and families have equal access to needed services.

Whereas we recognize the unique needs of young children with disabilities and those at high risk and their families, we believe that early intervention should be comprehensive, interdisciplinary, and holistic in order to meet a child's physical, developmental, emotional, and social needs. The interdisciplinary team approach is endorsed to encourage the collaborative process among professionals and parents who facilitate the child's development.

Whereas we recognize that young children must be viewed in the context of the family, we believe the parent must be an equal partner in assessment, determining the provision of services, and evaluating the appropriateness of the plan. The family must maintain a sense of dignity and control over the child's life and the decisions that are made. The primary service coordinator shall work closely with the family to ensure well-coordinated services and proper implementation of the plan.

Whereas we recognize that families have unique characteristics and cultural differences, we believe that services should be individualized, based on need, and based on equal access without regard to socioeconomic status, place of residence, diagnosis, or the family's ability to pay.

Whereas we recognize that early intervention services should encourage patterns of normal development, prevent conditions from becoming more debilitating, and decrease family stress, we believe that services should be provided at the time the need is identified rather than being determined by availability of resources.

Whereas we recognize that children with disabilities and those at high risk should be in the least restrictive setting, we believe that services should be in the most normal setting whenever possible and in special settings only to the extent necessary.

Whereas we recognize that agency resources are often limited and fluctuating, we believe that agencies have a responsibility to refer children and families to other agencies in the event that they are unable to provide them immediately. Providing the most appropriate services is important—which agency provides them is not.

Whereas we believe that no single agency, program, provider, or funding source has the capability to meet all of the needs of young children with disabilities and those at high risk, and their families, we believe that funding is a shared responsibility of agencies.

This set of beliefs is designed to provide guidance and direction for a responsive system of services provided by early intervention programs in this county. These beliefs will serve to guide interagency planning to ensure comprehensive, high quality services to young children and families in need.

Figure 4. Sample philosophy statement for an interagency council.

Preschool Interagency Council
Beliefs About Services to Preschool Children Who Have Disabilities

Development and expansion of services should be based upon a guiding philosophy and set of beliefs about those factors that result in quality services. In the provision of services to very young children, we believe:

Young children with disabilities or those at risk of later disabilities should be in typical settings whenever possible and in special services and special settings only to the extent necessary.

The least restrictive environment for very young children is the home, with the family, with a baby-sitter, in a childcare center, or in those settings where typical infants may be found. Every effort should be made to provide needed services in the most typical setting, within the context of the family, and with consideration of social/cultural values.

Coordination of agency services (medical, social services, educational, childcare, referral, parent education) is essential and in the best interests of the child and family.

No single agency, program, provider, or funding source has the capability to meet all the needs of a young child with disabilities and his family. Funding is a shared responsibility.

The role of agencies is to help families—not judge them.

Each child should have a designated case coordinator to coordinate the roles and services of agencies. The case coordinator may change over time but should be within the agency, program, or profession most relevant to the child's current needs.

The parent is an equal partner in determining provision of services and respective responsibilities. Active family participation is needed in assessing the child's needs, designing a service plan, and evaluating the appropriateness of the plan.

The parent and family must maintain a sense of dignity and control over their child's life and the decisions that are made for intervention.

While every child with disabilities has the right to a free, appropriate public education, families have choices in service options and may select a private provider.

Emphasis should be placed on actual "services" needed rather than simple placement in a "program" or being an "active" case.

Planning for services should be based on individual needs, not on the availability of resources. Agencies have a responsibility to recommend the most appropriate services and to refer to other agencies when they are unable to provide them.

Planning and services must consider the whole child rather than specific needs in a fragmented manner. Likewise, the child must be seen in the context of the family.

Providing the most appropriate services is important—which agency provides them is not.

Services should be tailored to the needs of the child and family, not to preconceived program designs or convenience.

An integrated therapy model rather than "pull-out" services is most appropriate for preschool children.

Assessment must be interdisciplinary and based on a solid understanding of child development rather than isolated test scores.

Services to families should be designed to foster problem solving and independence, rather than dependence on the service delivery system or case manager. A primary goal is to empower families with the skills they need to facilitate maximum development in their child.

Figure 5. Sample statement of beliefs about services.

erences regarding potential meeting date, time, location, and length. Tentative meeting plans can be made, although they may be changed within the first few months as schedules adjust, membership stabilizes, and time considerations become clear.

Discussion and consensus are needed regarding other organizational issues, such as agenda development, written records, meeting minutes, leadership, and council composition. For the newly organized council, planning and organizing activities represent safe and early opportunities for an increasingly complex interactional process. These activities permit the council members to maintain a safe and acceptable distance until working relationships, communication skills, trust, and cohesiveness begin to form and the foundation for future collaborative efforts is established.

Operating procedures may be informal and by verbal agreement. Written council guidelines may be developed if a more formal organization is desired or if the council is the result of a mandate or requirement (see the appendix at the end of this chapter for sample procedural guidelines). If agency personnel are overly cautious about the role of the council and legal issues, the initial use of informal procedures may be wise. The group may display a greater willingness to commit to written, formal procedures after trust and cohesion have developed.

Meeting Schedule and Agenda

Regular monthly meetings should be scheduled with a specified date and time. The first few meetings allow members to become acquainted, develop understanding of the other agencies and programs, initiate effective working relationships, establish trust and mutual respect, and create a common goal and vision for children within the community. More frequent meetings may be needed in the initial stages of council development and later when critical issues arise. Meetings held bimonthly or quarterly do not allow sufficient time to develop as a group, identify problems, and generate feasible solutions.

Procedures for meeting locations must be determined. Rotation among agency sites offers repeated opportunities for members to become familiar with services, programs, and personnel. It also serves to create good will and increase mutual respect.

The meeting agenda should be the re-

sponsibility of the council coordinator. It is based on the outcomes of the previous month's meeting and council input. If the group identifies agenda items, continuity across meetings and cooperation in reaching goals and objectives in an effective and timely manner are enhanced. An agenda distributed in advance with the meeting notice is helpful to members in their preparation and participation. Without this planning, the meeting is more likely to be rambling and unproductive. Group members should follow the agenda and keep the meeting on task.

Minutes

The manner of maintaining minutes of each council meeting must be determined. Writing, typing, and distributing detailed minutes require time, concentration, skill, secretarial assistance, and copying and mailing resources. If any of these are not available, an alternative may be needed, perhaps only on a temporary basis. Council members could be responsible for writing their own mintues. Although an informal means of keeping minutes, this method may result in a better understanding of the information and meeting proceedings by the members. A standard form for meeting minutes and meeting notes, as shown in Figure 6, can be developed for the council.

If greater formality and printed minutes are desired, the coordinator should be responsible for their completion and distribution. A member who is skilled at keeping minutes may be willing to provide a copy of his or her notes after the meeting. The coordinator can then summarize the information and have the summary typed and distributed. If the effort is exerted to print and disseminate the meeting minutes, they should contain the actual specifics of information discussed so that they may be used in a functional manner. Minutes should be regarded as a communication and coordination strategy and not an independent activity. Most importantly, the minutes should list the recommendations and specific as-

```
┌─────────────────────────────────────────────────────────────────────┐
│                    Preschool Interagency Council                      │
│                         Meeting Minutes                               │
│                                                                       │
│   Location: _____    Date: _____          │
│                                                                       │
│   Attending:                           Not in attendance:             │
│                                                                       │
│                                                                       │
│                                                                       │
│   New agency information shared:                                      │
│                                                                       │
│                                                                       │
│                                                                       │
│                                                                       │
│   ─────────────────────────────────────────────────────────────      │
│                                                                       │
│   Agenda issue 1                       Action to be taken             │
│                                                                       │
│                                                                       │
│   Agenda issue 2                       Action to be taken             │
│                                                                       │
│                                                                       │
│   Agenda issue 3                       Action to be taken             │
│                                                                       │
│   ─ ─ ─ ─ ─ ─ ─ ─ ─ ─ ─ ─ ─ ─ ─ ─ ─ ─ ─ ─ ─ ─ ─                     │
│                                                                       │
│   Case conferences:                                                   │
│   Child                    Issues                      Action         │
│   1                                                                   │
│                                                                       │
│   2                                                                   │
│                                                                       │
│   3                                                                   │
│                                                                       │
│   4                                                                   │
│                                                                       │
│   Follow-up for which I am responsible:                               │
│   1. _____            │
│   2. _____            │
│   3. _____            │
│   4. _____            │
│   Next month's meeting:                                               │
│   Date:          Time:         Location:                              │
│   Materials needed:                                                   │
│                                                                       │
└─────────────────────────────────────────────────────────────────────┘
```

Figure 6. Sample form for recording council minutes and meeting notes. (The information above the dashed line would be included on the front of this form; the information below the dashed line would be included on the back.) (Used with Permission of the Florida Department of Education, Bureau of Education for Exceptional Students, from *Building interagency teams,* [1990], pp. 83–84)

signments relative to any children discussed without violating confidentiality. The council coordinator should follow up on recommendations made during the meeting, as well as ensure that the contents are used to achieve continuity in the development of the next agenda.

Rotating the responsibility of keeping minutes among members may not be successful and it may even result in friction and feelings of guilt or embarrassment. The coordinator should make every effort to prevent these possibilities so that the emotional energies of the interagency team are channeled into discussion and problem solving, rather than routine housekeeping tasks.

Interagency Council Stationery

Separate letterhead stationery for use by the council: 1) provides identity as a separate group, 2) develops cohesion of the members, and 3) confirms equality of the member agencies. The name of the council is formalized and assists in confirming the nature of the group as an independent coalition of member agencies. Under no circumstances must one agency be perceived to have ownership. A sample letterhead is shown in Figure 7.

Composition of the Council

Composition of the council is a critical issue. Each primary agency program must have one staff member designated to attend meetings on a consistent basis. A written list of the names, addresses, and telephone numbers of council members should be created and updated as necessary. Procedures should emphasize that the council is not an open group. Rather, members are designated to represent their agencies and to hold clear authority and responsibility.

Council Coordinator

The role and responsibilities of the council coordinator should be identified. They generally include the overall guidance and organization of the interagency team. The coordinator must ensure that members are

allowed to operate on an equal footing, are free of burdensome paperwork or documentation, and are able to devote energy to positive problem solving. Specific responsibilities for the mechanics of operation and arrangements for meetings include:

Making final arrangements for monthly meetings
Distributing meeting notices and tentative agendas
Preparing written material and information for meetings
Distributing copies of information as needed
Maintaining an updated membership list
Facilitating the monthly meetings
Providing updates on local, state, and federal issues and important developments
Finalizing and distributing meeting minutes
Orienting new members to the council
Maintaining the interagency child tracking system

Often, the initial organizer of a local interagency council is a person who serves as an agency liaison and works with a variety of agencies and programs. This person might be a program supervisor, a social worker, a child find specialist, or a service coordinator who is instrumental in bringing together agency personnel for the purpose of linking children to services. The organizer may effectively serve this initial purpose but may not possess the understanding of program administration or the skills needed to serve as council coordinator on a permanent basis. Within the first year of council activity, the leadership role may shift to a strong, objective, and effective leader who will be a critical ingredient of collaborative success (Kagan, Rivera, & Parker, 1991).

Kagan, Lonow, and Levin (1989) found that leadership sharing may happen informally, but usually one individual is recognized as the primary possessor of power and authority in a collaboration. This leader tends to be a seasoned professional who guides the collaboration's work with vision, passion, and knowledge. The study raised some questions about the use of a shared leader-

Scott County Preschool Interagency Council

522 22nd St. SW
P.O. Box 429
Scottsburg, FL 34264
813-776-2226

Memorial Hospital
Speech Pathology Department

Children's Center

Children's Medical Services

Easter Seals Society

Child Find

Developmental Disabilities

Specialized Family Services

Parent Training Program

Head Start

Health Department

County School District

Mental Health Center, Inc.
Child and Family Services

Parent to Parent

Migrant Services Preschool Center

Serving Young Children with Special Needs

Figure 7.   Sample stationery for an interagency council.

ship model, such as a rotational model where leadership changes among agencies each year.

In situations where the council coordinator changes periodically, lack of continuity and instability of the group are likely. A temporary coordinator lacks long-term investment, accountability, and motivation to produce. Rotating the responsibility for coordinating the interagency council may appear to be a strategy for fairness and coping with the time demands of the role, but it may prove to be a significant disadvantage in the long run (*Developing interagency councils,* 1989).

REFERENCES

Building interagency teams, (1990). Tallahassee: Florida Department of Education, Bureau for the Education of Exceptional Students.

Daniels, W.R. (1986). *Group power: A manager's guide to using meetings.* San Diego: University Associates.

Developing interagency councils. (1989). Tallahassee: Florida Department of Education, Bureau of Education for Exceptional Students.

Ford, D.L. (1975). Nominal group technique: An applied group problem-solving activity. In *The 1975 annual handbook for group facilitators,* San Diego: University Associates.

Foster, R.E. (1986). *An evaluation report on the state plan grant project to improve pre-kindergarten services to handicapped children in Florida.* Tallahassee: Florida Department of Education, Bureau of Education for Exceptional Students.

Kagan, S.L., Lonow, D., & Levin, J. (1989). *Study of early care and education collaborations in three states.* Unpublished manuscript. Yale University: The Bush Center in Child Development and Social Policy.

Kagan, S.L., Rivera, A.M., & Parker, F.L. (1991). *Collaborations in action: Reshaping services to young children and their families* (Executive Summary). Yale University: The Bush Center in Child Development and Social Policy.

Mosvick, R.K., & Nelson, R.B. (1987). *We've got to start meeting like this!* Glenview, IL: Scott, Foresman.

Sample Procedural Guidelines
for a Preschool Interagency Council

MISSION

The mission of the council is to develop a comprehensive and coordinated array of community services to ensure that all children with disabilities and those at high risk, birth through 5 years, and their families, receive appropriate early intervention regardless of their residence or ability to pay.

The council is dedicated to ongoing collaboration among agencies for planning and financing of needed services. It serves as a master planning group of program administrators who work internally and collaboratively to coordinate budgets, program expansion, delivery of services, and grant development. The council is committed to elimination of unnecessary duplication, fragmentation of services, and agency competition that are detrimental to a healthy and responsive service delivery system.

AUTHORITY

1. The council exists under the requirements in the Education of the Handicapped Act Amendments of 1986 (PL 99-457) for interagency collaboration in the delivery of services.
2. The council is an independent coalition of agency representatives, participating on a voluntary and equal basis. No single agency claims ownership of the council or greater benefit.

ORGANIZATION

1. The council operates as an independent coalition of agency representatives, functioning as equal members with respect to the concept of shared decision making. To reinforce this collaborative effort, the organization will not be characterized by officers or a traditional "top-down" hierarchical structure.
2. The council will be facilitated by a coordinator whose role is to provide a vision and guidance for the interagency team, maintain necessary written records, and handle routine organizational tasks.

MEMBERSHIP

1. Membership of the council will consist of a maximum of 15 agencies considered to be the primary providers for educational, medical, therapeutic, parent, and social services to children (birth through 5 years) and their families in the community. Member agencies must provide direct services to children or families.
2. Each participation agency will designate one staff member who will consistently attend all meetings of the council. The representative shall be a program administrator, coordinator, supervisor, or in a position to represent the program both with respect to policy and direct services.

MEETINGS

1. Meetings will be held at 8:00 A.M. on the second Thursday of every month. Members will designate this time on their calendar, and avoid scheduling conflicting meetings.
2. Meeting locations will be rotated among the member agency sites as appropriate. Location will be decided on a month-by-month basis and determined by need, coordination with other meetings or events, or by noteworthy circumstances (new facility, new program, new staff members, special events, etc.).
3. The council coordinator shall be responsible to confirm monthly meetings (date, time, location)

with the members in advance. Members will be notified of case conferences to be conducted (unserved children; complicated cases) so that appropriate preparation can be done. Children to be discussed should be called to the attention of the council coordinator at least 4 days prior to the meeting to permit sufficient advance notice to all the members.

4. A written agenda will be provided for each regular meeting. The agenda will be revised accordingly at the outset of each meeting.

5. The council coordinator will be responsible for the development of the agenda, based upon the outcome and recommendations of the previous meeting. Each agenda will include time for: 1) agency updates, 2) ongoing activities and projects, 3) case coordination, and 4) recommendations for the next meeting.

6. Informal minutes of the meetings will be maintained by each council member. Dissemination of formal, written minutes following the meeting will be the responsibility of the council coordinator who will be assisted by a note-taker for maximum accuracy and thoroughness.

7. Special or emergency meetings may be called as needed, scheduled mutually with the members by telephone to ensure maximum participation. These meetings may be for the purpose of assisting with grant development, transition planning, legislative issues, or other planning matters that have immediate deadlines or are too extensive for inclusion on the regular agenda.

ROLE OF THE COORDINATOR

1. The council coordinator shall be designated by general consensus of the membership. The coordinator shall be selected based upon expertise in administration of preschool services for children with disabilities, knowledge of group process, understanding of the mission of the council, and the ability to provide strong and objective leadership to guide the group toward its goals.

2. The council coordinator shall provide stability and continuity of leadership for the group; no rotational process will be used.

3. The council coordinator shall be responsible for the overall guidance and direction, including routine and paperwork tasks that facilitate operation of the group. Responsibilities include:

    Making final arrangements for monthly meetings
    Sending out the meeting notice and tentative agenda
    Preparing written material and information for meetings
    Facilitating the monthly meetings
    Distributing information and copies as needed to members
    Maintaining an updated copy of the membership list
    Providing updates on local, state, and federal issues and important developments
    Finalizing and distributing meeting minutes
    Orienting new members to the council
    Facilitating informal networking
    Assisting committees as needed
    Ensuring use of the interagency release form
    Monitoring the interagency child tracking system
    Facilitating case conferences on unserved children

Chapter 10

Information-Sharing Activities

One of the first tasks of a newly established interagency council during stage 1 is to open the lines of communication and facilitate exchange of information among the agencies. (Various information-sharing activities are shown in Table 1.) Agency representatives have the opportunity to communicate with their counterparts, gain an understanding of the abilities and constraints of other programs, and see the roles of their own agencies with a perspective that includes the roles of others. They begin to realize that each program is only a part of the community service delivery system for young children and families. Often, this is the first, sometimes painful, step in the transition to a view of the entire system and the role of each agency within it. This awareness confirms the importance of working with others.

Information sharing is essential for interagency understanding. Discussion among council members about the roles, responsibilities, procedures, capabilities, and constraints of each agency can resolve long-established misconceptions that have interfered with the ability to work together effectively (Morgan & Swan, 1988).

The local interagency council establishes a network of people who work both informally and through the formal structure of the council. As council members become acquainted, they develop valuable contacts and sources of information and assistance. When questions or problems arise, they know whom to ask for assistance and support. Council members quickly learn how to use this valuable network to solve everyday service delivery problems.

Information-sharing activities of council

Table 1. Information-sharing activities

Exchange agency information
Explain program procedures
Explain eligibility criteria
Explain funding sources
Identify contact people
Explain terminology and definitions
Share agency literature and brochures
Develop interagency form for release of records
Develop procedures for records exchange
Develop directory of services
Share newsletters and mailing lists
Visit various agencies and programs

members include descriptions of each agency's programs, procedures, terminology, and eligibility criteria; exchange of information and printed material; and development of a monthly update procedure and interagency release form.

AGENCY PROGRAMS AND PROCEDURES

Along with the development of the council's operational procedures during the first stage, members should learn about other community agencies and programs. The first three or four council meeting agendas can include time for designated members to provide detailed presentations about the services their agencies provide for preschool children with disabilities and those at high risk and their families. An example of a council meeting agenda is shown in Figure 1. Agency profiles should include a description of the agency program, location, contact persons, services, delivery models, availability, target population, special con-

```
┌──────────────────────────────────────────┐
│          Preschool Interagency Council     │
│               Meeting Agenda               │
│                  10/21/91                  │
│                 UCP Center                 │
│                                            │
│ 8:00 A.M.  1.  Welcome and introduction of │
│                guest: Dr. Norma Smith, Di- │
│                rector, United Cerebral Palsy│
│                Center                      │
│                                            │
│                Brief tour of UCP facility  │
│                                            │
│ 8:30 A.M.  2.  Interagency council procedures│
│                2.1  Formulation of philoso-│
│                     phy and mission state- │
│                     ment                   │
│                2.2  Completion of state-   │
│                     ment of purpose        │
│                2.3  Determination of month-│
│                     ly meeting date        │
│                                            │
│ 9:30 A.M.  3.  Agency presentations        │
│                3.1  United Cerebral Palsy  │
│                3.2  Developmental disabili- │
│                     ties parent training pro-│
│                     gram                   │
│                3.3  School district early in-│
│                     tervention program     │
│                                            │
│ 10:00 A.M. 4.  Next meeting                │
│                4.1  Date and time?         │
│                4.2  Agency site?           │
│                4.3  Agenda items           │
└──────────────────────────────────────────┘
```

Figure 1. Sample council agenda in stage 1 activities.

siderations, and program priorities. An example of an agency profile is shown in Figure 2. Referral, placement, and dismissal procedures and timelines should be clarified.

TERMINOLOGY AND DEFINITIONS

Misunderstanding often occurs among agencies as a result of a lack of knowledge of terms, definitions, labels, program requirements, grant constraints, funding and budget levels, chain of command, and procedures. Council members must share information in order to learn how other agencies function, to understand their capabilities and limitations, and to engage in problem solving.

Agencies tend to differ in terminology, and it is helpful for the council to identify troublesome terms and discuss their respective meanings. Definitions may be written in formal policy or kept informal. The terms include disabilities, at risk, high risk, eligible, case manager, screening, evaluation, assessment, evaluator, psychological evaluation, individualized education program (IEP), individualized family service plan (IFSP), treatment plan, school day, application for services, certification, placement, staffing, parent involvement, and dismissal or termination of services. This discussion guarantees more accurate communication and relates directly to policy issues.

ELIGIBILITY CRITERIA

Eligibility criteria differ across agency programs. The various criteria represent a strength, rather than a problem. The problem occurs only when agency personnel are not familiar with different eligibility criteria (e.g., age, income, category), and the results are inappropriate referrals, confusion, or inability to gain access to services. The differences in eligibility criteria provide for flexibility in placement—a child ineligible under a program with strict categorical criteria may be eligible for other community programs that do not require these labels. It is important for members to know the agency programs that have income eligibility criteria and those that do not. Fee schedules, including sliding scale fee structures and adjusted fees, should be carefully understood to ensure appropriate referrals.

EXCHANGE OF INFORMATION AND PRINTED MATERIAL

Personnel across preschool agencies receive different information, newsletters, publications, and conference notices. Communications from state offices and policymakers are routed to regional offices and finally to local district personnel. Rarely is agency information communicated to other agencies in

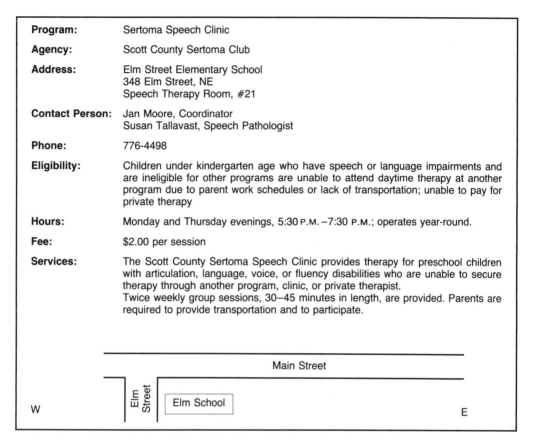

Program:	Sertoma Speech Clinic
Agency:	Scott County Sertoma Club
Address:	Elm Street Elementary School 348 Elm Street, NE Speech Therapy Room, #21
Contact Person:	Jan Moore, Coordinator Susan Tallavast, Speech Pathologist
Phone:	776-4498
Eligibility:	Children under kindergarten age who have speech or language impairments and are ineligible for other programs are unable to attend daytime therapy at another program due to parent work schedules or lack of transportation; unable to pay for private therapy
Hours:	Monday and Thursday evenings, 5:30 P.M.–7:30 P.M.; operates year-round.
Fee:	$2.00 per session
Services:	The Scott County Sertoma Speech Clinic provides therapy for preschool children with articulation, language, voice, or fluency disabilities who are unable to secure therapy through another program, clinic, or private therapist. Twice weekly group sessions, 30–45 minutes in length, are provided. Parents are required to provide transportation and to participate.

Figure 2. Sample profile for agency presentations.

a systematic manner. The local interagency council allows such information to be exchanged and cross-training to be conducted.

Brochures, fact sheets, and other printed materials are often distributed by council members during agency presentations. Each member should compile a notebook that contains helpful information for future reference, including maps, directions, and forms required by the various agencies. The notebook should be updated periodically.

To encourage council members to exchange information, particularly concerning conferences, national initiatives, legislation, and other items of mutual interest, sets of mailing labels may be printed and disseminated. With the use of these labels, each council member can more easily send copies of notices to the other members. Another method of information exchange is designation of the council coordinator or an agency representative who has access to clerical and mailing services to distribute all notices as they are provided by council members. The intent is to identify the best systematic and functional procedure for sharing this information.

MONTHLY UPDATE PROCEDURE

Agencies and programs constantly change. Funding levels, staff members, agency services, rules, and procedures fluctuate and adapt to new situations. As members gain a general understanding of procedures, roles, responsibilities, services, and abilities of each agency during council discussions, they must realize that the ability of each agency to meet its goals and provide services is continually affected by change. This is demonstrated by the agency update portion of the sample council meeting minutes, as shown in Figure 3, and the following examples:

An agency may be temporarily unable to provide physical therapy services while the therapist is on a 3- to 6-month maternity leave.

An agency may be temporarily unable to provide speech therapy services until it fills a vacant position.

An agency may be temporarily unable to purchase equipment that it normally provides until the new fiscal year or budget period begins.

A child with an atypical condition and abnormally high medical costs may temporarily deplete the budget for a local agency, such as children's medical services, which results in a delay or cut in other services, such as occupational, physical, and speech therapy, until the new budget period.

Because classrooms or program slots are at capacity, the program may be unable to serve more children until there is space.

Planned expansion of a program or construction of a new facility may be delayed, and placement of children may be postponed for an indefinite period.

Newly approved rules or procedures or a change in program philosophy may modify eligibility or services.

Statewide funding cutbacks may decrease or eliminate local programs.

State-level changes in program priorities or focus may result in program changes at the local level.

Grant funds may be lost or secured, which may result in termination or creation of services.

Personnel changes (e.g., administrators, teachers, therapists) may affect direct service capabilities.

When such situations occur within agencies, other agencies must adapt to maintain the balance in community services. Changes may be temporary or permanent, but compensatory action is needed when one program expands or becomes unable to provide certain services. In the case of the agency that is unable to provide physical therapy services while a staff member is on maternity leave, the referring agencies must be aware of this fact and not refer children and families during that time. If such a referral is made, the parent wastes time and energy in applying to an agency that cannot provide the service, the child may be placed on a waiting list for an indefinite period of time, and a time gap in service delivery needlessly occurs.

Regular updates on the status of services must be done at the community level. Recent statewide attempts to develop computerized information and referral services have received widespread interest and funding. The weakness of a computerized service, particularly at the state level, is its inability to account for continual program changes and fluctuations. Data entry is time-consuming and cannot adjust for daily or weekly changes in staff or resources. Referrals may be made in anticipation of services that an agency generally provides but are not readily available at the time. Furthermore, central information and referral services are not sensitive to unique personnel capabilities, specialties, and limitations. An agency program may report provision of physical therapy, for example, but not have a pediatric therapist. People working together on local interagency councils can better accommodate these situations.

INTERAGENCY RELEASE-OF-INFORMATION FORM

An essential outcome at this stage of council development is the use of an interagency release-of-information form, shown in Figure 4, that replaces existing agency-specific forms for the preschool population. Because the local interagency council coordinates services and agency roles, parental permission must be obtained to avoid violation of confidentiality. An interagency authoriza-

PRESCHOOL INTERAGENCY COUNCIL
Meeting Minutes
6-20-92

IN ATTENDANCE:

Jan Moore, School District
Cindy Smith, Child Find Specialist
Joan Weber, County Public Health Unit
Allison Roth, Children's Medical Services
Eddie Jones, Parent Training Program
Bob Bracken, Easter Seal Society
Mary Week, Preschool Migrant Program
Sally Payne, Parent to Parent

I   AGENCY UPDATES and INFORMATION SHARING

Joan Weber, Public Health Unit, reported on the new weekly staffing procedures at the County Hospital NICU that plan for newborn infants. Joan, and other Health Department nurses, will attend and link families to community services upon the infants' discharge (i.e., referral to Infant & Toddler Office, Parent to Parent, CMS, community programs, economic services, evaluation services). Sally Payne, Parent to Parent, will prepare packets of information that can be provided in the discharge packet.

Allison Roth, Children's Medical Services, distributed guidelines for state Medicaid changes allowing reimbursement for case management, skilled nursing care, equipment, occupational therapy, physical therapy, speech therapy. This result provides funding for early intervention services for children under 5 previously ineligible. Agencies should consider applying for Medicaid provider status. Bob Bracken reported that funding for therapy is at a higher level than the state funds generated by the school district.

Sally Payne, President and Referral Coordinator, described priorities and activities of Parent to Parent. New referrals should be made to her at 776-0035. Sally distributed copies of a brochure, a newly developed membership form, and a schedule for this year's parent groups. She encouraged wide distribution to all interested parents. Fourteen parents have been trained to provide workshops, including information on the IFSP, emotional needs of families, and development of communication skills to parents and professionals. Call Sally to schedule training.

Jan Moore reported that a competitive state grant would be available in October, funding innovative practices for case management and multiple disciplinary evaluation. She suggested the Council begin to draft content and prepare for submission of an application.

Human Resources has a vacant Parent Training position. Master's level early childhood or mentally handicapped certification is preferred. Refer applicants to Sandy Straight in the regional office until filled. Twelve families are not receiving these services.

Mary Week reported that funding for the preschool migrant program has been significantly reduced. Some services will be reduced or cut, particularly the home-based program for disabled infants. Referrals should be made to other agencies until further notice.

Bob Bracken introduced Hope Sullivan, the new case manager at the Easter Seal Society. Hope will be contacting each member to schedule a visit to each agency.

Jan Moore reported that new preschool classrooms for 3- and 4-year-old children at risk are being added at the following schools: Elm Street, Willow, and Spruce Elementary. Spruce Elementary will be "extended day," from 7:00 A.M. until 6:30 P.M. Ample space is currently available; refer children now.

Figure 3.   Excerpt from sample agenda showing agency updates.

```
AUTHORIZATION FOR RELEASE OF RECORDS

                                      Child's Name _____

                                      Birthdate: _____

I hereby authorize the following persons, agencies, programs, and/or the Scott County Preschool Inter-
agency Council to engage in verbal or written communication for my child. All pertinent records and
information can be released between agencies as necessary. I am aware that this information will be
strictly confidential and will be used in my child's best interest in order to plan and provide the best
program of early intervention services. I am aware that many agencies and programs will be working
cooperatively to provide my child's program, and that effective interagency communication between
them is essential.

I am also aware that I may deny consent for disclosure to any of the agencies or programs designated
below. The agencies and programs authorized to exchange information include:

Infant & Toddler Program, Interagency Intake        Child Find
Health & Human Resources                            Children & Adult Center, Inc.
Scott County School System                          Easter Seal Society
Developmental Disabilities (DD)                      Shadowbrook Child & Family Center
Children's Medical Services (CMS)                    Scott County Memorial Hospital
Scott County Public Health Unit                      Doctor's Hospital
Parent to Parent of Scott County                     Migrant Head Start Program
Other: _____                        Subsidized Child Care
Other: _____                        United Cerebral Palsy (UCP)

The following records may be exchanged:

_____Hearing Screening or Evaluation               _____Communication/Speech-Language
_____Vision Screening or Evaluation                _____Cognitive Development
_____Physical/Health/Medical                        _____Motor Development
_____Social/Emotional                               _____Social Work Assessment
_____Self-Help/Adaptive Behavior                    _____Family Assessment
_____Other: _____

This authorization includes release of information concerning HIV testing or treatment of AIDS, AIDS-
related conditions, drug or alcohol abuse, drug-related conditions, alcoholism, medications, and/or psy-
chiatric or psychological conditions.

Information will NOT be disclosed to any other party except personnel with a legitimate interest without
prior written consent of the parent or legal guardian. Both federal and state regulations require that you
be informed of your rights regarding assessment of your child and family. Those rights are described
for you in the attached form entitled "Procedural Safeguards." Please read this form carefully and ask
for an explanation of any part you may not understand.

I give consent for the agencies and programs listed to share information for the purpose of coordinating
services for my child. I understand my rights.


_____                      _____
Signature of Parent/Guardian                          Date of Consent

Attachment: Procedural Safeguards
```

Figure 4.   Sample interagency release-of-information form. (Adapted with Permission of the Florida Department of Education, Bureau of Education for Exceptional Students, from *Interagency problem solving,* [1990], p. 59)

tion for release of information is required for council members to: 1) engage in specific case coordination activities of children and families during council meetings, 2) facilitate the critical exchange of written reports and information, 3) eliminate exces- sive time delays during transmission of information, and 4) develop an interagency child tracking system (see chap. 14).

Potential violation of confidentiality appears to be one of the reasons most often cited by agencies trying to avoid interagency collaboration. It is essential that a procedure for sharing both written and verbal information be developed early in the council's development. The release form permits council discussion and coordination of complicated cases involving four or more community agencies (*Interagency problem solving,* 1989). The representatives can eliminate confusion; establish consensus on the most appropriate alternative courses of action; identify and eliminate duplication of services; distribute financial responsibility; and coordinate medical, educational, and therapy services. Most importantly, decisions and recommendations can be implemented in a short time frame without weeks of telephone calls and follow-up discussions with numerous agency personnel.

Because the interagency release form facilitates transmission of written records, two of the most common frustrations—difficulty and delay—encountered in securing records are avoided. Agency personnel, often with a need to "do things right," may create unnecessary demands on other agency personnel when records are requested. Release of records is often denied unless the agency's own release form is used, despite the fact that the requesting agency's form meets the same content criteria but looks different. Agency frustration is compounded by the greater frustration felt by parents when services needed by their child are delayed.

An interagency release-of-information form must contain at least the following four elements:

1. The member agencies, by name, that will exchange verbal and written information
2. Conformity with all requirements of the agencies
3. Blank spaces for the addition of other agencies or professionals from whom information specific to each child may be requested or sent
4. A means for the parent to deny authorization to any of the agencies listed if they so choose

The form must be implemented by adoption into the procedures of all participating preschool agencies. It should become part of the standard intake or application process and replace existing agency forms. After the release form has been implemented, the council should periodically verify its continued use. Personnel turnover, modifications in application or enrollment procedures, and changes in agency representation on the council make it necessary to ascertain that the form continues to be understood and appropriately used.

REFERENCES

Interagency problem solving. (1989). Tallahassee: Florida Department of Education, Bureau of Education for Exceptional Students.

Morgan, J.L., & Swan, W.W. (1988). *Local interagency councils for preschool handicapped programs: An effective strategy to implement the mandate.* Bloomington: Indiana University, Council for Administrators of Special Education, Inc. (CASE) (A Division of the Council for Exceptional Children).

Chapter 11

Analysis of the Existing Service Delivery System

Information sharing, a relatively basic task, dominates early interagency activities as the council functions like a learning or awareness group. This task is a mandatory initial step, but information sharing cannot remain the main purpose of the council. By about the fifth meeting, organizational and procedural issues have been tentatively resolved and members have a general overview of community agency programs. Trust among council members increases the comfort level and enables them to analyze the system critically and confront issues. The focus shifts to the needs of children and families who are unserved or underserved—the real reason for the council's existence. Later stage 1 activities include a more detailed analysis of agency information, existing resources, and constraints so that service delivery gaps can be remedied. Members initiate the complex process of developing a complete array of community services and recognize that a large number of service delivery options, both public and private, are necessary.

During the latter part of stage 1 in the council's development, members perform four primary functions: 1) analyze the existing service delivery system, 2) identify duplication and gaps in services, 3) identify the groups of children unserved or underserved, and 4) identify policy and procedural barriers. Council meetings are used for program updates, funding, and personnel changes so that the agency knowledge base remains current and accurate. The updating process is an ongoing, routine activity.

Activities relating to the identification and analysis of eight potential problem areas in the service delivery system are instrumental in laying the foundation of the council and establishing the rapport and trust necessary for the collaboration that will take place in stages 2 and 3. These activities focus on stabilization of the group, establishment of purpose and operating procedures, information sharing, procedures for exchange of records in accordance with confidentiality requirements, and an understanding of the current service delivery model. By the end of stage 1, council members will clearly identify the gaps in services. Trust and working relationships are developed to allow for interagency problem solving as the focus begins to shift to children and families.

EXISTING SERVICES

Brief agency presentations during the first three to five council meetings include an overview of existing services but do not provide an in-depth analysis of total services. This initial information eliminates misconceptions about programs and, more importantly, represents the beginning of a critical analysis of the current community service delivery system. At this stage, members continue to refine and internalize their knowledge by working closely with one another.

Council members should consider at least the following 13 parameters in their examination of existing services:

1. Types and variety of available services
2. Ages of children served

SERVICES	SCHOOL DIST.		DEVELOP. DISABIL.		UCP		ARC		EASTER SEALS		HEAD START	
	B-2	3-5	B-2	3-5	B-2	3-5	B-2	3-5	B-2	3-5	B-2	3-5
SOCIAL/DEVELOPMENTAL HISTORY												
FAMILY ASSESSMENT												
DEVELOPMENTAL SCREENING												
HEARING SCREENING												
VISION SCREENING												
MULTIDISCIPLINARY TEAM												
PSYCHOLOGICAL EVALUATION												
OT EVALUATION												
PT EVALUATION												
SPEECH/LANG. EVALUATION												
AUDIOLOGICAL EVALUATION												
VISION ASSESSMENT												
MEDICAL EVALUATION												
SERVICE COORDINATION												
IFSP/IEP												
SPECIAL EDUC. CLASSROOM												
INTEGRATED SETTING												
HOME-BASED PROGRAM												
OCCUPATIONAL THERAPY												
PHYSICAL THERAPY												
SPEECH/LANG. THERAPY												
VISION SERVICES												
TRANSPORTATION												
PARENT TRAINING												
PARENT COUNSELING/THERAPY												
PARENT SUPPORT GROUP												
PARENT LIBRARY/LOAN												
MEDICAL SERVICES												
DENTAL SERVICES												
SPECIALIZED EQUIPMENT												
CHILD CARE												
RESPITE CARE												
BEHAVIOR SPECIALIST												
NURSING SERVICES												
MEDICAID												
OTHER												

Figure 1. Community agency services matrix. (Adapted with Permission of the Florida Department of Education, Bureau of Education for Exceptional Students, from *Interagency problem solving*, [1989], p. 21)

3. Geographic distribution of services
4. Accessibility of services
5. Cost of services and funding options
6. Consistency of services with cultural values
7. Program times, hours of operation, and calendar year
8. Agency beliefs and philosophy
9. Provision of transportation
10. Time delays for service initiation

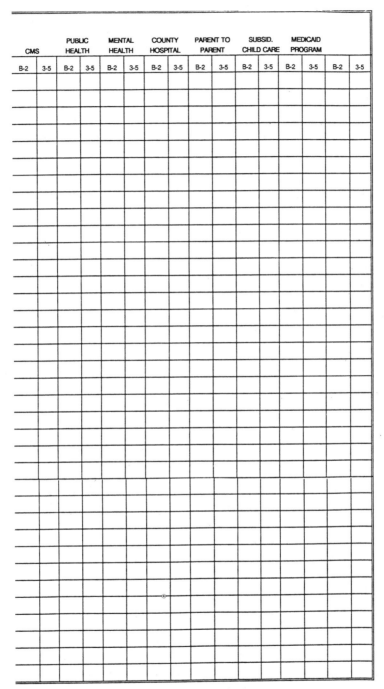

		PUBLIC HEALTH		MENTAL HEALTH		COUNTY HOSPITAL		PARENT TO PARENT		SUBSID. CHILD CARE		MEDICAID PROGRAM			
CMS															
B-2	3-5	B-2	3-5	B-2	3-5	B-2	3-5	B-2	3-5	B-2	3-5	B-2	3-5	B-2	3-5

Figure 1. (continued)

11. Availability of integrated programs
12. Most inclusive environment
13. Staff qualifications

Careful scrutiny of existing services can be accomplished through the use of two matrices that permit precise description of the services provided, age groups served, target populations addressed, and delivery models available (*Interagency problem solving,* 1989; Morgan & Swan, 1988). The community agency services matrix and the

SERVICES	SCHOOL DIST. B-2	SCHOOL DIST. 3-5	DEVELOP. DISABIL. B-2	DEVELOP. DISABIL. 3-5	UCP B-2	UCP 3-5	ARC B-2	ARC 3-5	EASTER SEALS B-2	EASTER SEALS 3-5	HEAD START B-2	HEAD START 3-5
SOCIAL/DEVELOPMENTAL HISTORY	✓	✓	✓	✓								
FAMILY ASSESSMENT	✓	✓	✓	✓								
DEVELOPMENTAL SCREENING	✓	✓	✓	✓								
HEARING SCREENING	✓	✓										
VISION SCREENING	✓	✓										
MULTIDISCIPLINARY TEAM	✓	✓										
PSYCHOLOGICAL EVALUATION	✓	✓	✓	✓								P
OT EVALUATION	✓	✓	P	P	✓				✓	✓		P
PT EVALUATION	✓	✓	P	P	✓				✓	✓		P
SPEECH/LANG. EVALUATION	✓	✓	P	P					✓	✓		P
AUDIOLOGICAL EVALUATION	✓	✓							✓	✓		P
VISION EVALUATION	✓	✓										P
MEDICAL EVALUATION												P
SERVICE COORDINATION	✓	✓	✓	✓			✓	✓	✓	✓		
IFSP/IEP	✓	✓	✓	✓			✓	✓	✓	✓	✓	
SPECIAL EDUC. CLASSROOM		✓					✓	✓				
HOME-BASED PROGRAM			✓		✓							
OCCUPATIONAL THERAPY		✓	P	P	✓		✓	✓	✓	✓		P
PHYSICAL THERAPY		✓	P	P	✓		✓	✓	✓	✓		P
SPEECH/LANG. THERAPY		✓	P	P			✓	✓	✓	✓		P
VISION SERVICES		✓										P
TRANSPORTATION	✓	✓					✓	✓				
PARENT TRAINING			✓									
PARENT COUNSELING/THERAPY												
PARENT SUPPORT GROUP							✓	✓	✓	✓		
PARENT LIBRARY/LOAN	✓	✓			✓				✓	✓		
MEDICAL SERVICES												P
DENTAL SERVICES												P
SPECIALIZED EQUIPMENT			✓	✓								
CHILD CARE							✓	✓	✓	✓		✓
RESPITE CARE			P	P								
BEHAVIOR SPECIALIST	✓	✓										
NURSING SERVICES												
MEDICAID					✓				✓	✓		
OTHER												

Figure 2. Completed example of a community agency services matrix. (✓ = provided by staff, F = fee, and P = purchase of services.) (Adapted with Permission of the Florida Department of Education, Bureau of Education for Exceptional Students, from *Interagency problem solving*, [1989], p. 23)

continuum of services matrix require one or two council meetings for detailed discussion and completion.

The community agency services matrix, shown in Figure 1, is the beginning point.

The names of the agency programs are written along the top and the range of services are written down the left column. Each program, including the services provided, is discussed in detail. Each service must be

CMS		HEALTH DEPT.		MENTAL HEALTH		COUNTY HOSPITAL		SPEECH CLINIC							
B-2	3-5	B-2	3-5	B-2	3-5	B-2	3-5	B-2	3-5	B-2	3-5	B-2	3-5	B-2	3-5
		✓	✓												
		✓	✓												
		✓	✓												
p	p														
p	p														
p	p					F	F								
P	P			F	F	F	F								
P	P														
✓	✓			F	F										
✓	✓														
P	P														
P	P			F	F										
P	P			F	F	F	F								
				✓	✓										
✓	✓	✓	✓			F	F								
		✓	✓												
✓	✓														
				✓	✓										
✓	✓	✓	✓												
✓	✓	✓	✓	✓	✓	✓	✓								

Figure 2.   (*continued*)

carefully defined so that terms are used consistently. A legend can be inserted at the bottom of the chart to provide a code that indicates if there is a fee for services or if services are purchased from other vendors, rather than provided by the agency staff.

The primary objective of the council is to clarify and understand the precise services provided, not judge them. Complaints and criticism should be withheld during the discussion; these will be dealt with later.

The matrix provides a clear, graphic display of services provided by each agency. When completed, it indicates: 1) appropriate referrals, based on the actual service needs of a child; 2) financial eligibility or fee requirements; and 3) an objective identification of service gaps within the community.

The completed sample of a community agency service matrix shown in Figure 2 demonstrates how the availability of information allows for more appropriate referrals. For example, if Head Start can provide dental services, whereas most other child care and educational programs cannot, Head Start is the viable placement option in the case of a financially eligible child requiring dental care. A physically disabled child who needs physical therapy can be referred to an agency that provides this service. When it is known that a private speech and hearing clinic charges hourly fees and is not a Medicaid provider, referrals will be limited to families who can afford to pay. If a family does not have transportation, only programs that provide it should be considered in order to prevent frustration and wasted time for the family. An understanding of the exact services provided by each agency results in a greatly improved referral system, greater parent satisfaction, and more confident agency personnel who can make appropriate referrals.

GAPS IN SERVICES

When the community agency services matrix has been completed, council members have an objective and precise picture of the kind, number, and geographic distribution of the various services in the community. The members can discuss each type of service and identify existing gaps. These may be specific to age groups (birth to 3 years of age or 3 through 5 years of age), types of services (e.g., hearing screening, multidisciplinary evaluation team, home-based programs, physical therapy, parent training), certain socioeconomic status (SES) populations, or particular geographic areas

of the community. The identified gaps will be addressed by the council in later activities and stated outcomes. Gaps or insufficient services seen in the sample matrix (see Figure 2) are listed in Table 1.

DELIVERY MODELS AND POPULATIONS SERVED

The continuum of services matrix shown in Figure 3 assists in identifying the various delivery models that comprise the community continuum of care and the populations of children served. The matrix provides a picture of how children are served within the most inclusive environment. It identifies full-time special education, part-time and part-day special education, mainstreamed or integrated settings, therapeutic options, home-based services, consultative programs, and residential care. For each delivery model, the matrix reveals the categorical population served, for example, developmentally delayed, high risk, mildly mentally disabled, moderately mentally disabled, profoundly disabled, speech-language disabled, physically disabled, traumatic brain injured, autistic, or hearing impaired. Overlaps in populations depend on definitions used by the various agencies. The same child, for instance, may be labeled high risk by one agency and trainable mentally handicapped by another.

A separate matrix should be completed

Table 1.   Gaps in services identified by sample community services matrix (Figure 2)

Insufficient home-based options

No home-based options for children 3 through 5 years old

No program for sensory impaired children under 3 years old

Insufficient multidisciplinary evaluation teams

Insufficient respite care providers

Insufficient screening activities

Insufficient therapy options

No services in north county area

Limited after-school care for children with disabilities

CONTINUUM OF SERVICES MATRIX

DISABILITY TYPE	RESIDENTIAL	FULL-TIME SPECIAL EDUCATION	PART-TIME SPECIAL EDUCATION	INTEGRATED SETTING	THERAPY	SPEECH/ LANGUAGE *ONLY	OT *ONLY	PT *ONLY	HOME BASED	CHILD CARE	CONSULTATIVE	PARENT TRAINING
DEVELOPMENTAL DELAY												
MILDLY MENTALLY HANDICAPPED (EMH)												
MODERATELY MENTALLY HANDICAPPED (TMH)												
SEVERE/PROFOUNDLY MENTALLY HANDICAPPED												
MILDLY PHYSICALLY IMPAIRED												
MODERATE TO SEVERELY PHYSICALLY IMPAIRED												
MILDLY VISUALLY IMPAIRED												
BLIND												
HARD OF HEARING												
DEAF												
MILD SP/LANGUAGE IMPAIRED												
SEVERELY LANGUAGE IMPAIRED												
BEHAVIORALLY DISORDERED												
SEVERELY EMOTIONALLY DISTURBED												
AUTISTIC												
TRAUMATIC BRAIN INJURY												

DIRECTIONS: IN THE BOXES, INDICATE THE AGENCY/PROGRAM THAT PROVIDES SERVICES TO EACH TYPE OF DISABILITY ACCORDING TO THE DELIVERY MODEL.

    * Services provided without a center-based classroom placement (i.e., the parent refuses a classroom program and wants only therapy at that time; or, the child needs only therapy.)

Figure 3.   Continuum of services matrix used to analyze disability groups served and available delivery models. (Adapted with Permission of the Florida Department of Education, Bureau of Education for Exceptional Students, from *Interagency problem solving*, [1989], p. 22)

CONTINUUM OF SERVICES MATRIX

DISABILITY TYPE	RESIDENTIAL	FULL-TIME SPECIAL EDUCATION	PART-TIME SPECIAL EDUCATION	INTEGRATED SETTING
DEVELOPMENTAL DELAY		ARC	ARC	Head Start, ARC, Easter Seals
MILDLY MENTALLY HANDICAPPED (EMH)		ARC School District	ARC School District	Head Start, ARC, Easter Seals
MODERATELY MENTALLY HANDICAPPED (TMH)		ARC School District	ARC School District	Head Start, ARC, Easter Seals
SEVERE/PROFOUNDLY MENTALLY HANDICAPPED		ARC School District	ARC School District	ARC, Easter Seals
MILDLY PHYSICALLY IMPAIRED			ARC, School Dist.	H.S., ARC, E.S.
MODERATE TO SEVERELY PHYSICALLY IMPAIRED		ARC School District	ARC School District	ARC, Easter Seals
MILDLY VISUALLY IMPAIRED			School District	H.S., ARC, E.S.
BLIND	State School	School District	School District	ARC, E.S.
HARD OF HEARING		School District	School District	H.S., ARC, E.S.
DEAF	State School	School District	School District	ARC, E.S.
MILD SP/LANGUAGE IMPAIRED			School District	H.S., ARC, E.S.
SEVERELY LANGUAGE IMPAIRED		School District	School District	H.S., ARC, E.S.
BEHAVIORALLY DISORDERED		School District	ARC, School Dist.	H.S., ARC, E.S.
SEVERELY EMOTIONALLY DISTURBED	Scott Palms Hospital	School District	School District	ARC, Easter Seals
AUTISTIC		ARC, School Dist.	ARC, School Dist.	ARC, E.S.
TRAUMATIC BRAIN INJURY		ARC, School Dist.	ARC, School Dist.	ARC, E.S.

DIRECTIONS: IN THE BOXES, INDICATE THE AGENCY/PROGRAM THAT PROVIDES SERVICES TO EACH TYPE OF DISABILITY ACCORDING TO THE DELIVERY MODEL.

* Services provided without a center-based classroom placement (i.e., the parent refuses a classroom program and wants only therapy at that time; or, the child needs only therapy.)

Figure 4. Example of a continuum of services matrix showing community providers. (Adapted with Permission of the Florida Department of Education, Bureau of Education for Exceptional Students, from *Interagency problem solving*, [1989], p. 29)

for each population: 1) birth through 2 years of age, and 2) 3 through 5 years of age. Some agencies may not serve the entire age span of birth through 5 years. Each column should be discussed in detail and accurately completed. Names of the agencies are placed in the appropriate boxes to indicate how services are provided to the type of children they serve.

Figure 4 is a sample continuum of services matrix, showing that two community options exist for a 3-year-old child with moderate mental disabilities whose family requests full-time special education: 1) the school district, and 2) The Arc. However, a family requesting only weekly physical therapy for a 2-year-old child with mild cerebral palsy has four options: 1) therapy provided at a nearby elementary school site; 2) therapy purchased from a private vendor by developmental services; 3) private therapy, paid for by the parent or insurance, at the local hospital rehabilitation department; and 4) therapy paid for by children's medical services and provided by a private practitioner or other agency. Financial considerations, program eligibilities, timelines, and such other considerations as transportation and parent preference may narrow the four options and indicate the best choice.

CHECK ONE: ___ B-2 OR ✓ 3-5

THERAPY	SPEECH/LANG. *ONLY	OT *ONLY	PT *ONLY	HOME BASED	CHILD CARE	CONSULTATIVE	PARENT TRAINING
UCP, Easter Seals Hospital	Easter Seals Speech Clinic	Easter Seals	Easter Seals		Head Start		Dev. Disab.
UCP, Easter Seals Hospital	S.D., E.S., Sph. Cl., Co. Hsp.	Easter Seals	Easter Seals		Head Start		Dev. Disab.
UCP, Easter Seals Hospital	S.D., E.S., Sph. Cl., Co. Hsp.	Easter Seals	Easter Seals		Head Start		Dev. Disab.
UCP, Easter Seals Hospital	S.D., E.S., Sph. Cl., Co. Hsp.	Easter Seals	Easter Seals		Head Start		Dev. Disab.
UPC, E.S. Hsp.	S.D., E.S., Sph. Cl., Co. Hsp.	E.S.	E.S.		H.S.		Dev. Disab.
UCP, Easter Seals Hospital	S.D., E.S., Sph. Cl., Co. Hsp.	Easter Seals	Easter Seals		Head Start		Dev. Disab.
UPC, E.S. Hsp.	S.D., E.S., Sph. Cl., Co. Hsp.	E.S.	E.S.		H.S.		
UPC, E.S. Hsp.	S.D., E.S., Sph. Cl., Co. Hsp.	E.S.	E.S.		H.S.		
UPC, E.S. Hsp.	S.D., E.S., Sph. Cl., Co. Hsp.	E.S.	E.S.		H.S.		
UPC, E.S. Hsp.	S.D., E.S., Sph. Cl., Co. Hsp.	E.S.	E.S.		H.S.		
UPC, E.S. Hsp.	S.D., E.S., Sph. Cl., Co. Hsp.	E.S.	E.S.		H.S.		
UPC, E.S. Hsp.	S.D., E.S., Sph. Cl., Co. Hsp.	E.S.	E.S.		H.S.		
UPC, E.S. Hsp.	S.D., E.S., Sph. Cl., Co. Hsp.	E.S.	E.S.		H.S.		
UCP, Easter Seals, Hospital	S.D., E.S., Sph. Cl., Co. Hsp.	Easter Seals	Easter Seals		Head Start		
UPC, E.S. Hsp.	S.D., E.S., Sph. Cl., Co. Hsp.	E.S.	E.S.		H.S.		Dev. Disab.
UPC, E.S. Hsp.	S.D., E.S., Sph. Cl., Co. Hsp.	E.S.	E.S.		H.S.		Dev. Disab.

H.S.–Head Start   Sph. Cl.–Speech Clinic
E.S.–Easter Seals   Co. Hsp.–County Hospital
Hsp.–Hospital   Dev. Disab.–Developmental Disability
S.D.–School District

GAPS IN DELIVERY MODELS AND POPULATIONS

With completion of the second matrix, council members have an objective and precise summary of the available delivery models and the manner in which children are served in the most inclusive environment. The matrix may show that some agency programs provide only full-time special education services, even for mildly impaired children who might be better served in a more normalized setting. It may also indicate a surprising lack of home-based programs or an insufficient number of parent-training options. It may reveal that the special needs of specific groups

of children, such as the visually impaired, deaf, or emotionally disturbed, are not addressed by any program.

Unnecessary duplication of services may be identified if the majority of agencies are targeting the same populations, such as children with mild developmental delays or physical impairments. Competition for these children may result, and programs for other children may not exist. Similarly, agency programs may have targeted the same age populations and left other age groups unserved. Completion and analysis of this matrix permits agencies to identify objectively the manner in which children are served and underserved. The information assists in determining the need for modification and expansion of programs.

CURRENT PRACTICES AND PROCEDURES

Practices and procedures currently used to identify and provide services needed by children and families in the community may also require thorough investigation. The council may choose to develop a needs-assessment procedure in order to obtain an accurate description of existing procedures.

Use of a brief, one-page mailed survey is not recommended. Although commonly used for a needs assessment, this practice generally is neither precise nor sufficiently structured to gather useful information. The council should identify the areas to be investigated, develop a list of questions to be answered for each area, identify the methods

or strategies to be employed, and determine the persons responsible for the investigation. Table 2 provides a sample needs-assessment process.

AREAS FOR POLICY MODIFICATION

As existing services and gaps are identified and analyzed, the council begins to isolate local policies and procedures that provide barriers to a comprehensive service system and coordinated care. Policy modifications may remedy problems and are often relatively easy to make after the problems have been identified. For example, an agency that has arbitrarily chosen not to serve 3-year-old children on the assumption that another agency is solely responsible for them may modify its policy accordingly. Discussion of other inaccurate perceptions about various

Table 2. Sample investigative questions used to identify current practices

Question	Member	Method
REFERRAL PROCEDURE		
1. What is the procedure used by the neonatal intensive care unit to refer newborns to local providers?		
2. How are newborns at Memorial Hospital identified and referred? Who is responsible for referrals?		
3. How are newborns at Community Hospital identified and referred? What persons?		
4. What is the knowledge level of area pediatricians about available services?		
5. What is the percentage of referrals received from pediatricians versus other sources? Who refers?		
6. Is there a local pediatric group? Who heads it? When and where does it meet?		
7. What is the current referral procedure for cocaine-exposed babies? Who is responsible for follow-up? How is it done?		
8. What are the primary referral sources?		
LOCATION AND IDENTIFICATION		
1. How do new residents to the county become aware of services? Where do they call? Where do they go?		
2. How are programs listed in the phone book?		
3. Where are the initial screening points?		
4. How well do daycare centers understand the referral process? Child find?		
5. Where are the infant daycare centers? Are all infants/toddlers screened? Who holds responsibility for referrals?		
6. What are the procedures at TAPP for infant screening and follow-up?		
7. How do offices, such as the Chamber of Commerce, county library, information and referral service, respond to inquiries?		

(continued)

Table 2. *(continued)*

Question	Member	Method

EVALUATION SERVICES

1. What agencies and programs evaluate 0-2? How are evaluation services funded? What are the procedures? The time delay?
2. Is the evaluation multidisciplinary, interdisciplinary, or transdisciplinary?
3. Are all needed evaluations provided or only portions provided?
4. What is the purpose of the evaluation? Does it serve to determine eligibility or is it prescriptive?
5. Is vision and hearing screening a routine part of the evaluation? Is this done prior to other evaluations? It is done early enough?
6. What is the role of the parent in the evaluation process?
7. How accessible are evaluation services? Location accessible? Time of day?
8. Does duplication exist? Where?
9. How many children were evaluated across programs/agencies last year? What was the outcome? Percentage into treatment and programs?
10. Is there reciprocity with regard to evaluation results and reports?
11. Where are the gaps in evaluation services? What are the problems?

INTERVENTION SERVICES

1. Who are the service providers? Medical, social services, educational, therapy, parent, and so forth?
2. What are the delivery models? Are there many options from which parents may select?
3. How many 0-2 children are served? In what settings? Are the settings least restrictive?
4. How many children are not currently provided services? What are the reasons?
5. What are the procedures for follow-up when children are not or cannot be served?
6. What are the numbers of cocaine-exposed babies identified and served? How are they served? Who are the providers?
7. How are social services provided by the various agency programs? What is the role of the social worker?
8. What are the current procedures for selection of a case manager to coordinate each case?
9. Are services complete? Are children underserved?

MEDICAL SERVICES

1. What services are covered by Medicaid? What are the constraints for use?
2. What percentage of 0-2 children have Medicaid? What are the procedures for application?
3. Who are the Medicaid providers in the county? Do they represent a sufficient number of pediatricians, dentists, specialists?
4. What is the percentage of 0-2 children who are patients of CMS? Clients of HRS/DS?
5. What does the Medically Needy Program provide? What percentage of children/families?
6. How many children have private insurance? What services may be covered?

TAPP, Teenage Pregnancy Program; HRS, Health and Rehabilitative Service; 0-2, children from birth through age 2; CMS, Children's Medical Services; DS, Developmental Services.

Funding source	Personnel	Evaluation	Therapy	Instructional materials
Local School Funds				
Preschool Entitlement PL 99-457				
PL 94-142				
Chapter 1, 89–313				
Chapter I, Disadvantaged				
Developmental Disabilities				
Migrant Head Start				
Head Start				
Medicaid				
CMS				

Figure 5.   Sample chart used to analyze funding sources.

agencies can result in clarification and often simple solutions to problems in service delivery. Examples of local policy changes include:

The health agency may agree to fund medically necessary occupational and physical therapy services on the realization that the schools provide educational, rather than medical, services.

A private center begins to require appropriate certification for its teaching staff to allow contracting options with the public schools.

A rehabilitation center decides to purchase psychological evaluation services from only certified school or clinical psychologists, rather than educational specialists, so that evaluation results can be used by the school district.

Agencies develop consistent evaluation procedures to allow reciprocity of evaluation results, thereby reducing duplication of testing.

The school district agrees to eliminate the requirement for a special school form and to accept other types of written therapy authorization from health agency physicians in order to shorten the time between recommendation and provision of therapy.

The subsidized child care provider agrees to fund before- and after-school care for children in educational programs, rather than considering them the total responsibility of the school system and ineligible for its program.

A rehabilitation center agrees to provide occupational, physical, and speech therapy to children at the child care center, preschool program, or caregiver's location in addition to the home.

The school district agrees to transport children after school to a location other than the home (e.g., child care center, rehabilitation center, specialized youth program).

A private center lengthens the school day to provide an option of extended care for working parents.

A program modifies its target population and eligibility to create an integrated preschool program.

GRANTS AND FUNDING SOURCES

Funding a comprehensive service delivery system depends on the most efficient use of available resources. Revealing information relative to budgets, grants, contributions, and other fiscal allocations is perhaps one

Equipment	Facilities	Transportation	Parent services	Counseling	Respite care

Figure 5. (continued)

of the most difficult and threatening activities in which agency personnel may participate. Particularly in the case of a small program with limited resources, revealing funding sources, levels, and allocations may place the program in a sensitive and vulnerable position. This information is essential, however, in developing interagency agreements and restructuring payment for services (Linder, 1983). Again, the use of a chart that shows how program and grant funds are allocated (and how they may not be spent) permits analysis and identification of unnecessary duplication and gaps. A sample chart to analyze funding sources is shown in Figure 5.

REFERENCES

Interagency problem solving. (1989). Tallahassee: Florida Department of Education, Bureau of Education for Exceptional Students.

Linder, T.W. (1983). *Early childhood special education: Program development and administration* (pp. 63–94). Baltimore: Paul H. Brookes Publishing Co.

Morgan, J.L., & Swan, W.W. (1988). *Local interagency councils for preschool handicapped programs: An effective strategy to implement the mandate.* Bloomington: Indiana University, Council for Administrators of Special Education, Inc. (CASE). (A Division of the Council for Exceptional Children.)

Chapter 12

Coordination of Agency Services

During stage 2 of interagency council development, the focus shifts abruptly from information-sharing activities to coordination of services. Turnover in membership and perhaps leadership results in a smaller, more stable and committed group. Through informal networking and teamwork, problems are solved as they occur. Council meeting agendas designate agency updates, case conferences, and ongoing interagency coordination projects.

The community service delivery system begins to undergo rapid change as council members define and realign their roles and responsibilities with respect to one another. Coordination activities span the components of the delivery system as shown in Table 1.

REVIEW OF COUNCIL STRUCTURE AND MEMBERSHIP

Council members have a clearly defined sense of purpose at this stage and have committed to collaboration. They understand the importance of regular council attendance, consistency of representation, and authority to represent and commit agency resources. An interagency team has emerged and operates as an independent consortium of agency representatives without ownership by one agency. The interagency team must now be assessed and appropriate changes made in

membership and procedures. Members who are frequently absent, unable to commit resources, or unable to participate effectively in the group process should be replaced. It is essential to understand the critical contribution of the members to the success of the collaborative efforts.

AGENCY ROLES AND RESPONSIBILITIES

Coordination in Program Planning

No single agency can provide all the services needed by a young child with disabilities and the family. These services require the coordinated efforts by a combination of agencies. Development of an individualized education program (IEP) should include personnel from all agencies that provide services to the child and family (Smith, 1988). This is the intent of the individualized family service plan (IFSP) described in the Education of the Handicapped Act Amendments of 1986 (PL 99-457) for the birth through age 2 population. Interagency planning is also important for the 3- through 5-year-old age group. It permits sharing of the financial responsibility for services and accommodates various program eligibilities. Services that cannot be provided by one agency are contributed by another. For example, if speech-language therapy services are not provided by the school program they may be available from developmental disabilities or the Easter Seal Society. Medically necessary physical therapy prescribed on a daily basis following surgery may be provided by the crippled children's bureau or United Cerebral Palsy (UCP). In col-

Table 1. Coordinating activities during stage 2

Reassess council membership
Coordinate services
Coordinate identification services
Coordinate case management
Coordinate referral and transition

laborative planning, program eligibility is considered and providers are determined through a decision-making process. Conflicts and misunderstandings among agencies are avoided and solutions determined more easily.

Agreement on needed services (e.g., adaptive equipment, audiological services, respite care) and the agencies that will provide them can be accomplished in a single meeting, rather than requiring months of letters, forms, and telephone calls. Joint decision making also ensures a fair division of cost sharing among the agencies.

Examples of outcomes resulting from coordinated interagency IFSP and IEP planning are:

Discussion and consensus ensures the determination of the respective role and responsibility of each agency in providing all of the needed services to a child and family.

Services are provided with improved organization, speed, and communication.

Frustration for the family or case manager that can result from searching for and securing agency approval of the needed service is reduced or eliminated.

All services are recorded in a single, comprehensive written program. Benefits to the child, the family, and the agencies are obvious.

Coordination in Providing Services

Analysis of the community service delivery system using the community agency services matrix and the continuum of services matrix (see chap. 11, this volume) identifies the types of disability groups, age groups, delivery models, and geographic distribution of services, along with the number of agencies that target the same population or provide similar services. Both necessary and unnecessary duplication and service gaps are determined. When unnecessary duplication is found, agencies have the option of shifting the program focus, modifying the age

groups served, or reallocating funds to eliminate waste and cover deficit areas.

The matrices provide an objective method of distributing children throughout the agency programs to ensure that each program has a sufficient number of clients and to avoid the need for competition. Analyzing the range of community programs clarifies priorities, preferences, capabilities, and limitations. For example, The Arc center may be designated to focus on the profoundly disabled population, birth to 3 years of age; United Cerebral Palsy to serve children in the same age group who require home-based occupational and physical therapy; the speech and hearing clinic to provide intensive speech and language therapy in a center-based program; Head Start to serve children with disabilities who function successfully in a mainstreamed setting; and the school district to serve 3- through 5-year-old children with disabilities who meet their eligibility criteria. Furthermore, clarification can be made about the roles of medical, social services, and parent education providers.

Realignment of Resources

When the analysis of needed community services has been completed, the council can identify the strategies needed to fill service gaps and create the complete array of services as desired. A number of solutions are possible.

Reduce or Eliminate Unnecessary Duplication If the analysis reveals that many agencies are attempting to serve the same age group or same population of children, the agencies may decide to redirect their efforts. Competition for the same age group of children in the presence of unserved groups is counterproductive.

Direct Program Expansion Agencies undergoing program expansion can be encouraged to develop programs for unserved children or underserved populations.

Redistribute Children Agency programs often enroll children who might be more appropriately placed in other settings. Although they may be well intentioned, program personnel must recognize the importance of placing youngsters in the most appropriate and most inclusive setting. For example, a mildly developmentally delayed child should be placed in a normal setting as opposed to a special school serving the profoundly impaired. Likewise, a severely physically impaired child may be unable to receive therapy services if served only by a home-based parent-training model or placed in day care. Identifying underserved and overserved children and realigning them into more appropriate services results in a better use of program slots.

Use Transportation Wisely Given several appropriate placement options, the deciding factor might be the need for and availability of transportation services. Program slots in centers providing transportation could be reserved for children who cannot participate without transportation. Filling these slots with children whose families can provide transportation may not represent the most effective use of placement options.

Utilize the Most Inclusive Setting Special education settings are often at capacity levels when children with mild impairments are enrolled on a full-time basis, rather than only for the amount of time required for special services. Overserving children in this manner results in unavailability of services for those in greater need. Children who require part-time special education services or therapy should be placed in settings less restrictive than full-time special education classrooms.

Create Therapy Options Programs should develop therapy options in a variety of settings for children who do not need full-time special education. Parents may bring children to neighborhood or other designated schools for speech, occupational, or physical therapy. During the school day, therapy can be provided to children whose parents can transport them. Transportation should be a related service only when it is necessary. Therapy provided at the school during early evening hours can accommodate parents' work schedules and eliminate transportation problems. Private centers can institute evening or Saturday morning schedules. Home-based services can be provided. Private therapy (funded by Medicaid, insurance, or the parent) can be provided within the educational or child care setting or during evening and Saturday hours. If families cannot provide transportation, children can be enrolled in community programs, such as Head Start, daycare centers, and child migrant programs. Therapy services may be provided by community agencies or by the school district through contractual agreements. Other creative alternatives can be identified.

Substitute Funding Sources Agencies often pay for services that can be funded by another source. Substitution of funding sources frees dollars that can be diverted into expansion of services. Medicaid-reimbursable services (e.g., audiological evaluations, medical consultations, vision examinations, therapy evaluations, glasses, hearing aids) are often funded by educational and community agency programs from operational funds, rather than a Medicaid provider. Awareness of the services covered by Medicaid results in new avenues for funding needed services, referrals to other providers, collaborative endeavors, and fund diversions to other areas of need.

CHILD IDENTIFICATION AND ASSESSMENT

Developing a comprehensive child location and identification system is far more complicated than it appears on the surface. Because it must accommodate a variety of community agencies, the procedure can be particularly complex. A process for ongoing review, revision, and evaluation of collaborative child find activities should be considered early in the council's planning activities (Smith, 1988). The development of a comprehensive child location and identification system requires the effective functioning of five interactive components:

1. Case finding and community awareness
2. Referral
3. Release of information and records
4. Screening
5. Evaluation

Identification of Existing Child Find Activities

Existing case-finding activities of community agencies should be identified. Together, council members can determine the populations to target for these efforts. A thorough cataloging of existing activities should be part of the initial planning. It may reveal duplication of effort that is not only wasteful to the system but confusing and discouraging to parents.

Local sources of information include parents; hospitals; child care and preschool facilities; the Early and Periodic Screening, Diagnosis, and Treatment Program (EPSDT); pediatricians, family physicians and other health care specialists; birth registries; women's, infants' and children's (WIC) services; and community health departments and clinics. The council may identify a list similar to the sample in Table 2.

Coordination of Child Find Activities

Community agencies should explore their public awareness and case-finding activities. They can be easily coordinated across agencies. The child find coordinator may be designated the person primarily responsible for the following five activities:

1. Disseminate brochures and other information about available services.
2. Develop an interagency brochure on the importance of early intervention.
3. Inform area physicians and other health care specialists of available services.
4. Coordinate mailings and awareness activities.
5. Identify other programs where high-risk children may be located, such as teenage pregnancy programs, drug and alcohol programs, nutrition and health programs, and deaf service centers.

Every community agency and program serving preschool children with disabilities and those at risk engage in some type of case-finding and public awareness activities. The specific term *child find* had its origins in the Education for All Handicapped Children Act (PL 94-142), but case-finding activities are not exclusively conducted by school personnel. Child find activities are also used for the purpose of "finding" or locating children who may need special services. An agency's case-finding activities represent a necessary first step in locating potential candidates for its program. Case-finding or child find activities are a means of accessing the target population of children and soliciting referrals (Peterson, 1987). Case finding alerts parents, professionals, educators, and the general public to children who may have special needs and encourages their help in referring children for screening. It refers to the initial location of these children and is followed by screening that identifies children who require more thorough evaluation to specify needed services.

Child find is often considered to consist of public awareness activities, such as media campaigns, but it should be much broader in scope. Two main spheres of activity can be identified for child find (Smith, 1988). The first, public awareness, relates to informing the right people (those who need early intervention services and those who refer children to these services) about available services. The second sphere involves screening and registry activities that identify children who may need the services. A comprehensive child find system must include the entire range of activities that span the period from birth through 5 years of age and that link with activities under the preschool portion of PL 99-457. It must be remembered that the largest portion of these

Table 2. Excerpt of a sample list of identified case-finding activities across community agencies

Agency	Activity
School district	Mails notice to pediatricians and specialists each fall with information about program
	Notice sent home with all special education students informing parents about preschool services
	Posters in all school offices with information on preschool services and referral information
	Speech-language screening of all preschool children in subsidized daycare each fall
	Developmental follow-up of all babies from the teenage pregnancy program
	Information sent to deaf parents through the deaf service center each year
	Information to programs serving adults with disabilities who may have high-risk children
Head Start	Newspaper recruitment articles
	Newspaper/information in area churches and stores
	Enrollment notices sent to agencies
	Door-to-door searches in designated areas
Easter Seal Society	Free speech/hearing screening to daycare centers
	Periodic newspaper articles
	Mailing campaign twice each year to physicians
	Distribution brochures
	Appearance on morning television talk show twice each year to explain program
Department of human resources	Telephone hotline; information on referral
	Linkages with single intake, child abuse investigators, alcohol and chemical dependency treatment centers
Migrant Head Start	Social workers visit the field
	Door-to-door canvassing in migrant camps
	Worker assigned to rural clinic to do developmental screening
	Notices distributed at churches, migrant camps, and clinics about services
	Posters on telephone booths and store fronts

(Adapted with Permission of the Florida Department of Education, Bureau of Education for Exceptional Students, from *Interagency problem solving,* [1989], p. 44)

children may not be identified at the time of birth but will display needs during the infant, toddler, and preschool years. This delay requires targeting those areas of the community where high-risk youngsters and their families are found. If community agencies coordinate their efforts, more effective location strategies will result in an increased number of children who are identified and served at an earlier age. Coordination is especially effective because the various agency programs: 1) have specific target populations, 2) reach different kinds of families, 3) differ in service capabilities, and 4) engage in significant duplication of screening and evaluation.

Identification of Areas Where Children at High Risk Are Found

The purpose of this strategy is to identify all of the areas where children at high-risk are found in order to create a network of referral sources. Identification of these programs, agencies, and facilities results in information necessary for the referral process, including screening procedures and the availability of on-site screening.

Parents are the critical element in case-finding and child find activities. Their knowledge of their children's skills, abilities, strengths, and areas of need must be included in any child find protocol. Identifying appropriate methods of reaching target groups of parents may prove difficult. An analysis of the child's development in relation to the local norms (Meisels, 1984) is important in determining how to encourage parents to refer their children. The stigma of disability or that attached to community agencies and programs may interfere with the willingness of parents to do so.

Hospitals identify children who are born with identifiable disabilities or risk factors commonly associated with developmental delay. Predischarge services for infants in neonatal, perinatal intensive care, and other specialized units can permit case management activities to begin prior to their discharge. Metabolic and high-risk screenings, including screening for hearing impairment, can be important resources in expanding identification efforts if they are linked with programs that provide direct intervention for identified children. A relatively small number (perhaps 20%) of the children served under PL 99-457 can be identified at birth (Smith, 1988).

Birth certificate data are inadequate for identification of infants with existing or potential disabilities. Numerous problems with accuracy of the data have been cited (Frost, Starzyk, George, & MacLaughlin, 1984). Such conditions as cleft palate and spina bifida, although easily diagnosed at birth, are often omitted from birth certificates because of inconsistencies in their completion.

Pediatricians and family physicians are essential to identification of children during the early years, particularly the immunization period. Studies have indicated, however, that only 50% of the nation's children receive regular health care at 2 years of age (Blackman, 1986).

Other sources of health care within the community must be identified and targeted for child find activities. Hospital emergency rooms are often substituted for primary care physicians by families who cannot afford regular medical care. Community health departments, indigent and rural health clinics, and walk-in clinics are primary care providers for many families with children who are at high risk for developmental delay. Routine developmental screenings may be provided to children as a part of their care and are important in case-finding activities. EPSDT was initiated in 1967 to provide Medicaid-eligible children with ongoing health and developmental monitoring and treatment. The program resulted from the only federal legislation mandating developmental screening for the purpose of prevention (Meisels, 1984). EPSDT activities should be incorporated into the comprehensive child find system at the local level.

The WIC special supplemental food program remains an underutilized and potentially significant resource for case finding because the target population consists of low-income mothers and children who are at increased nutritional risk. The link between adequate nutrition and normal growth and development has been well documented. Failure to thrive, feeding difficulties, weight gain, or growth problems may be the earliest indicators of potential disabilities in some children.

Protective services, foster care programs, human resources departments, mental health services, and chemical dependency programs are instrumental in locating abused and neglected children, many of whom have emotional, behavioral, or other developmental delays.

Childcare and community preschool programs provide excellent case-finding options. Linkages and public awareness activities with these centers can generate referrals of children with potential disabilities. Head Start, a federally subsidized day care program, and preschool programs for migrant children routinely provide developmental screening. Children identified in these screenings should be referred for additional assessment in accordance with appropriate referral procedures.

Many other community programs can be identified as targets in case-finding activities. The interagency council should consider adult treatment programs that may lead to children with disabilities and those at risk. Examples are programs for alcohol- and drug-dependent adults and teenage pregnancy programs. The council can list the target programs and categorize them by types, such as medical, prenatal, educational, and mental health. The list may include programs and agencies that provide the following services:

Education to the public on the causes of disabilities (e.g., community seminars, advocacy groups, March of Dimes)

Education to the public about child development and parenting skills (e.g., health department, community college, parent groups, local hospital, mental health center, women's center)

Family planning programs (e.g., health department, family planning clinics, indigent clinics, teenage pregnancy programs)

Comprehensive prenatal care for low-income women

Perinatal intensive care and follow-up programs

Developmental training, parent training, and follow-up services for neonatal intensive care center graduates

High-risk registries

Preventive health care for indigent preschool children

Nutritional programs for indigent preschool children

Alcohol-, drug-, and chemical-dependency programs serving parents of preschool children

Walk-in medical clinic services for families that do not have access to routine medical care

Special education for students who may have preschool siblings also in need of services

Counseling by psychologists and other specialists in private practice

Audiology and other therapy (private practice)

Vocational, work, and sheltered workshop programs for adults with disabilities

Deaf and blind adult programs (e.g., deaf service center, resource center, church programs, sign language clubs, blind services, public libraries, support groups)

Mental health and counseling centers

Foster care, respite centers, and adoption agencies

Daycare programs for indigent children

Abuse prevention and crisis management programs

Centers for the homeless

Preparing such a list by program name and contact person helps to identify all areas where children in need of special services may be found. An organized and structured plan that focuses on case-finding activities is then developed. A sample listing of locations for preschool children at high risk is shown in Table 3.

Areas with high concentrations of indigent children, migrant farm workers, non-English speaking children, and refugees may be targeted for awareness activities that are not dependent on newspaper and other printed notices.

Expansion of Case-Finding Activities

After the council has completed its case-finding plan and the high-risk populations have been identified, the council is ready to expand the case-finding activities. Council agencies may collaborate in the development and joint funding of a brochure or community directory of services that explains the services available to preschool children and their families and perhaps an interagency brochure on the importance of early intervention. A special mailing or a meeting for area physicians and specialists might be organized. The council can coor-

Table 3.   Excerpt from a sample listing of locations for preschool children at high risk

Type	Program	High-risk group
Medical	Health department	Indigent children needing medical care
	Rural health clinic	Indigent children needing medical care
	Medical clinic	Indigent children needing medical care
	Children's medical services	Chronically ill, disabled, and high-risk children
	Hospital and emergency room (social work department)	Medically impaired, accident victims, failure to thrive, families without medical care
	Developmental disabilities	Premature, high-risk infants
Social services	Foster care	Abused, neglected children
	Protective services	Abused, neglected children
	Shelter home	Homeless children and families
Mental health	Mental health center	Children of psychotic and severely emotionally disturbed adults
	Chemical dependency program	Children of adults with alcohol and drug dependencies

(Adapted with Permission of the Florida Department of Education, Bureau of Education for Exceptional Students, from *Interagency problem solving,* [1989], p. 48)

dinate regular mailing and fund-raising campaigns of member agencies.

Council members can make presentations to parent-teacher organizations and civic, church, and other parent groups. In some communities, the annual county fair provides an excellent opportunity to distribute brochures; educate the public about programs and services; and offer free vision, hearing, or developmental screenings. Brochures and screening information can be provided throughout the community. Appropriate locations vary with the community but may include public libraries, health clinics, hospital emergency rooms, social services offices, community centers, social security offices, drivers' license bureaus, county information centers, and referral programs.

The council must identify various avenues for reaching parents and families who:

Are new to the community
Are nonreaders or non–English speaking
Have family members with disabilities
Do not have access to medical services
Live in remote or rural areas
Have a family history of disabilities

COORDINATION OF REFERRAL SERVICES

Council members gain information and increased understanding of existing programs, services, and delivery models through analysis and discussion. More appropriate referrals occur as a natural result of this knowledge. The referral process focuses on identification of specific services needed by children and families and consideration of the least restrictive environment. The former system of referring children to programs based on nonspecific criteria (e.g., age, location) is replaced by referring children to the agencies that can provide the appropriate services, such as speech therapy, vision services, dental services, physical therapy, and home-based services.

An understanding of eligibility criteria that relate to income, category, age and other factors increases the appropriateness of referrals and reduces the frustration of families in their attempts to secure services. Familiarity with intake personnel and procedures shortens both the time required to make a referral and the delay between referral and initiation of services. An ongoing, informal, network of agency personnel can improve with time and, in conjunction with specific council activities, result in a streamlined referral system.

Identification of Agency Characteristics

Through identification of agency services and delivery model characteristics (as shown by the matrix analysis in chap. 11, this volume), the council becomes increasingly knowledgeable about appropriate referrals. A comparison of agency features offers an additional focus on available options. The comparison should consider such factors as the family's ability to pay, the time element in providing the service, transportation needs, work schedules of the parents, most inclusive environment, and program location.

Placement Options for Various Disabilities

When council members have an understanding of the roles of agencies and programs as they relate to the various types of disabilities, they can appropriately match them with children's needs. A 4-year-old child who is blind, for example, would not be referred to a program that does not have personnel with expertise in visual impairment. The child with severe cerebral palsy would not be referred to a program that does not provide occupational and physical therapy. The 4-year-old child whose parents will not agree to a placement requiring a classification of retardation could be referred instead to the local UCP center or a nonpublic school or rehabilitation program that is not required to provide categorical labels.

The council can establish a process to direct referrals to appropriate agencies based on identification of the need for services. This redirection results in six beneficial outcomes in a relatively short period of time:

1. The time between referral and initiation of services is shortened.
2. The time spent by parents and agency personnel to process ineligible children is reduced.
3. Parent frustration is minimized.
4. The system is streamlined and less frustrating for the service coordinator.
5. Confusion over agency roles is minimized.
6. Frustration and hard feelings among agencies that result from misunderstanding each agency's roles and procedures are minimized.

Development of Interagency Referral Procedure

In developing an interagency referral procedure, the council should carefully describe and clarify the referral requirements, including the necessary forms and attachments, of the various agencies so that referrals can be processed in an expeditious manner. Misunderstanding the forms used by other agencies can create a time delay or an inappropriate response to referrals. Program offices deal with exchange of extensive records and information every day. It is easy to understand how secretarial or other program personnel may not recognize a request for information or a referral form used by another agency. Unknowingly, the request may be filed away instead of being processed.

The willingness and ability of programs to provide reciprocity in child assessment are important. The conditions under which evaluation reports may be accepted and used for the purposes of placement should be clarified. Unnecessary evaluation should be eliminated. In addition, procedures for proper release of information and confidential records must be established.

The council can also develop standardized procedures for making referrals among the various community agencies. Standardized procedures eliminate questions about expectations, forms, and consent procedures, and minimize the time between the referral and the intended outcome. Clarifying reports or information that should accompany referrals facilitates the process, and communication between parties improves. A sample interagency referral form is shown in Figure 1.

INTERAGENCY REFERRAL FORM

Referral Date:_____

Child: _____

D.O.B: _____Age:_____

Address:_____

_____

REFERRED BY:

Phone: _____(Home)

_____(Work/Other)

Name

Medicaid Number:_____

Title

Agencies Known to:

Agency

Phone

Address

DESCRIBE REASON FOR REFERRAL:

Other Information:

____ Parents are aware of the referral.   ____ The child is served by our program.
____ Parents are awaiting your call.   ____ The child is not receiving our services.
____ Parents will contact your office.   ____ The case has been closed.
____ Transportation may be a problem.   ____ The child is ineligible for our services.
____ An interpreter will be needed.
____ Protective Services Worker:_____
____ Primary Service Coordinator:_____

Records:

____ A release form is attached.   ____ No records are available.
____ A release form is on file   ____ Records will be sent.
____ All records are attached.
____ Consent for evaluation, signed by parent, is attached.

____ Send a copy of your report(s), when completed, to:

Figure 1. Sample interagency referral form. (Adapted with Permission of the Florida Department of Education, Bureau of Education for Exceptional Students, from *Interagency problem solving*, [1989], p. 66)

Identification of Contact People

The council should identify personnel who handle referrals in each agency. Knowing the name of a contact person who can answer questions about the appropriateness of possible referrals facilitates the referral system and minimizes inappropriate referrals.

A telephone call about requirements can prevent wasted time and frustration for both parents and agency personnel.

Exchange of Agency Brochures and Information

Agency brochures and other written information are helpful when referring parents to other agencies. The interagency council facilitates the exchange of brochures and ensures that representatives maintain sufficient supplies. As brochures become outdated, monthly council meetings allow for the dissemination of revised copies and a description of significant changes in procedures and services.

Many agency programs have developed videotapes that explain their history, mission, and services. These materials also help parents to understand the federal, state, and local agencies that serve their children.

Updates on Program Openings, Waiting Lists, Expansions, and Cutbacks

The current status of an agency must be considered in making a referral. The availability of resources constantly changes during any given year. Vacancies occur as families move away and withdraw their children from local programs; expansions of programs and services create new resources. On the other hand, there will be times when some agencies may be temporarily unable to serve new children because classroom programs or caseloads are at capacity. Funding cutbacks or temporary deficits in agency budgets often result in a short-term "hold" on commitments for additional services.

As these changes in available resources occur, agency personnel should be alerted so that referrals can be redirected. The ability of the council to identify shifts in resources prevents delays in providing services, and the frustration of parents and agency personnel can be minimized or eliminated.

COORDINATION OF SCREENING SERVICES

A lack of resources for providing developmental and sensory (vision and hearing) screenings to preschool children at referral is a common problem. Most preschool programs provide health or developmental screening to children enrolled in the pro-

grams but do not screen children who are not enrolled. As a result, a social worker in a protective services program may find it difficult to secure a developmental screening for a young child suspected of developmental delays.

It is important to know where and how to refer the child who needs screening services. If the council has identified the agencies and programs that provide these services by using the community agency services matrix (see chap. 11, this volume), members will be aware of screening resources. When an inadequate number of such services exists, the council can identify ways to increase the number of options through coordination of services or new interagency collaborative efforts.

EVALUATION SERVICES

Identification of Existing Evaluation Activities

Evaluation activities constitute the primary area of duplication of services. It is easier to provide evaluation services than services required for treatment. A child often receives duplication in evaluation without the family realizing that the same service was provided by another specialist or agency weeks or months earlier. Both time and funding are spent needlessly.

Duplication arises from several sources. Most often, an evaluation is conducted by an agency that has no knowledge of a previous evaluation. Lack of communication among agencies or the absence of a functional tracking system may be the cause. Parents, eager to cooperate with recommendations, are unaware of duplication and the resultant time delay in eventual provision of services.

Some duplication of evaluation, however, is deliberate and is based on an attitude that the evaluations provided by personnel of other agencies are inferior. Or, a policy denying reciprocity with regard to evaluation reports may exist. In considering the best interest of the child, such attitudes and policies are not defensible. Duplication results in waste of time, money, energy, and efficiency by agency personnel and a delay in providing actual intervention services to the child. It also imposes additional and unnecessary burdens on parents to take time off from work, schedule appointments, and subject their child to additional testing.

Where unnecessary duplication exists, its sources should be identified and corrected. The council can discuss each agency's requirements related to evaluation and placement. An eligibility checklist can be developed to clarify required evaluation components and ensure that appropriate information is available. Programs (e.g., school district, Head Start) that require psychological evaluations to be completed by properly certified psychologists must make these requirements clear to other agencies. If evaluation personnel of an agency are educational specialists rather than certified psychologists, for example, it is important for them to know why their reports are not used for placement purposes in these cases. This knowledge will make it clear that the decisions are based on state or federal program requirements rather than what may be misinterpreted as territorial issues.

Discussion of these requirements and procedures can result in agreements, informal or formal, among agencies relative to evaluation procedures and utilization of reports. The agencies can develop interdisciplinary evaluation procedures for young preschool children, share recommendations for the preferred or most appropriate instruments and procedures, and provide cross-training.

Coordination of Evaluation Activities

When the council reviews the manner in which preschool children are evaluated and referred, it generally finds significant duplication of effort. Fragmented evaluation activities that consume considerable time and effort are also detected. Agencies are often unaware of evaluations conducted by other agencies, are unable to secure them easily, or even refuse to accept them and deliberately duplicate the effort. The evaluation process requires coordination and streamlining to avoid this unnecessary duplication and drain on resources. Coordination benefits the child, the family, and the agencies.

The interagency council can improve the evaluation process through the following five activities:

1. Identify current evaluation practices.
2. Standardize the best evaluation practice.
3. Identify evaluation personnel who specialize in infants and preschool children.
4. Clarify evaluation requirements, such as tests, procedures, and examiner credentials.
5. Encourage acceptance of evaluations performed by other agencies.

TRANSITION SERVICES

The need for systematic interagency activities for transition of children between agencies is often overlooked. Agency programs spend considerable time on identification of children with disabilities but often fail to plan for the transfer or transition of children between agencies (Gallaher, Maddox, & Edgar, 1984). A number of questions must be answered. Who will be involved in the transition? How will it take place? When will it occur? What is required to accomplish it? How will it change the child's program? Properly planned transition activities require understanding, precise coordination between agencies, and effective communication. Transition includes planning activities involving three primary target groups: 1) agency personnel, including teachers and therapists; 2) the child; and 3) the parents or family.

Transition procedures will emerge as a natural consequence of effective interagency relationships. In the spring of each year, the council should address the transition of children from program to program. Establishing timelines and understanding agency procedures and constraints result in a good foundation for transition procedures. Information available in a child tracking system (see chap. 14, this volume) can also alert agencies to the type and number of children requiring transition each year.

Although the primary time for transition activities is in the spring as agencies prepare for the start of the next school year, not all children are transferred at that time. There are many reasons why a child's intervention program may require modification and transition services during other times of the year. The activities and needs of the child, parents, and agency staff members remain the same and should be considered in the procedures established for transition.

Development of Agency Procedures and Timelines for Effective Transition

In January or February of each year, personnel of preschool programs begin plans for the following year, including an assessment of the number of children who will leave programs, the number of vacancies to be filled, the assessment and staffing time needed prior to placement of children, the type of expansion or program modification needed, personnel changes, and funding needs. The interagency council provides the optimal setting for discussion of transition plans related to these considerations and future program planning.

Council discussions can include clarification of agency roles, timelines for transition, and general procedures relating to the following eight issues:

1. The children who require transition services
2. Procedures for notifying parents
3. Timelines for referral to the receiving agencies
4. Requirements for placement and enrollment (e.g., evaluations, forms, birth

records, physical examinations, immunizations)
5. Evaluation requirements and responsibilities
6. Personnel responsibilities
7. Staffing and IFSP/IEP development procedures
8. Transfer of records and case files

Use of a Child Tracking System

If a child tracking system is operational, the council coordinator can generate lists of children who require transition services. Several groups can be included. For example, one list identifies 5-year-old children who are expected to enter the school district kindergarten or primary exceptional student education programs. A second list identifies children who will be age-eligible for transfer from community programs to preschool programs of the school district. A third includes children who may need transition from home-based to center-based models. Any number of alternatives are possible, depending on the need. If a new program is being developed for children with multiple disabilities or with physical disabilities, for instance, the child tracking system can generate a list of potential enrollees.

This use of the child tracking system can be important for school district programs in projection of full-time equivalents (FTE) by exceptionality for the coming year. It can assist each community program in more precise planning, allocation of units and space, and hiring or preparation of staff.

Identification of Transition Activities for Parents

The transition of a child from one agency to another represents a critical time for parents and a period of potential stress (MacKeith, 1973). Separation from a program and staff members who have provided considerable support can be an anxious experience for parents. Not knowing what lies ahead in the new program may produce even greater anxiety. The presence of the child with disabilities and his or her unique educational needs may affect the family's perceived control (Bailey & Simeonsson, 1984). Not knowing what to do, how to access needed services, or to whom to turn is frustrating for parents and affects their feelings of competence. To recognize this critical period and the needs that parents have, particularly in the planning process, obligates both the sending and receiving agency programs to organize activities that will assist the parents in making a smooth transition.

Parent orientation meetings can be scheduled to explain the series of upcoming events. The receiving program coordinator or administrator should meet with the parents as a group to explain the program and the services provided and ensure them that they will be involved in the planning process. The meeting can relieve the anxiety of parents and give them an opportunity to ask questions about the program. Common parental concerns include transportation, distance of the program from home, continuation of the existing individual educational program, staff–child ratio, program hours, and continuation of therapy provided in the current program.

It is critical that parents realize that the services and programs provided by the agencies naturally change as the child grows. The home-based parent training program gives way to more direct child intervention in a center-based program. Programs and services that are focused on a medical model and provide individual therapy early in the child's life eventually give way to an educational model and group therapy as the child becomes older and more independent. The differences in these programs must be explained to parents in a positive manner. Otherwise, parents often confuse these appropriate differences in program models with qualitative differences and have the mistaken notion that the new program will not be as effective for their child. Because of its rapport and credibility with the parents, the sending agency plays the key role in helping

parents to understand the changing needs of their child with respect to appropriate program models.

Development of Transition Activities for Children

Children also must be prepared for a change in programs. Agency personnel often underestimate the knowledge and needs of children. Classroom activities may be introduced to help explain the change. A field trip to the playground or other facility of the receiving center can gradually expose the child to the idea of moving to a new place. Preschool graduation ceremonies often provide a sense of closure, positive progression, and pride in the transition that is about to occur. These ceremonies are important for both the child and the parent. They symbolize in a concrete manner the notion that the child is growing and moving on to greater independence. *A Transition Kit: Transition from Preschool to Kindergarten* (1988), available from the Chapel Hill Training-Outreach Program, Lincoln Center, Chapel Hill, North Carolina 27514, provides a multitude of parent and child activities, as well as curricular activities for the classroom that can help children to make a smooth transition.

Development of Transition Activities for Agency Staffs

Some of the most effective transition activities developed for parents and children can be quickly undermined by the actions or comments of teachers, therapists, and other staff. Staff members must be aware of the impact of their comments to parents about other programs and agencies. "Letting go" is often very difficult for teachers and therapists. They have invested a significant amount of time, care, and effort in the child and the family. Their natural inclination to be protective often has unintentional but negative effects. If they give parents the impression that the receiving agency will not provide the kind of services the child requires or if they criticize staff members, parental trust may be unfairly undermined and negative expectations established. Staff members must realize that they may be doing the family a great disservice by creating a sense of caution or mistrust toward the receiving agency.

Staff members of the sending agency should have the opportunity to participate in the educational or service plan developed by the receiving agency. Their knowledge of the child must be taken into consideration and utilized in the transition. They should be encouraged to assist parents with the transition in a positive manner. Teachers and therapists should help parents to have realistic expectations about their child and the new program. They can be supportive of the parents' feelings about the change and perhaps arrange a meeting or telephone conference with staff members of the receiving agency.

Elimination of Unnecessary Duplication in Evaluation

A time delay frequently occurs within the transition sequence when agencies require additional evaluations of children despite the fact that thorough evaluation services have already been provided by the agencies currently serving the children. The interagency council is in a position to identify and discuss these potential sources of duplication and determine how they can be resolved. Through determination of appropriate timelines and provision of evaluation reports to the initial referral, much of this duplication can be avoided.

Development of a Transition Guide

The interagency council may demonstrate its commitment to the concept of effective transition by developing a booklet or brochure to assist parents during transition. It might describe the differences among various community program delivery models as they relate to the needs of the child and the family. The guide might also explain the differences between medical and educational models, and indicate when each is most appropriate in the child's life.

A transition guide can inform parents about entrance procedures of various agencies and their requirements, including physical examinations, immunizations, and documentation of birth date. It can provide helpful information on how these requirements are met. Parents need to know, for example, if the health department regularly schedules appointments for preschool physical examinations 2 months in advance. Otherwise, they may wait until the week before the child is scheduled to begin the program, only to find that the physical requirement will significantly delay the initiation of services. This type of assistance helps parents to avoid confusion and stress and to save time as they search for resources in the community.

REFERENCES

Bailey, D.B., & Simeonsson, R.J. (1984). Critical issues underlying research and intervention with families of young handicapped children. *Journal of the Division for Early Childhood, 9*(1), 38–48.

Blackman, J.A. (1986). *Warning signals: Basic criteria for tracking at-risk infants and toddlers.* Washington, DC: National Center for Clinical Infant Programs.

Frost, L., Starzyk, P., George, S., & MacLaughlin, J. (1984). Birth complication reporting: The effect of birth certificate design. *American Journal of Public Health, 74*(5), 505–506.

Gallaher, J., Maddox, M., & Edgar, E. (1984). *Early childhood interagency transition model.* Seattle: University of Washington.

Interagency problem solving (1989). Tallahassee: Florida Department of Education, Bureau of Education for Exceptional Students.

MacKeith, R. (1973). The feelings and behavior of parents of handicapped children. *Developmental Medicine and Child Neurology, 15,* 524–527.

Meisels, S.J. (1984). Prediction, prevention and developmental screening in the EPSDT program. In H.W. Stevenson & A.E. Siegel (Eds.), *Child development research and social policy.* Chicago: University of Chicago Press.

Peterson, N. (1987). *Early intervention for handicapped and at-risk children.* Denver: Love Publishing Co.

Smith, B. (Ed.). (1988). *Mapping the future for children with special needs: PL 99–457.* Washington, DC: Administration on Developmental Disabilities.

A transition kit: Transition from preschool to kindergarten. (1988). Chapel Hill, NC: Chapel Hill Training-Outreach Program.

Chapter 13

Parent Services
and Staff Development

During stage 2 of interagency council development, activities acknowledge family involvement as a well-established component of early intervention programs. In its broadest context, parent involvement implies shared responsibility for the child's educational process. It also implies that the child with a disability, as a member of a dynamic family unit, has as great an impact on the family as the family has on the child; it is a reciprocal relationship (Linder, 1983).

PARENT EDUCATION AND SUPPORT

Family-Focused Intervention

Research in parent training has demonstrated that when specific aspects of family involvement are targeted for intervention, positive results are obtained. Despite data obtained from a meta-analysis that suggest this interpretation is questionable (Casto & Lewis, 1984; Casto & Mastropieri, 1986), a number of arguments in favor of strong parental involvement exist (Linder, 1983; Peterson, 1987). These include:

Parents and primary care givers are the key teachers and socializing agents for children in the early years.
Parents can be effective teachers of their own children.
The child's home environment can facilitate learning; early intervention services help parents to create an optimal learning environment in the home.
Parents of young children with disabilities typically face additional demands and

stresses that test their coping abilities and parenting skills.
Intervention works best when parents and professionals work toward common goals and apply compatible strategies.
Parent involvement helps to build parent and community support for early intervention programs.
Parents have a right to be informed about and participate in educational programming for their child; involvement in planning and decision making ensures that needs are addressed at all levels.
Parents increase sensitivity to the role of cultural and religious beliefs that affect the family's ability to cope with the presence of a child with disabilities.
Parent involvement increases parent knowledge and ability to gain access to community resources.

An understanding of the significance of the family in the child's total development has increased emphasis on parent education, training, and support programs. Some state and federal programs require parent participation as a program component. Development of effective parent components requires substantial effort, knowledge, resources, and time. Large early intervention programs with considerable resources often find it easier to provide a wide range of parent services than small community programs that lack sufficient staff, time, and funding to implement the desired activities. Without coordination of the various parent education efforts that emerge, however, duplication and confusion may result.

Because the provision of parent services and support is common to all preschool programs, a coordination of efforts and combination of resources among the community agencies can result in a successful and comprehensive continuum of parent services. In this manner, agencies identify their strengths and make reasonable contributions, rather than attempting to create their own assortments of parent education activities. Unnecessary waste, duplication, and underutilization of resources are avoided.

Continuum of Parent Services

The parents of young children with disabilities and those at risk form a heterogeneous group. Parents differ widely in their personal resources, family support systems, educational backgrounds, literacy levels, socioeconomic status, and their abilities to cope with the unique needs of their children. No two parents or families are exactly alike; the needs of each require an individualized approach. All parents do not want or need to be involved in early intervention programs in the same way or to the same degree. Families also change over time and may move along a continuum of possible levels of participation, depending on the level of stress, environmental crises, and the developmental stage of their children (Nash, 1991). A wide range of activities can be developed through interagency coordination so that parents have a choice of options for participation.

Parent activities and services can be represented as points along a continuum that vary by the type and extent of participation. Five overlapping dimensions of parent services can be defined (Lillie & Trohanis, 1976):

1. *Parent Involvement:* Assistance from the parents in ongoing program activities, educational planning, and activities and interaction with the child is sought. Involvement enhances parental self-worth, increased understanding, and a broader repertoire of experiences with their child. Participation in volunteer activities, parent advisory groups, fundraising events, staffings, conferences, educational plan development, and implementation of activities for home are examples of parent involvement. Most all early intervention programs incorporate this broad level.

2. *Parent Information:* Assisting a family to understand the terminology, rationale, activities, and objectives of its child's program provides the parents with more accurate knowledge of the program and the child's unique needs and development. Parent information can be provided through newsletters, flyers, mailings, calendars of events, pamphlets, directories, and handouts. The extent of information provided to parents by agency programs varies according to personnel time, budgetary considerations, and other resources.

3. *Parent Education:* This field of study is composed of workshops, training sessions, seminars, and courses that teach new material. Parent groups often meet in the evenings and utilize a variety of teaching methods, including lectures, participatory instruction, and audiovisual materials. Workshops are generally organized and taught by professionals. Parent education activities are frequently organized through school programs, community colleges, mental health agencies, and parent resource programs.

4. *Parent Training:* Actual demonstration of effective child-rearing practices and skills is an important component that can be done as a home-based or center-based activity. The training is usually done on an individual basis, rather than in a group. Often costly, these services are used as a service delivery model to reach families of infants and toddlers with disabilities or those at high risk.

5. *Parent Support:* Parents often have social and emotional needs for support to

reduce anxieties caused by the feelings of inadequacy, guilt, or anger within the family. Support also serves to increase positive feelings about the family as a unit. These activities are provided on an individual basis or through a parent support group. They encourage support, advice, understanding, comfort, motivation, information, and nonjudgmental listening. Parents, rather than professionals, usually conduct the activities.

Services provided to parents must be matched to their needs at any given time. Various types of parent services (e.g., support, training, education) are appropriate at different times in their lives. No one type of parent activity is superior to others—activities can be appropriately matched according to the particular needs of the par-

ent. The mother of a newborn child with Down syndrome, for example, may have the greatest need initially for support, comfort, and understanding from another parent who has experienced the same situation. The need for guidance, empathy, and advice plays a critical role in parents' growth toward accepting the disability of a child and developing realistic expectations for the future. In addition to support, parents need information that helps them to understand the child's condition and the roles they play in maximizing his or her progress. Over a period of time, the parents' need for emotional support may decrease and the role of home-based parent training may become their primary interest. The need for various kinds of information may remain high as the child grows, particularly in relation to an understanding of community resources; laws concerning the education and rights of children

---

Agency Survey: Parent Services

Agency: _____

Agency's target population: _____

Parent services provided: _____

_____

Times and days of parent groups: _____

Responsible staff member: _____

Groups open to other parents?   Yes _____ No _____

Does a lending library exist?   Yes _____ No _____

The library contains: Toys _____ Books _____ Videos _____

Instructors with expertise in conducting parent groups and workshops:

_____

_____

Indicate facilities that could be used for parent groups:
   When available? _____

   Accommodates _____ parents.

   Restrictions / conditions on use: _____

Other comments:

Return to:

Figure 1.   Sample survey to identify existing parent activities.

AGENCY	FOCUS	TARGET POP.	LOCATION
SCHOOL DISTRICT	PARENT EDUCATION AND SUPPORT GROUP	PARENTS OF PRE-SCHOOL DEAF CHILDREN	BAYSIDE ELEMENTARY
SCHOOL DISTRICT	INFANT STIMULATION FOR DISABLED AND DEVELOPMENTALLY DELAYED CHILDREN	PARENTS AND 0-3 YEAR OLD DELAYED INFANTS & TODDLERS	CHRIST EPISCOPAL CHURCH NURSERY
PARENT RESOURCE PROGRAM	GENERAL & DISABILITY SPECIFIC PARENT EDUCATION	COMMUNITY	VARIOUS SITES AROUND COMMUNITY
PARENT TRAINING	PARENT TRAINING	PARENTS OF B-5 DEVELOPMENTALLY DELAYED CHILDREN	HOME BASED
HEAD START	GENERAL PARENT INVOLVEMENT	PARENTS 3-5 YEAR DISADVANTAGED CHILDREN	CENTER OR HOME VISITS
PARENT CARE PROGRAM	PREVENTION SERVICES	COMMUNITY	CENTER AND COMMUNITY
PARENT SUPPORT GROUP	PARENT SUPPORT, INFORMATION, EDUCATION	PARENTS OF DISABLED, 0-10 YEARS	EASTER SEAL SOCIETY
PARENT-TO-PARENT	PARENT SUPPORT	PARENTS OF NEWBORNS WITH DISABILITIES	HOSPITAL/HOME
SPECIAL BEGINNINGS	PARENT SUPPORT	PARENTS OF PREEMIES AND HIGH RISK INFANTS	HOSPITAL/HOME
COMPASSIONATE FRIENDS	PARENT SUPPORT	BEREAVED PARENTS	BLAKE HOSPITAL
F.A.C.E.	PARENT SUPPORT AND EDUCATION	PARENTS OF CHILDREN WITH CRANIO-FACIAL DISORDERS	SARASOTA MEMORIAL HOSPITAL
PROJECT RAINBOW	FAMILY SUPPORT	CHRONICALLY ILL CHILD, YOUNG ADULTS AND THEIR FAMILIES	HOME

Figure 2. Excerpt from a sample chart showing community parent groups.

with disabilities; such services as speech, occupational, and physical therapy; and other available programs. Formal parent education workshops and groups provide another avenue for learning about the child's disability, general parenting skills, and related issues. General parent involvement can be encouraged in every aspect of decision making and educational planning.

Coordination of Parent Services

The role of the interagency council in coordinating parent services relates to eight areas of activity.

Identification of Existing Parent Services
Almost every early intervention program provides some type of parent service. These activities may be general or specific to a

TIME/DAY	SIZE	COST TO PARENT	CONTACT
PARENTS SCHEDULE EVERY OTHER MONTH: 3:00 PM	UNLIMITED	NONE	DEBBIE JONES 555-3456
10:00-NOON, EACH FRIDAY	SMALL GROUP	NONE	JAN LOGAN 555-5678
SCHEDULED	GROUPS OF 15 OR MORE	VARIES WITH CLASS	CRYSTAL HENRY 555-9876
SCHEDULED WITH PARENT	INDIVIDUAL AND GROUP	NONE	CATHY SPRING 555-8347
7-8:30 PM SCHEDULED AS NEEDED	UNLIMITED	NONE	LISA WATERS 555-1234
SCHEDULED	GROUP	NONE	CONNIE SMITH 555-0000
4TH TUESDAY 7:00-9:00 PM	GROUP	NONE	KIM BAGLEY 555-4567
SCHEDULED AS NEEDED	INDIVIDUAL	HOME	MYRIAM RAINS 555-7654
WHENEVER NEEDED	INDIVIDUAL	NONE	LAURA HEAR 555-0987
4TH MONDAY 7:30 PM	INDIVIDUAL OR GROUP	NONE	ANITA UPSTER 555-4823
2ND TUESDAY 7:30 PM	INDIVIDUAL OR GROUP	$5.00/YEAR	BARB EASON 555-5904
WHENEVER NEEDED/24 HOURS/DAY	INDIVIDUAL AND GROUP	NONE	JUDY ROBERTS 555-9999

Figure 2. (*continued*)

condition, such as Down syndrome, cleft palate, or cerebral palsy. The interagency council can compile information about existing parent groups, lending libraries, cooperatives, support groups, respite services, and babysitting services. Possible locations and instructors for workshops can be identified through a survey as shown in Figure 1. This information is needed before the council can implement a comprehensive, coordinated system of parent services.

Identification of Related Community Services Parent resources that address broad age ranges or target groups also exist in communities. Parent groups providing support to parents of premature infants, abused children, terminally ill children, and bereaved families can be identified. The March of Dimes, United Way, Easter Seal Society, Epilepsy Foundation, and local hospitals may also provide support, information, and educational groups for parents.

PARENT SURVEY

Dear Parent:

Below is a list of possible topics for workshops. Please check up to five topics that would be of most interest to you. Add any other suggestions that are not listed. Return this form by _____ to:

_____ Mainstreaming
_____ Understanding individualized education programs (IEPs)
_____ PL 94-142: Your rights as a parent
_____ Play: How children learn
_____ Understanding mental impairment
_____ Wills, trusts, and guardianship
_____ Adapting your home for the physically impaired child
_____ Learning materials to make at home
_____ Building family strengths
_____ PL 99-475: Services to preschool children
_____ Parent-to-parent support: Benefits and involvement
_____ Understanding psychological evaluation of children
_____ Helping brothers and sisters to understand siblings with disabilities
_____ Respite care
_____ Sibling rivalry
_____ Sign language
_____ Behavior management
_____ Building self-esteem
_____ Genetic counseling
_____ Understanding physical and occupational therapy
_____ Adaptive equipment
_____ Stress reduction
_____ Communicating with your physician
_____ Language experiences at home

Best days for workshops?   Monday   Tuesday   Wednesday   Thursday   Friday   Saturday

Best times?   8–11 A.M.   Lunch hour   1–4 P.M.   7–8 P.M.

Best location?   Elm School   Library   Easter Seal Society   United Cerebral Palsy
                   Other: _____

Have transportation?   Yes   No   I would be able to bring someone without transportation

                                                    Parent: _____

                                                    Phone: _____

Figure 3.   Sample needs assessment for parent workshops. (Used with Permission of the Florida Department of Education, Bureau of Education for Exceptional Students, from *Interagency problem solving,* [1989], p. 100)

After these groups have been identified, information relating to how they are accessed and used can be gathered. Council members may be surprised at the extent of parent resources available in the community. The information can be compiled in the form of a directory, list, or other type of handout. Figure 2 is an example of a chart showing available community parent groups. Linkages with these groups can be created and parents encouraged to participate in the most appropriate groups.

Needs Assessment for Parent Services Agency personnel must be cautious about imposing their values and expectations for parent education on families. Lack of attendance at organized parent meetings may be an indication that the meetings do not meet the needs or interests of families. If feedback is requested from parents about their actual needs and interests, a better planning base can be established. The interagency council can develop and administer needs assessment for parent services across preschool agencies. This information can assist the council in coordinating activities on a community basis. A sample needs assessment for parent workshops is shown in Figure 3.

Designation of a Lead Agency for Parent Services The first step in developing a coordinated system of parent services may be to identify one agency to assume responsibility for coordination. A community parent resource or parent education program, a parent support group, a community college, or an agency program may possess the personnel and expertise to develop this comprehensive effort.

Development of Workshops and Groups Based on Parents' Needs As parents' needs and interests are identified, the council can develop activities and designate appropriate agency personnel or parents to conduct them. Parent activities should be scheduled at the times, days, and locations identified in the needs assessment. Possible workshop topics are listed in Table 1. The locations for parent groups and workshops should be distributed across the various agency programs to maximize accessibility and attendance.

Encouragement of Parent Support Groups Parents of young children with disabilities often need a support group of caring, understanding parents with whom they can identify and discuss their feelings. They need friendship and emotional support in addition to help and information. The need for

Table 1. Suggested topics for parent education workshops

Child growth and development (language, motor, physical, social, emotional, behavioral, cognitive)

Teach a tot; developmental activities for infants and toddlers

Play and learning

Enhancing language development

Disciplining toddlers

Behavior management techniques

Systematic training for effective parenting (STEP)

Developing mealtime and bedtime routines

Enhancing self-esteem of young children

Understanding early intervention services

Access to community resources

Parent-to-parent support services

Understanding your feelings

Dealing with family stress

Sibling rivalry

Family budgeting

Sibling acceptance of disabilities

Single parenting; divorce and separation

Building family strengths

Community economic services

Understanding occupational and physical therapy

Adaptive equipment and toys

Appropriate books and toys that teach

Parent/professional partnerships

Understanding specific disabilities and syndromes

Education for All Handicapped Children Act (PL 94-142); Education of the Handicapped Act Amendments of 1986 (PL 99-457)

Understanding the individualized family service plan (IFSP)

Procedural safeguards

Least restrictive environment

Medical concerns of children with disabilities

Understanding Medicaid and private insurance

Chronic otis media and hearing impairment

Cardiopulmonary resuscitation (CPR) and first-aid procedures

Nutritional needs of young children

support is best met by other parents, not professionals. The interagency council can identify parents capable of organizing effective parent support groups and assist them by providing meeting places, clerical help, funding, printing, and postage. Preschool agencies and programs funded by federal or state grants can include grant objectives that support the needs of such groups. The council should proactively encourage this support.

The interagency council can also search the community for existing support groups that provide valuable resources to families and programs. Identifying these groups prevents needless duplication in the development of additional efforts.

Coordination of Parent Newsletters Newsletters are effective in communicating with parents. They can provide information and parenting tips, and they also enhance public awareness. Most early intervention programs publish a newsletter that is sent to parents, professionals, and perhaps other members of the community. The interagency council can identify existing newsletters, facilitate agency exchange for communication purposes, recommend elimination of duplication, or merge independent newsletters into a common publication that can be used by all programs. A parent resource organization, support group, or community college might assume the responsibility for coordinating the effort across the various early intervention programs.

Coordination of Lending Libraries The development of lending libraries for parents has become a popular activity and is often supported by federal or state grants. In developing these libraries, agencies may purchase expensive materials that already exist in the community. Unnecessary expense and duplication may result in addition to underutilization of the materials if parents are not aware of the location and borrowing procedures of the libraries.

The interagency council can identify existing libraries, compile lists of available materials and books, and develop a directory. A directory provides information on the location of the various lending libraries, procedures for borrowing materials, the length of time materials may be kept, and the names of contact persons. Figure 4 provides an example of a parent lending library directory. Parent trainers, in particular, may be interested in access to this information for use in home programs. Procedures should also be developed for parent evaluation of materials and books and suggestions for the purchase of other materials.

PERSONNEL DEVELOPMENT

Staff Training and Education

Well-prepared, enthusiastic staff members make a program work (Peterson, 1987). As a result, staff training and preparation con-

---

Parent Lending Libraries

Agency: United Cerebral Palsy

Location: 544 24th Avenue,
               Scottsburg

Telephone: 755-4786

Contact: Mary Ellsworth

Hours: 8 A.M.–5 P.M.

Lending Procedures:

Materials may be borrowed by parents whose children are clients of United Cerebral Palsy. Parents may make arrangements by calling Mary Ellsworth or one of the therapists on staff. The loan period varies and is based on need. Most materials may be kept until they are no longer needed.

Materials:

The lending library contains books for parents, videotapes, adaptive equipment, adaptive toys, specialized switches, and miscellaneous therapy and developmental materials. A listing by category can be seen on the following pages.

Figure 4.   Example of a page from a parent lending library directory.

stitute a critical component in the administration of any early childhood program and perhaps one of the most pressing issues related to successful implementation of the Education of the Handicapped Act Amendments of 1986 (PL 99-457) (Bruder & McLean, 1988).

Staff training and in-service education for early childhood programs, particularly those including children with disabilities, present a special challenge. Personnel working with infants and toddlers with disabilities or conditions of risk and their families have unique training requirements (Bricker & Slentz, 1988; McCollum & Bailey, 1991). In the case of infant programs, close meshing of intervention efforts by personnel from different disciplines and transdisciplinary efforts is needed. In an ideal preschool program situation, staff members have training and experience in both early childhood programs and special education. With the current absence of such training programs, personnel with this type of background may be difficult to find.

Because instructional approaches may differ for preschool children, the development of unique teacher and therapist competencies is needed. Emphasis on teams, interdisciplinary intervention (Linder, 1983), interagency collaboration (Bricker & Slentz, 1988), integration of therapy into the classroom activities, and family focused intervention (Bailey & Simeonsson, 1984) provides a need for training that special educators have not been previously afforded.

A notable void in university training programs for educators has been in the area of working with parents. Professionals agree that parent participation and involvement are a vital part of effective early intervention. The most successful programs are those that support parents in their parenting efforts and strengthen the parent–child relationship (Peterson, 1987). Parents, however, are not always welcome parties to educational activities. Lip service has often been paid to parent involvement, but actual practices have often failed to reflect a true commitment.

Recruiting a sufficient number of appropriately trained personnel, such as speech, physical, and occupational therapists, may be difficult, especially in remote or rural areas. The existing staff members may need to acquire special skills to compensate. The rapid expansion of preschool programs and services has further compounded the staff recruitment problem.

The need for personnel training is also obvious in the area of assessing infants, toddlers, and preschool children. School psychologists and social workers with experience in the evaluation of older children may find their skills, assessment instruments, and competencies inadequate to deal with the unique characteristics of very young, multiply impaired children. Every psychologist will not possess the patience, skills, or desire to assist in the evaluation of young preschool children. Some psychologists, accustomed to making a diagnosis on the basis of scores from a standard intelligence test, may become frustrated when they are faced with the motor, speech and language, and behavioral problems displayed by preschool children with disabilities. Also, they may find it difficult to function as a member of an interdisciplinary team and to share the responsibility of diagnosis and recommendation with other professionals. They may be unwilling to place a classification, such as retardation, on a child because of their discomfort with assessment tools and the complicating factors of the child's characteristics.

The need for training administrators of early childhood special education programs should not be overlooked. Leadership is critical in the development of sound programs to assess and intervene in child and family needs. Programs must be built on a thorough understanding of federal and state requirements, least restrictive environment and similar concepts, and competency in collaborating with other agencies. Without this leadership, programs for preschool children with disabilities and those at risk may not develop in a sound, logical manner (see chap. 6, this volume for more information).

As a result of these conditions and the immediate need for qualified, competent, and effective personnel, the in-service training program has a critical role in staff development.

Coordination of Staff Development

The interagency council can be effective in coordinating agency staff development through council activities in nine areas.

Identification of Consultants and Professional Expertise Members of the interagency council, who represent various aspects of intervention, can analyze the need for local staff training in a comprehensive manner. They can pool their knowledge of available consultants and the professional expertise required for successful staff development.

Use of Training Materials Council representatives should identify in-service training materials and kits used within their agencies that might be of interest and use to staff trainers in other agency programs. Sharing these materials can provide needed resources and perhaps avoid excessive expenditure of funds. Such programs as the March of Dimes, Head Start, United Cerebral Palsy, and regional diagnostic and learning resource centers may be valuable sources of training materials.

Identification of Local Agency Training Experts As an alternative to incurring considerable expense for outside consultants and trainers, the agencies should look for experts within their own programs who can provide training. Teachers, therapists, social workers, psychologists, parents, and other staff members with expertise or exemplary practices can be identified and shared with other agencies.

Identification of Local Training Resources The council should attempt to identify any local agencies that have special funds, grants, and other resources earmarked for staff training. Often, an agency has a designated staff trainer or educational specialist whose services can be used. Several agencies might be interested in contributing a portion of the trainer's salary in order to utilize the services to a greater extent.

Available resources may include special training grants given to local agencies. As new training grants are developed, they can be written with the input of multiple agencies.

Opportunities for Observation and Visitation A valuable form of training for staff members may be the opportunity to spend several days in observing teachers and therapists in other agency settings. A useful training activity for a Head Start teacher who has a child with a behavior disorder in her class, for example, might be observation of behavior management skills and techniques used by a trained teacher working with preschool children with emotional disabilities. Likewise, a speech-language pathologist can model strategies to expand and enrich the communication of young children and an occupational therapist demonstrate development of fine motor skills within daily classroom activities. These types of observation and on-site training can provide insight, opportunity for questions, and a richer level of meaning than might be gained from lecture-type training sessions.

Cross-Agency Training Conferences have a way of being notoriously segregated in terms of the participants. Department of education conferences are typically advertised and attended by educators. Health and medical conferences are typically advertised and attended by medical professionals. Conferences dealing with concerns of the family, emotional and social development of children, and family support services are typically attended by social services workers and counselors. An insufficient amount of cross-training is the result of this type of segregation. For agencies to promote an understanding of the whole child in the context of the family requires reaching out to other professional conferences and meetings.

Interagency council members should regularly share notices of conferences and training opportunities they receive. They should also actively encourage participation in the conferences held by related agency programs to secure a well-rounded understanding of the needs of the young child with disabilities and the family.

The individualized family service plan (IFSP) may represent the heart and soul of the Part H program. Effective strategies for interagency planning of a process for IFSP development are essential if the necessary array of services for a given child is to become a reality. The degree to which interagency planners are able to provide simultaneous training of early intervention teachers, therapists, service coordinators, and other

staff members in the IFSP process and the nature of family-focused intervention will directly influence the effective implementation of council decisions, related to these services.

Coordination of Interagency Staff Training The interagency council may wish to consider a comprehensive plan of staff development across agencies. An interagency needs assessment could be completed such as the sample shown in Figure 5. Based on the results of the assessment, staff training activities can be identified and developed. Local agency experts and outside consul-

---

In-Service Needs Assessment

Name of agency: _____

Name of agency representative: _____

I. Please compile and summarize the results of the in-service needs assessments completed by teachers and staff from your agency. Present the information below, along with your comments in regard to priority in-service needs.

Summary:

Identified priorities (in order):
1.
2.
3.
4.
5.

II. List the in-service days that your agency has designated:

_____

_____

III. Can your staff be released on other days to attend countywide in-service? Explain: _____

_____

IV. What are the best times for your staff to attend in-service (full days, half days, specific days of the week, etc.)? _____

_____

(continued)

Figure 5. Sample needs assessment form for in-service activities. (Used with Permission of the Florida Department of Education, Bureau of Education for Exceptional Students, from *Interagency problem solving*, [1989], pp. 89–91)

Figure 5.   (*continued*)

V. Would your agency be willing to allow other teachers and aides to visit and observe your program?
Yes _____No _____
Comments: _____

_____

VI. Does your agency have a suitable facility for an in-service program? Yes _____No _____
If yes, would you be willing to house select programs?
Describe the meeting space available:

_____

_____

VII. Does your agency have some financial resources with which to jointly fund a consultant?
Yes _____No _____
Comments: _____

_____

VIII. List personnel at your agency who could provide an in-service program:

Name: In-service topic:

_____

_____

_____

_____

_____

IX. List outside consultants whom you would highly recommend for specific training areas:

Name   Program/Location   Topic   Fee

_____

_____

_____

_____

_____

tants can be identified and chosen. Training should be scheduled mutually by the agency representatives to ensure accessibility. Agencies can share financial and organizational responsibilities. Some may contribute to the actual cost of the consultant or trainer and others contribute in another way, such as providing the facility, refreshments, or materials, so that training is a joint venture.

Interagency Procedures for Certification of Teachers in Nonpublic Programs   In order for teachers to secure certification, they must meet certain training and internship requirements. Small nonpublic schools and centers, such as The Arc center, private preschool programs for children with disabilities, clinics, and rehabilitation centers may have only a few teachers and need assistance to meet state internship and supervision requirements.

Training of supervisors and peer teachers under public school beginning-teacher or internship programs should be extended to personnel in the nonpublic school settings. The council can develop procedures to assist agencies in devising their plans and to ensure that agency personnel have the same opportunities for certification as public school teachers.

Central Directory of Trainers and Consultants To assist in staff development through in-service workshops and consultation, the interagency council can pool its knowledge of available agency experts and private consultants who can be used as re-sources. These individuals may be found in public and private agencies, training and technical assistance programs, demonstration projects, personnel training centers, colleges, and universities. The council can compile a central directory that contains a range of personnel and expertise from multiple disciplines and professions.

REFERENCES

Bailey, D.B., & Simeonsson, R.J. (1984). Critical issues underlying research and intervention with families of young handicapped children. *Journal of the Division for Early Childhood, 2*(1), 38–48.

Bricker, D., & Slentz, K. (1988). Personnel preparation: Handicapped infants. In M.C. Wang, M.C. Reynolds, & H.J. Walberg (Eds.), *Handbook of special education: Research and practice* (pp. 319–345). Elmsford, NY: Pergamon.

Bruder, M.B., & McLean, M. (1988). Personnel preparation for infant interventionists: A review of federally funded projects. *Journal of the Division for Early Childhood, 12*(4), 299–305.

Casto, G., & Lewis, A.C. (1984). Parent involvement in infant and preschool programs. *Journal of the Division for Early Childhood, 9,* 49–56.

Casto, G., & Mastropieri, M.A. (1986). The efficacy of early intervention programs: A meta-analysis. *Exceptional Children, 52,* 417–424.

Interagency problem solving (1989). Tallahassee: Florida Department of Education, Bureau of Education for Exceptional Students.

Lillie, D.L., & Trohanis, P.L. (1976). *Teaching parents to teach.* New York: Walker & Co.

Linder, T.W. (1983). *Early childhood special education: Program development and administration.* Baltimore: Paul H. Brookes Publishing Co.

McCollum, J.A., & Bailey, D.B. (1991). Developing comprehensive personnel systems: Issues and alternatives. *Journal of Early Intervention, 15*(1), 57–65.

Nash, J.K. (1991). Public Law 99-457: Facilitating family participation on the multidisciplinary team. *Journal of Early Intervention, 14*(4), 318–326.

Peterson, N. (1987). *Early intervention for handicapped and at-risk children.* Denver: Love Publishing Co.

Chapter 14

Coordination of Case Management

Based on the premise that young children with disabilities and their families require comprehensive services that are unlikely to be available through any one agency, the Education of the Handicapped Act Amendments of 1986 (PL 99-457) emphasize the role of the case management function and the case manager. The individualized family service plan (IFSP), exemplifying the concept of coordination of public and private sources to meet child and family needs, requires case management services to ensure full and proper implementation. These services are also required to ensure that support to the family provides opportunities for enhancement of the family's ability to become independent, active, and a partner in early intervention. Congress intended for case management practices to support and strengthen families in order to increase their ability to mobilize resources to meet their needs (Dunst & Trivette, 1989).

NEW PERSPECTIVES ON CASE MANAGEMENT

The yet undefined process of case management under PL 99-457 creates a number of possibilities for implementation of various practices and models. Many traditional case management models have been based on the assumption that families and children are passive recipients of resources and services. Such models are clearly inconsistent with the intent of the law (Dunst, 1991). As such, professionals must ensure that the manner in which case management is conceptualized, operationalized, and implemented under PL 99-457 is designed for optimal influence on the child, parent, and family functioning.

A new paradigm of case management has emerged under PL 99-457. The term *case management,* implying that children and families need to be "managed," has been replaced by the term *service coordination.* Contemporary models of service coordination are transforming previous practices from an agency-driven to a family-driven focus. As a result, implementation of the IFSP creates opportunities to develop enabling and empowering models of service coordination. The effectiveness of the model of service coordination, however, depends on the ability to maintain an ongoing, supportive relationship with the family and an understanding of local services and options. Local interagency councils will play a critical role in the development of local family supports, including case management or service coordination strategies, across programs.

Developing a system of service coordination under PL 99-457 will involve a host of community agencies, public and private. Furthermore, an effective system will require that the agencies share a common set of principles and practices that will enable multiple service providers involved with the same family to work concurrently in implementing the IFSP. If a primary focus involves assisting families to gain access to necessary agency resources, those agencies must be committed to a system that is responsive to parental attempts at access. A bilevel (community and family) system of case management or service coordination must consist of two components:

1. A community system of comprehensive and coordinated services that is responsive and easy for families to access
2. A family-focused system of necessary

167

supports to enable and empower families in obtaining available community services needed for their children

The bilevel system is imperative. It is not sufficient to provide service coordination designed to strengthen families and avoid dependence on the service coordinator alone. If families are to be empowered, the community system of providers must be coordinated and responsive to their needs and preferences.

CASE MANAGEMENT APPROACHES

Traditional Approaches

Historically, case management emerged out of the casework practices of social workers during the 1920s and 1930s and, more recently, from the deinstitutionalization movements in the fields of mental health and mental retardation (Dunst & Trivette, 1989). Case management practices have occurred largely in response to the fragmented and uncoordinated system of human services, medical, and educational programs. Various models of case management exist, but they all involve coordination and integration of services and serve to match the needs of the client to service providers.

The term *case management* has traditionally referred to facilitating a comprehensive assessment of client needs, developing an individualized service plan, providing access to the needed services, and monitoring the appropriateness and effectiveness of those services. The case manager usually has a large caseload and tells the family what it needs and what services it can have. Two traditional approaches to case management, the role-focused approach and the resource procurement approach, have been identified by Dunst and Trivette (1989). The role-focused approach has emphasized the functions and role of the case manager as they relate to securing and controlling the services for the client. This approach regards clients generally as incompetent, passive recipients of services who are unable to make appropriate decisions and must depend on the case manager and the system. These services are agency-driven and characterized by agency allocation of available resources. The resource procurement approach has been typically characterized by the coordination and integration of services. Although the case manager may be highly sensitive to provide or mobilize the services and supports needed, clients are not actively engaged in accessing the resources and they remain passive recipients.

Contemporary Approaches

Through the passage of PL 99-457 and amendments, Congress intended that comprehensive and community-based early intervention and preschool services, including procedures for case management, be instituted. The language of Part H implies a focus on the enhancement of family functioning (Dokecki & Heflinger, 1989), thus creating an opportunity for development of a system of case management or service coordination that views parents and service providers as equal partners in assessment, decision making, and intervention. This gradual shift from a child-centered approach to a family-centered approach in early intervention and service coordination has been witnessed during the past several years (Dunst, Trivette, & Deal, 1988; McGonigel & Garland, 1988; McGonigel, Kaufmann, & Johnson, 1991).

The alternative to the traditional approach reverses the roles and encourages direction by the family with the assistance of the professionals. In this role, the professional helps the family to identify the short- and long-term outcomes and support services needed and assists the family to gain access to these services (Duwa, Kassack, & Graham, 1990). If the services do not exist, the case manager works with community-based agencies to utilize existing services or create new services. The local interagency council may be the primary vehicle for organizing new and collaborative programs to meet the needs of children and families.

At the heart of the family centered philosophy are the concepts of enablement and empowerment. *Parent enablement* is the primary means of strengthening families. The term refers to the creation of opportunities and means for families to apply their present abilities and current competencies while acquiring new abilities to meet the needs of their children (McGonigel et al., 1991). A *client empowerment* approach emphasizes the enhancement of a client's ability to negotiate service systems and to acquire needed services (Dunst & Trivette, 1989; Levine & Fleming, 1984; Weil & Karls, 1985), rather than the promotion of a passive and dependent role. The client empowerment approach to service coordination represents both a process and an outcome that may take different forms in different families. The empowerment process refers to interaction with a family that enables the family to maintain or acquire a sense of control over its family life and perceive its own strengths, abilities, and actions as the reason for the positive changes resulting from early intervention services (Johnson, McGonigel, & Kaufmann, 1989).

Service coordination incorporates the functions and efforts concerned with mobilization of resources and services required to meet the needs of children with disabilities (Austin, 1983; Dunst & Trivette, 1989; Erickson, 1981; Weil & Karls, 1985). Other definitions, emphasizing the importance of family-focused services, have emerged:

> Services provided to families of handicapped infants and toddlers to assist them in gaining access to early intervention . . . and other services identified in the . . . Individualized Family Service Plan. (Education of the Handicapped Act Amendments of 1986, House of Representatives Report 99-860, p. 8)

> A set of goal-oriented activities which organize, coordinate, and monitor service delivery based on measurable objectives intended to meet the needs of . . . children and their families. (Freedman, Reiss, & Pierce, 1987, p. 2)

> The process by which early intervention needs of children and families are linked and monitored in order to ensure that the early intervention needs of children and families are addressed in a systematic manner. (Smith, 1987, p. 2)

Client empowerment approaches emphasize three factors: 1) integration and coordination of services, 2) identification of needs and provision of supports in response to client needs, and 3) use of procedures that empower clients by enhancing their abilities to function as independently as possible to assume an active, rather than a passive, role in the case management process (Dunst & Trivette, 1989; Levine & Fleming, 1984; Weil & Karls, 1985).

SERVICE COORDINATION AT TWO LEVELS

If service coordination refers to those functions designed to assist families in securing access to early intervention services, two levels might be described: 1) the community level that is coordinated by the interagency council, and 2) the family level. Although each level offers a different perspective of service coordination, the two levels are interdependent. The desired outcome for both is provision of a coordinated and comprehensive program for each child and family, based on the expressed needs and priorities of the family.

Coordination at the Community Level

The complex service delivery system has fostered the traditional role-focused and resource procurement approaches of case management. These approaches have been precipitated by a fragmented system, lack of coordination, and overprotection of limited agency resources. Resource procurement approaches, generally well-intentioned, have resulted from the overwhelming maze of services and eligibilities that families have been unable or too frustrated to negotiate. Case managers themselves, however, have been unable to comprehend and navigate the system in their attempts to assist families.

The current professionally driven nature of the service delivery system, where professionals determine the services to be provided, must be transformed. Agency personnel must take the leadership and responsibility for repairing the uncoordinated and unresponsive system that exists. This is the level of case management for which the interagency council is responsible: to identify existing community resources, coordinate resources, complete the array of needed services, and define the respective roles and responsibilities of the various agencies and programs. The council must also identify program and policy constraints that restrict family access to needed services. Policies must be adopted and implemented that can enable parents to maintain and enhance their capabilities for making intelligent choices, manage resources in the interest of their children, and make competent decisions for their families (Hobbs et al., 1984). As such, these new policies should aim to strengthen the family; enhance the well-being, developmental status, and rights of all family members; and avoid family dependence on the service coordinator or service delivery system.

The role of the council is to create an organizational framework within which the agency programs, operating in synchrony, integrate their services as necessary for the benefit of children and families (*Interagency problem-solving*, 1989). This framework is the cornerstone of an approach that will enable each family to select and mobilize the community resources of its own choice.

A system that promotes parental involvement in the treatment of children must be based on the assumption that family members are capable caregivers whose judgments can be trusted. To establish this system, the council must meet the following three objectives:

1. Creation of a coordinated, comprehensive array of services that meets the needs of children and families

2. Establishment of an effective interagency process for development and implementation of IFSPs
3. Establishment of service coordination principles, policies, and training that support and strengthen families

The interagency council must commit to an effective process for developing and implementing the IFSP. To succeed, the council must create a rich assortment of service options from which families may choose. The council must reaffirm its responsiveness to families and to a belief that services should be available when families need them.

Coordination at the Family Level

Service coordination at the family level rests with the individual or primary service coordinator selected to assist specific families in the ongoing process of coordinating and monitoring services across the various providers. The role of the individual service coordinator should be to assist families in gaining the knowledge and skills necessary to seek appropriate resources and become effective decision makers in matters relating to their children's needs and care (Dunst & Trivette, 1989). In this role, the coordinator changes from one who allocates services to one who supports a family, is sensitive to the family unit, understands the function of a family as caregiver, and is knowledgeable about community resources (Moroney & Dokecki, 1984, p. 234).

COORDINATION ACTIVITIES

The activities of the interagency council are crucial to the establishment of a communitywide system that develops and implements IFSPs, offers a range of accessible service options from which families may choose, and operates a system of case management that supports and empowers families. These activities encompass 10 specific areas.

Service Options

A primary role of the interagency council is the development of a comprehensive array of community service for children with disabilities and those at risk and their families (see chaps. 11 and 12, this volume). The council must identify existing programs and services, as well as constraints and service gaps. Through coordination and collaboration, the agency representatives refine and align the community system of programs and services to more adequately meet the needs of children and families. The council also promotes the philosophy that a wide assortment of programs, services, and delivery models must be available and that parents may choose the most appropriate services at any given time.

Family-Focused Policies

The interagency council should focus on policies, procedures, roles, and overall coordination of programs to ensure easily accessible services. Families are often frustrated in their attempts to secure services as a result of competing policy mandates or agency procedures—procedures that can often be changed when they are identified. For example, an arbitrary policy may be developed by a local United Cerebral Palsy (UCP) center to serve children to only 3 years of age, based on the assumption that all children will be served by the school district program beginning on their third birthday. Such a policy, however, does not consider that some children may not meet the school's categorical eligibility. Furthermore, it fails to give parents the option of UCP services. The policy is agency-directed and operates on the basis of allocating services in a manner that is inconsistent with the needs and desires of families. After policy constraints have been identified and resolved, the results are improved access to needed services, greater service options, and considerably less frustration to parents and agency personnel.

Interagency Release-of-Information Form

A uniform interagency release-of-information form (see chap. 10, this volume) developed by the local council can provide a strategy for an efficient exchange of reports and records. The exchange of records, including evaluation reports and individual educational or service plans, is an important service coordination function.

Interagency Procedures for Individualized Family Service Plans

With the participation of multiple agencies that serve young children, the IFSP can be developed through discussion and joint decision making relative to the roles, responsibilities, and contributions of the agencies. The council can mobilize the efforts of the agency programs to establish local procedures and values that will guide IFSP development and implementation. Consensus on procedures is critical if the IFSP is to coordinate services, both public and private, as Congress intended. The council can facilitate use of a uniform IFSP form across all agencies to ensure that the written plan is child- and family-focused, rather than agency-focused.

Interagency Procedures for Service Coordination

The interagency council can facilitate the development of appropriate, consistent, and family focused service coordination procedures across community agencies. Discussion and clarification of various service coordination approaches used by the programs can result in a definition of what constitutes service coordination and how it can be accomplished most effectively in a given locale. The council may consider creating a task force or committee to develop interagency procedures. Professionals and parents representing a wide range of disciplines; perspectives; racial, cultural and ethnic groups; and geographic regions can assist in developing service coordination principles and practices that are sensitive to the needs and values of families in the community. Procedures can be established for identifying the primary service coordinator for each child and family and determining expectations for the role. Coordination activities and best practices to be discussed include referral, evaluation, transition, and implementation of services described in the IFSP.

Procedures for Selecting a Primary Service Coordinator

PL 99-457 requires identification of a primary service coordinator who should "assist in gaining access to early intervention . . . and other services" (Committee on Education and Labor, 1986, p. 8). Multiple agency providers and program case managers often result in unnecessary duplication of services. Consistent with a coordinated case management system and the intent of the IFSP, designation of a service coordinator to hold primary responsibility for the implementation and coordination of services is required. Furthermore, the service coordinator is to be named from the profession most immediately relevant to the needs of the child and the family. Given this clear intent, the council may wish to discuss and identify the manner in which these personnel will be selected and the conditions under which the designated service coordinator will change.

The council can identify existing state laws, statutes, policy, and certification requirements that may dictate who can serve as a case manager. For example, agencies may require social work certification or mental retardation specialties. This type of information assists in the development of interagency procedures and prevents later penalties in an audit or monitoring situation. The council should identify procedures for recording the name of the primary service coordinator in a child's case records. Agency forms, such as individualized education programs, service and treatment plans, and referral forms should be revised to include a space for the coordinator's name.

Training for Professionals and Parents

McGonigel et al. (1991) maintained that a broad-based, family centered approach to the IFSP component is possible only when a comprehensive system of personnel development prepares individuals to cross disciplinary and agency boundaries and to work in partnership with one another and with parents. Strategies for personnel development described by the authors include:

Providing opportunities for families and professionals to attend workshops, conferences, and training together

Encouraging and facilitating joint teaching by families and professionals at pre-service and in-service levels

Providing cross-disciplinary and cross-agency training

Creating opportunities for professionals to learn about successful family centered approaches, services, and programs

Using outreach fairs, parent-to-parent networks, and other groups that offer training and technical assistance

The interagency council can identify training strategies that increase parent support, build family strengths, and enable parents to participate fully in the development of the IFSP.

Central Referral System

Variations in eligibility requirements and lack of coordination among service providers are major concerns and reasons for duplication of effort. The intent of coordinated services under PL 99-457 may result in new or revised structures for identification, referral, determination of eligibility, planning, service delivery, and transition. Central referral systems (see chap. 15, this volume) have been proved an efficient means of identifying and facilitating delivery of services to families and children (Lynch, Mercury, DiCola, & Widley, 1988). Central interagency intake procedures can streamline the eligibility process and make services more accessible.

Interagency Child Tracking System

A major problem within the community service delivery system is the frequency with which children are "lost" among the eligibilities, mandates, and follow-up procedures of agency programs. Multiple service providers for the preschool population make tracking of children a difficult task. After initial identification and elaborate assessment activities, it is not unusual for agencies to lose track of children for such reasons as transportation difficulties, work schedules, family crises and priorities, changes in residence, inability to pay, and parental hesitancy before services are initiated. Services may be discontinued for the same reasons. Children and families then often go for extended periods of time without needed services.

An effective child tracking system can prevent this gap in services by following the children, identifying when services are interrupted, and initiating new contacts with the family to determine their continued interest in services. A tracking system places responsibility on agencies to identify the reasons that services are not provided and to seek appropriate remedies.

A tracking system differs significantly from a central registry or a data entry system (Morgan & Swan, 1988; Smith, 1988). Registries, student/client information systems, and data base systems are designed to collect and record data on the number, type, and severity of children identified. They are used for such purposes as collecting research data, generating state and federal reports, and transmitting data to state-level systems. A child tracking system, however, is designed as a functional system to hold agencies accountable and provide a mechanism for the continued provision of services to children and families. A genuine child tracking system continually monitors services provided to children. It is an effective strategy for community-level service coordination.

Interagency Case Conference Procedure

The interagency council does not engage in placement or staffing activities or develop IFSPs for specific children. Its functions, however, include improving communication among agencies, identifying and discussing general procedures to improve service coordination, and identifying the respective roles and responsibilities of agencies in the provision of services to complicated cases or children who are unserved. For example, the council may discuss complicated cases to prevent duplication of effort and contradiction of information that is provided to families.

An effective child tracking system maintained by the council coordinator can identify complex cases that require periodic council updates to ensure that consistent services and information are provided to families. A tracking system should be designed to identify any child who is unserved or any child who presents unusually complicated coordination problems. The coordinator assumes the responsibility of organizing and facilitating an exchange of communication among providers and agency-based service coordinators regarding these children. Most problems can be resolved simply by telephone conversations between service coordinators. More complex cases, however, may be placed on the council meeting agenda so that agency personnel can devise problem-solving strategies for service coordination and funding. When all of the primary agencies are represented at the table, discussion can generate consensus on the agencies that will assume responsibility for each case. Financial, program, and resource responsibilities can be identified and mutually agreed upon.

INTERAGENCY CHILD TRACKING SYSTEM

The development of a comprehensive array of services within the community is not sufficient. Interagency strategies are required to ensure that the children and families identified as needing services actually receive them. Monitoring the services provided to preschool children with disabilities throughout the community can be accomplished only through implementation of an interagency child tracking system. To be effective, this system must have the commitment and participation of all primary agencies that serve preschool children with disabilities. It is a sophisticated collaborative program that is based on trust among the agencies. An efficient tracking system represents an affirmation of interagency service coordination and accountability of the council as coordinator in the IFSP.

Essential Elements

An interagency tracking system is designed to identify cases requiring more precise agency communication and discussion by council members to ensure proper coordination of services, avoidance of duplication, and elimination of contradictory or inconsistent messages that could be sent to families. Case conferences during council meetings are critical to problem solving and decisions related to the respective role of each agency.

To serve as a strategy for interagency service coordination, a child tracking system must contain eight essential elements:

1. Interagency release-of-information form that is used by all community agencies participating in the council
2. Adoption by the primary community agencies that identify and serve preschool children with disabilities and those at risk
3. Procedures for reporting every child in the target population who is identified as needing services
4. Continuous monitoring of the services provided to children and families
5. Proper transition of children from programs for birth through age 2 to programs for ages 3 through 5 years
6. Indication when needed services are terminated, for whatever reason
7. Identification of unserved or underserved children who require service coordination by the interagency council
8. Reinstating services to a child and family when appropriate

Objectives

The specific objectives of an interagency child tracking system must be considered by the interagency council.

Ensure that Identified Children Are Not Lost to the System Many children, after lengthy and thorough assessment efforts by agencies, are not enrolled in preschool services. The reasons vary; they include lack of transportation, schedule conflicts, parental preferences, family problems, and day care needs. The cases are generally closed, leaving the children to be "identified" again by other agencies or programs. Children may be withdrawn or discharged from services because of sporadic attendance, inability of the family to pay for services, transportation difficulties, or changes in residence or work schedules. An effective tracking system is designed to report children when they are initially identified, pinpoint the time when services cease or are not provided, and ensure that families are aware of alternative services.

Identify Unserved Children Proper procedures should be established to identify children who are both unserved and underserved. Interagency procedures for service coordination can be developed to ensure that all children receive appropriate services.

Minimize Duplication of Services Screening and evaluation services are often unknowingly duplicated by agency programs. Parents who are eager to comply with agency recommendations for the benefit of their child may submit to unnecessary evaluations and referrals. They are generally unaware that similar or identical procedures have already been done. A tracking system that contains evaluation information can prevent duplication and unnecessary expense.

Ensure Provision of All Needed Services A tracking system that reflects the disabilities or primary diagnosis of each child can result in provision of a complete array of needed services. For example, a red flag can indicate a physically impaired child whose tracking data reveal that occupational and physical therapy evaluation or treatment services have never been provided. This allows notification of the primary service coordinator or parent and determination of the reason for the gap in services.

Identify Sources of Funding   A tracking system should identify the programs for which each child is eligible and the potential sources of funding for services. Medicaid eligibility or eligibility for public programs that provide educational, therapeutic, and related services is a critical component in service coordination. Knowledge of all potential combinations of resources assists in providing a coordinated array of services for each child.

Facilitate Service Coordination   A tracking system should reveal the agencies and programs with which the child is involved so that proper coordination is achieved among all providers.

Assist in Transition and Long-Range Planning   A tracking system can generate information on the number and type of cases requiring transition each year from programs serving children from birth to 2 years of age to those serving 3- to 5-year-old children. This information also can be used in long-range planning to identify, by age and disability, the number of children who will enter school programs during succeeding years so that sufficient services are available for each geographical area.

Organization

The use of a manual tracking system, maintained in a card file, or a computerized system may depend on the size of the community, financial resources, or access to computer technology. Advantages and disadvantages exist for both methods.

A school district not exceeding 20,000 students can probably develop a successful card file tracking system, but a larger district usually needs a computerized system. A manual system is flexible and can be im-

mediately accessed by staff members despite their levels of computer literacy. A computerized system provides a major advantage in its capability to generate forms, lists, and reports. If the tracking system is exclusively computerized, however, access is limited to those who have a terminal and knowledge of the program. The computer itself cannot "track" services provided to children. The computer can only report the information that people put into it. Computerization requires extra time, additional financial resources, and special expertise.

Development of a Card File System

A manual tracking system can be readily devised by the council and implemented across all participating agencies. The contents of the card file should be simple and limited to essential information needed to accomplish the primary goals. Information requested for each child must fill a specific need, such as biographical data, type of disabilities, long-range planning, funding sources, evaluation and services to be provided, kindergarten entrance date, or agency references. It can be tailored to coincide with data required for periodic interagency reports. Basically, the card file should help to eliminate fragmentation and duplication and enhance coordination in planning, funding, and delivering services.

A sample tracking system card (5″ × 7″) is shown in Figure 1. An analysis of the information to be recorded on this card shows the following:

1. Birth date and age yield information on age eligibility for programs.
2. Disabilities or diagnoses yield information on program eligibility and possible needed services.
3. Current program placements are identified.
4. The primary service coordinator is identified.
5. Agencies that have records, evaluation

```
┌─────────────────────────────────────────────────────────────────────────┐
│                         Preschool Tracking Card                           │
│                                                                           │
│                                        Turns 3 years old on: _____    │
│                                             K-Entrance: _____         │
│                                                                           │
│   Name: _____ Address: _____ │
│   Parent/Guardian: _____ Phone: _____ │
│   DOB: _____ Age: _____ Gender: _____ │
│                                                                           │
│   Disabilities: a) _____ b) _____  │
│                                                                           │
│      Current Placements        Initiated        Discharged        Service Coordinator │
│      _____        _____      _____      _____ │
│      _____        _____      _____      _____ │
│      _____        _____      _____      _____ │
│                                                                           │
│      Program Eligibility:       Physicians                Evaluations     │
│                                                                           │
│   CMS       yes  no   _____    _____Developmental   _____Audiology │
│   HRS/DS    yes  no   _____    _____Psychological   _____Vision  │
│   Schools   yes  no   _____    _____Speech          _____Medical │
│   Medicaid  yes  no   _____    _____OT              _____PT      │
│   SSI       yes  no   _____    _____Social history              │
│   Chapter 1 yes  no   _____    _____Other: _____  │
│             yes  no   _____                                     │
│             yes  no   _____                                     │
└─────────────────────────────────────────────────────────────────────────┘
```

Figure 1. Sample card for an interagency child tracking system. (CMS, children's medical services, HRS/DS, Health and Rehabilitative Services/Developmental Services, SSI, Supplemental Security Income, OT, occupational therapy, PT, physical therapy.) (Used with Permission of the Florida Department of Education, Bureau of Education for Exceptional Students, from *Interagency problem solving,* [1989], p. 81.)

reports, and other information on eligibility and services are identified.

6. Funding sources, such as Medicaid, insurance, Chapter I, or school district programs, are identified.

7. Physicians who can provide needed medical services, information, reports, or recommendations for therapy are recorded.

8. Evaluations previously provided are revealed to avoid duplication in testing.

9. Kindergarten entrance date allows for identification of children for transition activities and for projection of full-time equivalents (FTE) and future unit needs.

The card file is organized by sections. A tab or divider is created for each of the agency programs in the community (e.g., school system, UCP, The Arc, Easter Seal Society, speech clinic, parent training program). At the front of the drawer, a series of tabs is included for children in various situations (e.g., being evaluated, pending placement, unserved, annual follow-up, parent not interested in services, unable to locate). The organization of the card file, at a glance, reveals the number of children served across the various agencies and programs and the number of children who are yet unserved and need the attention of the service coordinator or the council.

Staff Responsibility and System Location
The interagency council must identify who will have responsibility for maintenance of the child tracking system. It may be the council coordinator, a child find specialist, a service coordinator, or another professional who is motivated to engage in the time-consuming tasks involved. Often, a

school district program coordinator takes responsibility because almost every child ultimately enters the school district.

The council coordinator requires access to the card file to determine the unserved children who will be the subjects of case conferences during the monthly meetings. The council must identify others who need access to the system and also develop a standard procedure for updating it.

Sufficient cards and direction must be provided to each participating agency so that it can establish procedures and designate the personnel responsible for proper completion of the cards. It is often appropriate for each agency to incorporate this function into its standard intake or application procedure.

Agency Participation Cards must be completed by all agencies that provide direct intervention services to children in order to identify the children who are currently receiving services and those who are not. Agencies that provide related services (e.g., audiological services, equipment) or serve almost every child (e.g., health department, children's medical services [CMS]) may be referenced on the cards, rather than each making separate cards.

Interagency Release Form Before implementing the interagency child tracking system, the council must develop a uniform interagency release-of-information form (see chap. 10, this volume). This release is required for discussing and sharing information contained in the tracking system. The release form may be printed on the reverse side of the tracking card for easy reference.

Procedures Development, implementation, and updating procedures for the child-tracking system must be established by the council (see appendix to this chapter). A tracking card must be completed and sent to the council coordinator (or person in charge of the system) when each child is initially identified by any agency program. This procedure alerts the coordinator to the child, and the child is entered into the tracking system. The card file is organized by agency program, rather than alphabetically according to the child's last name. This type of organization reveals the location in which the child is currently served.

If the child is currently being served by a

MEMORANDUM

TO: Interagency Council Members
FROM: Council Coordinator
DATE: 5-15-92
RE: Update of Preschool Tracking Information

Please assist me in updating the preschool tracking system. Below is a list of all children currently identified as served by your agency. Review it for accuracy and notify me *only* of changes or additions.

Notify me, by phone or mail, of:

1. Any child who *has withdrawn* from your program or *has transferred* into another agency program
2. Any *new child* who was identified despite whether he has been formally enrolled yet
3. Any *changes* in address, phone, program, foster parent, or other information

Thanks for your help. Review this list and notify me of changes as soon as possible:

Alice Smith
John Maten
Sarah Boots
Allison Delgato
Leanne Simmons
Ralph Lopez

Figure 2.   Sample memorandum for updating child tracking system data.

program, the card is filed in the corresponding section of the card file. If the child is not being served, the council coordinator must be responsible for stimulating efforts to identify and provide the services needed by the child and family. For many children, a referral to appropriate agency programs based on the wishes of the family will suffice. For others, evaluation may be needed prior to referral for services. For a small number of children, the interagency council may need to discuss available resources and strategies in order to provide the appropriate combination of services required by each family.

A procedure for periodic updating of the card file is needed to identify changes in services that agency representatives may have forgotten to report. A bimonthly memorandum containing a list of the children served by the various agency programs is a simple and effective strategy to identify unreported changes (e.g., moved, discharged, withdrawn, transferred, or newly enrolled). A sample of such a memorandum is shown in Figure 2.

When a child is dismissed or drops out of a program, agency personnel must immediately notify the council coordinator by telephone or in writing. The card is pulled, and efforts are made to enroll the child in another appropriate program. Likewise, the council coordinator is notified of a child's transition from one program to another so that the card can be relocated in the card file.

Evaluation The council coordinator may want to maintain monthly child-count records to document the number of children served across agency programs. This will provide feedback to the agencies and demonstrate the increase in the numbers served, partially as a result of effective interagency collaboration.

REFERENCES

Austin, C.D. (1983). Case management in long-term care: Options and opportunities. *Health and Social Work, 8,* 16–30.

Committee on Education and Labor. (U.S. House of Representatives). (1986). *Report 99–860—Education of the Handicapped Act Amendments of 1986.* Washington, D.C.: Author

Dokecki, P.R., & Heflinger, C.A. (1989). Strengthening families of young children with handicapping conditions: Mapping backward from the "street level." In J.J. Gallagher, P.L. Trohanis, & R.M. Clifford (Eds.), *Policy implementation and PL 99-457: Planning for young children with special needs* (pp. 59–84). Baltimore: Paul H. Brookes Publishing Co.

Dunst, C.J. (1990). Implementation of the individualized family service plan. In B.H. Johnson, M.J. McGonigel, & R.K. Kaufmann (Eds.), *Guidelines and recommended practices for the individualized family service plan* (2nd ed.). Washington, DC: Association for the Care of Children's Health.

Dunst, C.J. (1991). Implementation of the individualized family support plan. In M.J. McGonigel, R.K. Kaufmann, & B.H. Johnson (Eds.), *Guidelines and recommended practices for the individualized family service plan* (2nd ed.) (pp. 67–78). Bethesda, MD: Association for the Care of Children's Health.

Dunst, C.J., & Trivette, C.M. (1989). An enablement and empowerment perspective of case management. *Topics in Early Childhood Special Education, 8*(4), 87–102.

Dunst, C.J., Trivette, C., & Deal, A. (1988). *Enabling and empowering families: Principles and guidelines for practice.* Cambridge, MA: Brookline Books.

Duwa, S., Kassack, C., & Graham, M.A. (1990). *Enhancing family support.* Tallahassee: Florida State University, Center for Policy Studies in Education.

Education of the Handicapped Act Amendments of 1986, PL 99-457, Sec. 677, (September 22, 1986). 20 U.S.C. Sec. 1477.

Erickson, K. (1981). *Human services today* (2nd ed.). Reston, VA: Reston Publishing Co.

Freedman, S.A., Reiss, J.G., & Pierce, P.M. (1987). *Focus and functions of case management for child health policy.* Gainesville: University of Florida.

Hobbs, N., Dokecki, P.R., Hoover-Dempsey, K.V., Moroney, R.M., Shayne, M.W., & Weeks, K.H. (1984). *Strengthening families.* San Francisco: Jossey-Bass.

Interagency problem solving. (1989). Tallahassee: Florida Department of Education, Bureau of Education for Exceptional Students.

Johnson, B.H., McGonigel, M.J., & Kaufmann, R.K. (1989). *Guidelines and recommended practices for the individualized family service plan* (2nd ed.). Washington, DC: Association for the Care of Children's Health.

Levine, I.S., & Fleming, J. (1984). *Human resource development: Issues in case management.* Baltimore: Center of Rehabilitation and Manpower Services.

Lynch, E.C., Mercury, M.G., DiCola, J.M., & Widley,

R. (1988). The function of a central referral system in interagency identification, eligibility, and service delivery: A case study. *Topics in Early Childhood Special Education, 8*(3), 86–97.

McGonigel, M.J., & Garland, C. (1988). The Individualized Family Service Plan and the early intervention team: Team and family issues and recommended practices. *Infants and Young Children, 1*(1), 10–21.

McGonigel, M.J., Kaufmann, R.K., & Johnson, B.H. (1991). A family-centered process for the individualized family service plan. *Journal of Early Intervention, 15*(1), 46–56.

Morgan, J.L., & Swan, W.W. (1988). *Local interagency councils for preschool handicapped programs: An effective strategy to implement the mandate*. Bloomington: Indiana University, Council for Administrators of Special Education, Inc. (CASE) (A Division of the Council for Exceptional Children).

Moroney, R.M., & Dokecki, P.R. (1984). The family and the professions: Implications for public policy. *Journal of Family Issues, 5,* 224–238.

Smith, B. (Ed.). (1987). *Position statements and recommendations relating to PL 99-457 and other federal and state early childhood policies*. Position paper. Reston, VA: Council for Exceptional Children, Division for Early Childhood.

Smith, B. (Ed.). (1988). *Mapping the future for children with special needs: PL 99-457*. Washington, DC: Administration on Developmental Disabilities.

Weil, M., & Karls, J.M. (1985). *Case management in human service practice: A systematic approach to mobilizing resources for clients*. San Francisco: Jossey-Bass.

Sample Procedures for Child Tracking System

WHICH CHILDREN ARE INCLUDED?

A card should be completed for any child, birth through 5 years, who is identified as having any disability, risk factor, or special need that warrants the provision of special services. The card is completed at the time the child is *identified,* regardless of whether the agency is providing services to the child. A signed parent release-of-records form must be secured in order for any child to be submitted to the system.

WHO COMPLETES THE CARD?

The cards should be completed by all agencies or individuals who are providing direct services in the form of programs, evaluation, therapy, counseling, or other. Cards do not need to be completed by health agencies, such as children's medical services or the health department, because they will be referenced in the program eligibility section. The first agency responsible for identification or intake should complete the card. It may be the child find specialist who later refers the child to an agency or it may be the social worker at the agency who first becomes aware of the child as the parent inquires about services. Each agency should determine the procedure for completion of the cards. It is recommended that they become part of each agency's regular procedure for enrollment.

HOW ARE THE CARDS COMPLETED?

Use pencil to fill out the information requested.

1. K-Entrance: Leave this box blank. It will be completed when received by the council coordinator and will indicate the year the child will enter kindergarten.
2. Name: Child's name, list last name first.
3. Identifying information: Complete child's address, date of birth, gender, telephone, age, name of the parent/guardian
4. Disabilities: List disabilities, with the primary first
5. Placements: List programs in which the child is currently enrolled, the initiation date, and the service coordinator or contact
6. Agencies: Check or list every agency involved
7. Physicians: Past and current physicians and specialists working with this child
8. Evaluations: List most recent evaluation dates
9. Comments: On the reverse side of the card, list any comments or additional information that should be known

WHERE ARE THE CARDS SENT?

When completed, mail or deliver cards to the council coordinator or turn them in at the monthly council meetings. Keep a photocopy of the card for future reference and for updating.

HOW IS THE FILE UPDATED?

Whenever there is a change in the information provided on the card (e.g., address, program placement, disability, service coordinator), indicate the change in *red* on the photocopy of the card that you retained and send it to the council coordinator.

WHAT HAPPENS WHEN A CHILD IS WITHDRAWN FROM A PROGRAM?

When a child is withdrawn or terminated from services for any reason, the council coordinator must be notified by telephone contact, or by sending an update to the card. Indicate the reason (e.g., moved, transportation). If the child is in need of continued services, it is critical that immediate notification is made. The family will be contacted to determine other methods of providing needed and desired services.

Chapter 15

Interagency Collaboration

Activities in stage 3 represent interagency collaboration and are characterized by a willingness of the agency representatives to solve problems by a creative combination of agency resources. Instead of adhering to their individual agendas, the agencies form a partnership and establish common goals.

ADVANTAGES OF COLLABORATION

In order to solve problems that single agencies cannot solve alone, council members agree to pool resources and jointly plan, implement, and evaluate new ventures and procedures. A sophisticated interagency system emerges as agency programs become interdependent and mutually supporting. The council functions as a family of related agencies and prioritizes quality services to children and families in the most efficient manner. Written agreements, contracts, and mingling of dollars and personnel are used to create new services and programs that did not previously exist (Morgan & Swan, 1988).

The activities at this stage of council development represent continued refinement of the efforts in stage 2. Ventures at the agency or system level are empowered politically by virtue of the members' collective clout (Melaville & Blank, 1991). Council members can advocate and negotiate changes in policy and procedures that result in a more comprehensive and responsive service delivery system. Council members must have the authority to commit resources, such as staff, facilities, and funding, that are required to alter existing procedures and services. At this stage, members are able to exceed the informational and advisory activities characteristic of the previous stages of cooperation and coordination. What sets collaboration apart from the earlier ventures is the commitment of the council members to use their power and leverage to accomplish common goals. They assert their authority and call for new directions in system-wide programming and make the budgetary, administrative, and personnel changes necessary for implementation.

The collaborative ventures of the council are focused on common goals articulated in specific action plans that guide each step. These common goals include a detailed plan to identify and fill service gaps, refine information exchange, implement a child tracking system, develop contracts and agreements, and create new collaborative programs and other foci requiring major investment of energy. Relationships among the agencies continue to require nurturing to maintain their strength and motivation when fluctuating resources and periodic setbacks occur. Table 1 contains examples of collaborative ventures.

The system- or agency-level collaboration of a mature interagency council creates tangible change at the system and service delivery levels. The advantages of collaboration result from the council's ability to restructure the expertise and resources of member agencies. Collaboration provides the opportunity to alter existing services, design and deliver new services, and realign the existing roles of the agencies. It offers the potential for real movement toward the creation of an integrated and comprehensive service delivery system.

Table 1. Examples of collaborative ventures

Co-location and integration of services

Co-location of administrative or supervisory staff

Employment of a paid council coordinator

Contracts and written agreements

Mutual development of grants and budgets

Single point of entry

Interagency intake process

Standardized referral procedures

Collaborative community screening program

Interagency child tracking system

Interagency evaluation team

Uniform policies and procedures

Collaborative public awareness activities

Collaborative parent services

Consolidation of parent newsletters and libraries

Establishment of a parent resource center

Standardization of individualized education program (IEP) and individualized family service plan (IFSP) forms

Interagency transition procedures

COLLABORATIVE ACTIVITIES

Interagency partnerships hold great potential for reorienting the manner in which schools and human services agencies do business. Interagency collaboration offers the opportunity to bring together a broad range of professional expertise, knowledge, and services on behalf of children with disabilities and their families. Interagency initiatives have the capacity to harness and combine the substantial financial resources available within institutional budgets. These interagency initiatives can create the structure and mechanisms necessary to coordinate existing services and, by tapping into current funding sources, reorganize available resources to create more effective prevention, treatment, and support services.

Creating an array of comprehensive, flexible services from over a dozen community health, education, therapeutic, social services, and parent services programs requires time, skill, and a vision of substantial change in the way services are traditionally delivered. Five factors strongly influence all interagency efforts: 1) the climate in which the initiatives exist, 2) the processes used to

build trust and manage conflict, 3) the people involved, 4) the policies that support or inhibit partnership efforts, and 5) the availability of resources to enable the efforts to continue (Melaville & Blank, 1991).

The necessary linkages among these agencies and providers demand not just one leader, but many, with each working in concert. The local interagency council, composed of representatives with power and position to create changes within their programs, has the necessary authority to alter the delivery of services or to negotiate systemwide changes. As the process of creating the shared vision evolves, joint efforts on the part of the council members will shape and realign the resources, expertise, and operation of the delivery system to create the shared system of services intended by the Education of the Handicapped Act Amendments of 1986 (PL 99-457). These efforts will include collaboration among the areas of activity described below.

Collaborative Programs Through Co-Location and Integration of Services

Contracts and written agreements allow agencies to combine their resources to take advantage of respective strengths and program components. Co-location and integration go one step farther by bringing programs and services together at the same site to improve access for families. For example, a collaborative program could be created by the school district, The Arc center, United Cerebral Palsy (UCP), and subsidized day care. Vacant space might be provided by The Arc and the staff contributed by the other agencies to provide multiple programs and components at the same site. A teacher could be provided by the school district, therapists by UCP, and after-school care by the subsidized day care program. A written agreement among the agencies describes the eligible population, agency contributions, responsibilities, procedures, and financial considerations. Unless the staffs that provide various services formulate common goals on behalf of the children and families and integrate these services, however, the actual care and follow-up are likely to differ little from what children and families would receive at separate locations (Melaville & Blank, 1991). Other examples of co-location of services include the following:

Occupational and physical therapy is provided by UCP to eligible children during the day in their classroom at The Arc, rather than requiring them to travel to the UCP center for therapy.

The school district provides speech therapy at the subsidized child care centers and Head Start.

The Easter Seal Society audiologist schedules the mobile hearing assessment van to visit community sites (e.g., health department, rural clinics, schools, The Arc) on specific days each month.

The community mental health center schedules parent education and counseling sessions at the preschool program sites.

The school district child find specialist is based at the county health department to participate in early and periodic screening, diagnosis, and treatment (EPSDT) program screenings.

A school district preschool classroom is located in vacant space at The Arc.

Children's medical services schedules a quarterly orthopedic clinic at the UCP center to allow exchange among physicians, specialists, parents, therapists, and teachers. Children can be observed in the classroom setting to assess levels of functioning, positioning, and use of adaptive equipment.

The subsidized child care program provides before- and after-school childcare at the UCP center, The Arc, and the school site instead of requiring children to be transported to community daycare centers.

Physical examinations, immunizations, and health screenings are conducted by health department personnel at the preschool sites.

The Arc locates a classroom within a church-operated preschool program to provide opportunities for integration of children with disabilities among their nondisabled peers.

The Arc and subsidized childcare program create a day program at the public health department facility for medically complex preschool children where medical, nursing, nutrition, and social services are readily available.

The Arc and Easter Seal Society pool funding to buy several vans, hire drivers, and create transportation services for use by both agencies.

Contracts for Expansion of Services

Agencies may choose to contract with others to provide a wider range of program and location options. A school district, for example, might contract with the local branch of The Arc and a speech and hearing clinic to provide additional options for special education, therapy, and related services to supplement existing school-based programs. A variety of contracts with community programs multiplies the number, type, and locations of settings where children may be served.

Written agreements and contracts (see chaps. 17 and 18, this volume) can result in valuable options that compensate for resource constraints, maximize available resources, provide more cost-effective delivery of services, offer flexibility in placement, minimize student transportation time, utilize the strengths and special expertise of other programs, and provide education in a most inclusive environment.

Co-Location of Administrative Staff

Co-location of administrative staff, supervisors, and service coordinators improves information exchange, program and service planning, working relationships, familiarity with procedures, and trust. Bringing together agency personnel at the same work site eliminates the time constraints that have been reported as primary barriers to effective collaboration. Agency procedures, forms, policies, parent contacts, data entry, educational planning, and record keeping can be coordinated and streamlined. As trust and working relationships grow, new and innovative solutions are identified for old problems.

Single Point of Entry Model

Another alternative is the single point of entry model (Anderson, 1977). It provides a specific structure, such as a central or interagency evaluation team, through which children enter the service delivery system. A case manager is assigned at entry to assist the family in proceeding through the screening and evaluation system in an organized manner to the stage where intervention services are initiated. The single point of entry model is designed to avoid duplication of effort and to streamline service delivery.

Interagency Intake Team

An interagency intake team eliminates the duplicative application procedure often imposed on families and consolidates the intake process across the primary public agencies as shown in Figure 1. A team of public agency representatives (e.g., school district, developmental disabilities, children's medical services) and a consolidated application form provide a family with "one-stop shopping." A single application is shared by the various educational, social services, medical, economic assistance, and therapeutic programs. Multiple social and developmental history, consent, release-of-information, and biographical forms are avoided. The parent is required to contact or visit only one central program office, rather than numerous offices located in different areas of the community. Parents do not have to cancel significant work time or travel long distances to gain access to needed services. This model is particularly helpful for those with transportation problems.

An intake team coordinator receives all referrals, schedules an initial contact with the family, assists the family in completing the necessary forms, requests medical and agency records, and conducts a develop-

mental and social history (plus a family assessment, with the approval of the family). The team coordinator explains the eligibility determination process, timelines, and possible service options and begins to prepare the family for its role in the IFSP process.

The interagency intake team meets at least weekly to review all new referrals, coordinate roles and responsibilities, determine eligibility for interim services, schedule assessments and appointments, and discuss follow-up. Intake forms, reports, and other necessary information are kept by the respective agency personnel who will serve the child. The intake team represents a highly efficient manner of coordinating agency roles and services. It avoids needless duplication, maximizes exchange of information, coordinates eligibility, and shortens the time between intake and delivery of services.

Standardization of Referral Procedures

Implementation of a standardized interagency referral form (see chap. 12, this volume) streamlines written requirements, avoids misunderstanding, and hastens the child's entry into services. A standardized form eliminates the practice of agencies insisting on the use of their own forms in accepting referrals.

Collaborative Community Screening Program

To facilitate early identification of children in need of services, community agencies can collaborate to provide community developmental screening programs (Smith, 1988). A screening protocol can be developed that includes input from professionals across the various disciplines and agency programs. Large numbers of children can be screened at low cost and in an efficient manner. Personnel from the appropriate agencies can conduct screenings in such locations as shopping malls, grocery stores, and child care centers, thereby reaching children whose parents are not likely to discover screening services independently. A combination of

Interagency Intake Team

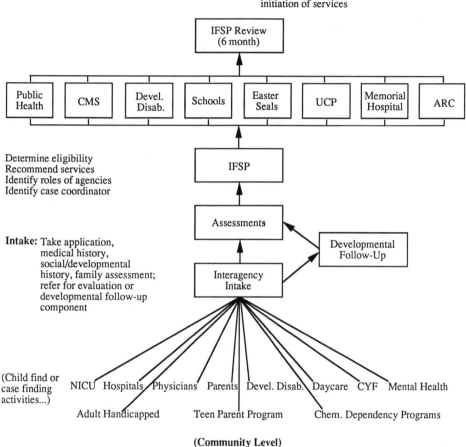

Agency Programs: Developmental Disabilities
School District
Children's Medical Services

Purpose: Simultaneous review, determination of eligibility,
& identification of services; earlier referral and
initiation of services

Figure 1. Flowchart of the interagency intake team process. (IFSP, individualized family service plan; CMS, children's medical services; UCP, United Cerebral Palsy; NICU, neonatal intensive care unit; CYF, Children, Youth, and Families.)

agency resources results in substantial screening efforts.

Interagency Preschool Evaluation Team

Insufficient evaluation services can be overcome through development of interagency preschool evaluation teams. Small communities often find comprehensive evaluation services difficult to provide because of shortages in funds and personnel, inadequately trained staffs, or an insufficient number of available therapists. Conversely, larger communities, where services are abundant, may be guilty of duplicating assessment services. To deal with these problems, many areas have developed interagency evaluation teams (Kazuk, 1980; Mulvenon, 1980) for the purpose of comprehensive assessments. The teams are organized through the collaborative efforts of several agencies that contribute one member each to the evaluation team. One agency may contribute a psychologist with expertise in testing preschool children; another agency may have a speech-language pathologist or an occupational therapist with appropriate experience and skills. With each agency contributing its expertise, a team of skilled professionals can effectively assess young children who need evaluation. Furthermore, no undue burden is placed on any one agency for these services.

Uniform Agency Procedures

Uniform procedures to improve and streamline referral, assessment, and placement can be developed by the interagency council and implemented by the member agencies. The procedures include policies, time frames, forms, personnel, and standards that are consistent with the requirements and regulations of each participating agency. Collaboration on procedural issues results in the most significant and lasting change required for an effective service delivery system.

Modification of Existing Agency Policies

The essence of collaboration is the ability to restructure and modify agency policies and procedures in order to realign agency roles and improve the system of services for children and families. Both formal and informal policies and procedures that have created barriers to services are identified by the council. They may relate to age eligibility, income criteria, entrance requirements, classification, mainstreaming, priorities, assessment, placement, referrals, location of services, parent involvement, waiting lists, days and hours, delivery models, curriculum and philosophy, and educational planning. Identification and resolution of these constraints can become a common goal for the interagency council.

Collaboration on Grant Development and Budgets

The ability to make administrative and budgeting commitments to implement and continue recommended changes sets collaboration apart from other ventures. Agency resources, particularly funding, are neces-

sary for collaboration. Budget development and allocation of funds are most effective when coordinated with the abilities of other agencies to ensure that gaps in services are eliminated. Yearly entitlement grants and other budgets should be developed with consideration of various agency initiatives. Resources of several agencies can be pooled to create collaborative programs through joint funding of staff and activities. Collaboration with respect to state and federal child counts can result in increased generation of funds for the various agencies.

With the current emphasis and requirement for interagency coordination, strength and support can be added to new applications for state or federal grants when collaboration among community agencies is evident in development of the grant.

Procedures for Resolution of Disputes

Interagency arrangements regarding the assignment of financial responsibility for provision of services to children and families under PL 99-457 require development of procedures for resolving disputes among and within agencies. An interagency agreement, jointly developed and adopted, creates mutual ownership of roles and procedures and results in a system that is more responsive to the needs of children and families.

Collaboration on Public Awareness

The interagency council can collaborate on public awareness through the use of media campaigns, interagency brochures and directory of services, public service announcements, videotaped materials, and other activities. These collaborative efforts are characterized by mutual development, common goals, shared funding, and follow-up.

A comprehensive directory of community preschool services provides a summary of the educational, medical, and social services available for children under 5 years of age (see chap. 10, this volume). The directory should be jointly developed and funded by member agencies. Copies can be directed to area physicians, clinics, hospitals, emergency rooms, social services offices, and other locations where concentrations of high-risk children may be found. The directories also can be used in child find activities jointly developed and funded by member agencies.

Collaboration on Parent Programs

The independent and duplicative efforts of each agency with respect to parent education and support services can be combined into a single, comprehensive system of parent services. The council may identify one agency, such as a community parent resource or parent education program, a parent-to-parent group, a local community college, or an agency with a primary focus of services to parents as the lead agency for these efforts. Existing expertise can be coordinated across all agencies. A comprehensive needs assessment, identification of resources, and shared funding by member agencies can guide the effort.

Parent newsletters are a particular area of extensive duplication. An overwhelming number of newsletters has appeared as agencies have attempted to increase school/home/agency communication. Similar content is common, and printing and postage are expensive. The interagency council may wish to consolidate multiple newsletters into one publication that is jointly published and funded by the agencies, or an existing newsletter might be selected, modified, and distributed to all parents across the community preschool agencies. A consolidated publication presents a cohesive, coordinated community image, provides interdisciplinary information to parents, and assists smaller preschool programs that lack resources to sponsor their own newsletters. A collaborative publication should clearly reflect joint sponsorship by using the names of the agencies, multiple agency logos, or the name of the interagency council.

Duplication of lending libraries for parents may be another concern of the council. Existing libraries could be identified and consolidated into one accessible site that is mutually determined by the agencies. This also may be advantageous to teachers, therapists, and parent trainers who use library materials for home-based programs with parents.

Consolidation of lending libraries and other parent education and support activities may be accomplished by establishing a parent resource center that is jointly funded, equipped, and supported by the various agency programs. The center could be used for formal and informal meetings, as well as providing accessibility to books, pamphlets, articles, videotapes, and similar materials. A bulletin board could be made available for a calendar of events, community information, current legislative issues, and other notices of interest to parents. A comfortable room containing a couch, overstuffed chairs, and a coffeepot provides a place for parents to gather (Linder, 1983).

A resource center can be staffed by various agency social workers, paraprofessionals, or parent volunteers, and designed to provide information and assistance to families. Interpreting, advocacy, information, referral, parent support, and counseling services could be offered.

Use of a Salaried Council Coordinator

Coordinating an effective local interagency council is an intensive, continuous, and time-consuming responsibility. The influence of the council may be directly related to the impact of the coordinator and his or her ability to facilitate collaboration. The "agency-neutral" aspect of the council coordinator may be a critical variable in the success and effectiveness of the council. A salaried coordinator, employed through shared funding and a written agreement, is an option to assume the massive responsibilities for guiding collaborative efforts and negotiating agency change.

Standardization of Program Forms

To ensure collaboration in the development and implementation of the individualized education program (IEP) and individualized family service plan (IFSP), the interagency council should standardize the forms and processes employed by all agencies. Hesitancy or reluctance in accepting an IEP or IFSP from another agency often occurs simply because of the differences in forms; as a result, a new plan is developed. A simple strategy of standardizing the form may eliminate this needless duplication and reinforce the interagency nature of the plans. Staff training and cross-training require joint planning and development.

Collaboration in IEP and IFSP Development

No single agency can provide all of the services needed by a family and a young child with disabilities. Collaboration in the development and implementation of the IEP or IFSP will ensure an array of services from which the family may select appropriate options. Services not provided by one agency can be contributed by another. Joint planning compensates for different eligibility criteria and capabilities of programs. Discussions of conflicts between recommended therapy and ineligibility, for example, may help to simplify solutions. This form of joint decision making can prevent misunderstandings among agencies. Discussion also clarifies which agencies have the ability to provide specific services, such as adaptive equipment. Agreement on providing services can be accomplished during a single meeting, rather than requiring months of letters, forms, and telephone calls.

Coordinated interagency planning has five results: 1) identification of the respective roles and responsibilities of each agency so that all needed services are provided; 2) more immediate entry into services; 3) improved communication and organization; 4) increased family and service coordinator satisfaction; and 5) development of one comprehensive, written plan. Benefits to the child, the family, and the agencies are obvious.

Interagency Transition Procedures

Collaboration among agency personnel is essential to prepare children, parents, and staff members for effective transition. Planning requires an assessment of the number of children who will be leaving programs, the number of vacancies to be filled, the assessment and staffing time needed prior to placement of children, the type of expansion or program modification needed, personnel changes, and funding needs. The interagency council provides the optimal setting for discussion of transition and future program plans. Careful collaboration by the agencies ensures smooth transition and allows agencies to anticipate areas where expansion of services will be needed to meet increasing demands. The council can identify and discuss potential sources of unnecessary duplication of evaluations and determine how to resolve the problem. Through identification and discussion of timelines and evaluation reports provided with initial referrals, much of this duplication might be avoided. Discussion during council meetings can include clarification of agency roles, timelines for transition, and general procedures in the following eight areas:

1. Children who require transition services
2. Procedures for notifying parents
3. Timelines for referral to receiving agencies
4. Requirements for placement and enrollment (evaluations, forms, birth records, physical examinations, immunizations)
5. Evaluation requirements and responsibilities
6. Personnel responsibilities
7. Staffing and IEP/IFSP development procedures
8. Transfer of records and case files

Transition of children from one agency to another represents a period of potential stress for parents. In recognition of this, both the sending and receiving agency programs have an obligation to organize activities to effect a smooth transition. Agencies can collaborate in planning parent orientation meetings to explain the series of upcoming events and provide opportunities for questions and discussion of concerns about transportation, program times and locations, procedures, educational planning, staff–child ratios, and therapy services. The sending agency program has established a sense of rapport and credibility with parents and therefore plays the key role in helping parents to understand the changing needs of their child with respect to appropriate program models.

Collaborative activities, such as field trips to the playground or facility of the receiving center, can prepare a child for the transition. Graduation ceremonies provide closure, positive feelings, and pride in the fact that the child is growing and moving on to greater independence. These activities may represent important steps for both child and parents.

Collaboration in staff transition activities also assists teachers and therapists in the difficult process of "letting go." Procedures should ensure their participation and input

in the educational plan developed by the receiving agency. Their knowledge of the child must be considered and utilized during the transition.

The interagency council can develop and publish a booklet or brochure designed as a transition guide for parents, children, and agency staffs. The guide can describe the differences in various community program delivery models as they relate to the needs of children and their families; for example, medical and educational models and the points in a child's life when each is most appropriate. Parents can be informed about entrance procedures and requirements of various agencies, including requirements for physical examinations, immunizations, and birth date documentation, and how to meet these requirements. If parents do not know that the health department requires an appointment 2 months in advance for a preschool physical examination, for instance, their child's enrollment in school will be delayed.

REFERENCES

Anderson, R.J. (1977). The human perspective. *The service integration project: Final report*. A report funded by the National Office of Child Development, Department of Health, Education, and Welfare. Chapel Hill, NC: Chapel Hill Training-Outreach Project.

Interagency problem solving. (1989). Tallahassee: Florida Department of Education, Bureau of Education for Exceptional Students.

Kazuk, E. (1980). Development of a community-based interagency model. In J.O. Elder & P.R. Magrab (Eds.), *Coordinating services to handicapped children: A handbook for interagency collaboration* (pp. 99–131). Baltimore: Paul H. Brookes Publishing Co.

Linder, T.W. (1983). *Early childhood special education: Program development and administration*. Baltimore: Paul H. Brookes Publishing Co.

Melaville, A.I., & Blank, M.J. (1991). *What it takes:*

Structuring interagency partnerships to connect children and families with comprehensive services. Washington, DC: Education and Human Services Consortium.

Morgan, J.L., & Swan, W.W. (1988). *Local interagency councils for preschool handicapped programs: An effective strategy to implement the mandate*. Bloomington: Indiana University, Council for Administrators of Special Education, Inc. (CASE). (A Division of the Council for Exceptional Children).

Mulvenon, J. (1980). Development of preschool interagency teams. In J.O. Elder & P.R. Magrab (Eds.), *Coordinating services to handicapped children: A handbook for interagency collaboration* (pp. 133–162). Baltimore: Paul H. Brookes Publishing Co.

Smith, B. (Ed.). (1988). *Mapping the future for children with special needs: PL 99-457*. Washington, DC: Administration on Developmental Disabilities.

Chapter 16

Evaluation of the Interagency Council

This chapter provides an overview of the reasons for evaluating interagency council efforts, an approach for conducting evaluation, and sample applications of this approach to council activities. The council should develop an evaluation plan that is consistent with the goals and objectives of the council and that assists in determining whether the council's activities are effective in achieving the goals and objectives.

REASONS FOR EVALUATION

Evaluation is an integral part of effective preschool interagency councils for five reasons (Huberty, Quirk, & Swan, 1973; Huberty & Swan, 1977; Smith, 1990; Swan, 1989; Travers & Light, 1982; Wolf, 1990). First, evaluation of public and private programs is either required by funding agencies or expected by the clients those programs serve. Council members expect that the council will be accountable for its actions and efforts. Second, the evaluation of the impact of council activities specified in action plans requires that council members communicate effectively concerning the expected results of these plans and activities. Evaluation is a vehicle to enhance communication among council members by defining common terms and expectations. Third, examining the results of council activities from action plans can improve the effectiveness of these activities. By examining procedures and outcome, the council can refine or redirect efforts to maximize the return on investment of human and financial re-

sources. Fourth, evaluation can be focused on the worth of the council in meeting its overall goals. Objective evaluation strategies can be used effectively as part of an overall evaluation plan to assist the council in reaching its goals and objectives. Fifth, evaluation can raise new questions concerning council procedures or services for preschool children with disabilities and those at risk and their families. This encourages the continued refinement of the development of community services for these children and their families.

EVALUATION APPROACH

The evaluation approach suggested for local preschool interagency councils is described as a decision-facilitation model and as a utilitarian, objectives-oriented approach focusing on internal and external perspectives with both formative and summative features (Popham, 1988; Worthen & Sanders, 1987). The approach is decision-facilitation as it focuses on specific council decisions concerning the investment of human and financial resources; it is utilitarian and objectives-oriented as it focuses on practical information and data for specific council goals, objectives, and activities. Because the evaluation is conducted by the council coordinator and the members, this approach is considered internal; it is also external because the results must be credible to relevant others in the community. It is formative because it emphasizes refinement and improvement of council efforts; it is summative because it provides statements of impact at the end of selected times (e.g., annually) on selected council activities, objectives, or goals.

Collection of Information and Data

This approach emphasizes the collection of practical and available information and data, generally descriptive in nature, that are related to specific council goals, objectives, and activities. Although some statistics are used for comparisons (e.g., ranges, means, standard deviations), few or no experimental studies are conducted and few or no inferential statistics are used to determine relative impact. The emphasis is on macromeasures of impact, such as reduction of unnecessary psychological evaluations or an increase in services provided, rather than on micro-measures of impact, such as individual child progress on an individualized family service plan (IFSP) in the area of fine motor development, or an increase in particular parent skills. Macro-measures are the focus for council efforts and are evaluated across agencies, whereas micro-measures are the focus of specific agencies and programs with results evaluated through annual, or more frequent, reviews of the individualized

education program (IEP) and the IFSP for individual children and families.

The evaluation approach, as shown in Table 1, has three components (Huberty et al., 1973; Smith, 1990):

1. *Planning* emphasizes identification of needs and the development of an action plan, including both specific evaluation criteria and data collection, to respond to those needs.
2. *Monitoring* emphasizes the collection and preparation of information and data for review by council members as the decision makers.
3. *Appraising* focuses on the council's determination of whether the actions, based on goals and objectives, have resulted in the intended impacts.

Three levels of information and data are suggested for implementing the evaluation approach (Swan, 1989):

1. *Documentation*—demonstrating that events occurred (e.g., council met as scheduled; joint community screenings conducted; directory of community ser-

Table 1. Overview of the evaluation approach

Type of activity	Sample functions	Sample methods
Planning	Identify/assess needs and problems State goals and objectives Develop action plans for objectives and activities Collect baseline information/data as necessary	Complete community services matrix Complete continuum of services matrix Discussion with council members
Monitoring	Collect information/data on implementing action plans Relate information/data to goals/objectives/activities	Council members provide information/data Summarize and analyze information/data Develop summaries of information/data
Appraising	Judge the information/data relative to goals/objectives/activities and expected outcomes Determine completion of activity/objective/goal or continuation of activity/objective/goal to achieve desired outcome If goal/objective/activity is continued, specify refinements in process, if any, revise action plan, and begin evaluation process again	Council members review and analyze information/data Council members discuss results as compared with original needs or new needs Council members suggest improvements for continued goal/objective/activity or celebrate achievement of goal/objective/activity

Adapted from Huberty, Quirk, and Swan (1973) and Swan (1989).

vices mailed; community-wide staff development program conducted; grant application for funding of a new, needed service submitted to funding agency; children served in a particular program)

2. *Satisfaction*—indicating that people were pleased with council efforts (e.g., perceptions of council members that council met their agencies' needs, agency personnel's perceptions of the council's effectiveness, parents' perceptions of timeliness and quality of services)

3. *Change*—indicating differences between one period of time and another (e.g., increased numbers of children and families being served in the community or by particular agencies or programs, percent of council members attending meetings, implementation of a central intake procedure, reduced unnecessary duplication of services, improved skills of service providers)

Only one level of information may be necessary for evaluating the impact of an action plan; more than one level may be used as determined by the council. The council and the council coordinator conduct the evaluation as an integral part of council activities.

The human and financial resources to plan, monitor, and appraise the information and data increase from the documentation (basic) level to the change (sophisticated) level. The level(s) selected to evaluate a particular council action plan should be based on the purposes of the action plan and the needs of the council. The information and data to be collected should be highly practical indicators of impact and relevant to the agencies represented on the council (Travers & Light, 1982). Existing data sources should be used as often as possible to minimize the need to collect new information.

Components of the Evaluation

The council has two organizational components: 1) operating procedures; and 2) goals, objectives, and activities. The operating procedures may be written, infor-

mal, or a combination of both. The goals, objectives, and activities are expressed in philosophy statements, action plans, and council minutes. The council should evaluate both components as they interact to produce results.

APPLICATION

The application of the evaluation approach should be based on three principles: 1) The approach is individualized to meet specific council needs; the goals, objectives, and activities, coupled with the action plan, are the vehicles for evaluation. 2) The evaluation produces objective and accurate (reliable and valid) information and data that have clear meanings, are relatively easy to collect, and have direct relevance to the council. 3) The evaluation effort is as simple as possible.

The application is divided into two sections—common examples and specific examples. The common examples focus on efforts that almost all councils should pursue—the overall council goal and council operations. The specific examples focus on council activities as expressed in action plans. These examples are representative of council operations or actions; they are not exhaustive in depicting all of the possible alternatives for a council. However, they should provide the council with sufficient guidance to individualize its own evaluation efforts. Each example is described in terms of action plan objective, the evaluation approach (planning, monitoring, and appraising), and the level(s) of information and data to be collected (documentation, satisfaction, change).

Common Examples

Overall Council Goal   The evaluation of the overall council goal is common to all councils—to provide a comprehensive array of community services to all preschool children with disabilities and those at risk and their families. This goal is the focal point for council efforts.

Examples of Evaluation Approach Planning: The council pursues the goal of providing a comprehensive array of community services to all preschool children with disabilities and those at risk and their families. The planning for council efforts is based on the goal, completion of the community services matrix and the continuum of services matrix (see chap. 11, this volume), case reviews, and child count. The council minutes and the action plans related to these items form the continuing means to review planning efforts.

Monitoring: The council reviews and refines the matrices, the case reviews for complex services (spanning four or more agencies or programs), and the child count on a monthly or quarterly basis. Other council activities relate to these indexes or to the quality of services.

Appraising: The council reviews the changes in matrices, the case reviews, and the child-count information to determine if the council's goal is being achieved. This appraisal is usually conducted twice a year but may be conducted more often if necessary. The council may choose to appraise all council activities (as specified in action plans) related to the overall goal at least once a year to determine if priorities should be changed; if particular activities should be continued, revised, or deleted; and if new programs are necessary to meet changing needs.

Examples of Information and Data Levels Documentation: The matrices can be updated on a monthly basis to reflect changing services in the community. The child-count data also can be updated on a monthly basis to identify available resources for new students; changes in staffing patterns; changes in funding sources; and changes in program priorities from the local, state, and federal levels.

Satisfaction: Because an important part of the council's goal is to support child and family functions by improving the coordination of services, parents' perceptions can be extremely helpful in determining the directions of the council. Figure 1 contains sample questions for a survey requesting parents' perceptions of council activities. The parents of a child with disabilities have the most intimate view of whether agencies are

---

HOW EFFECTIVE IS COORDINATION BETWEEN AGENCIES			
Directions: Read the following questions and respond by circling Yes, No, or DK (Don't Know).			
Do you feel that the various agencies that serve your child communicate sufficiently regarding their services and recommendations?	Yes	DK	No
Are individual educational programs or service plans developed mutually through participation of representatives from the various agencies that serve your child?	Yes	DK	No
Do the various agencies discuss and coordinate what each will provide so that your child receives *all* the needed services?	Yes	DK	No
Do the agency programs exchange records and reports regularly and with ease?	Yes	DK	No
Do the agency personnel mutually determine with you who the primary case manager will be?	Yes	DK	No
Do the agency personnel speak favorably about one another and about other agency programs?	Yes	DK	No
Do the agency personnel instill confidence in you about the other agency programs?	Yes	DK	No
Do the agency personnel attempt to avoid duplication of unnecessary services such as testing or therapy?	Yes	DK	No
Do the agency personnel appear to work together in a friendly and cooperative manner?	Yes	DK	No
Do you feel that the agency personnel prioritize quality services to your child rather than cumbersome paperwork and agency requirements?	Yes	DK	No
Do agency personnel eagerly refer you to the programs that can assist you if they cannot?	Yes	DK	No

Figure 1. Sample items for parent survey. (From *Interagency problem solving*, 1989; reprinted by permission.) (Adapted with Permission of the Florida Department of Education, Bureau of Education for Exceptional Students, from *Interagency problem solving*, [1989], p. 89.)

responsive to their needs and the needs of the child. A device such as this survey assesses these perceptions as they directly relate to the council's goal. A similar series of questions could be asked of agency representatives. Such questions also could be part of the council's review of particularly complex cases through comparison of agency personnel perceptions regarding the effectiveness of coordination efforts.

Change: The comparison of completed matrices from a prior time to the current time provides an index of change of the comprehensive array of community services and the continuum of services. These data are objective and indicate critical features of the impact of council efforts. No changes suggest that the council is not effective in reaching its goal. Desired changes, particularly as identified in action plans, should be reflected in the matrices during a particular period in time. Another means of evaluating the impact of council efforts is a review of the number of children served by agency programs; increases or decreases indicate the results of council activities. To conduct this evaluation of change, each agency must provide the names of children served each month to the council coordinator. Discussion could focus on the possible reasons for increases or decreases in the numbers of children served and the potential for resolution of problems that have resulted in decreases. An effective preschool child-tracking system is an objective method of maintaining these data, as well as other information about the children. The use of a child tracking system (see chap. 14, this volume) in which all agencies participate can result in a summary of children served by an agency, as shown in Table 2. Comparison of these data with those of prior years

Table 2. Sample chart of child-count data for interagency council child tracking

Agency	Enrollment (unduplicated)										
	Aug.	Sept.	Oct.	Nov.	Dec.	Jan.	Feb.	Mar.	Apr.	May	June
Memorial Hospital	2	2	2	2	2	6	8	9	9	10	11
County schools	10	10	21	40	42	40	40	40	41	42	42
The Arc	16	16	17	18	19	19	20	20	18	16	14
Parent training				(21)	(21)	(23)	(23)	(23)	(22)	(18)	(18)
				6	6	6	6	6	3	2	1
Easter Seal Society	17	17	18	17	17	17	17	18	18	19	20
Kiwanis Speech Clinic	4	4	8	8	8	8	10	12	13	10	8
Mother-toddler program	8	8	8	9	9	9	8	8	8	10	11
Head Start	4	4	6	9	9	9	9	9	8	8	8
Infant stimulation program	4	4	4	4	4	4	4	4	4	4	4
Migrant Head Start	2	2	2	2	2	2	2	2	2	2	2
Hospital speech center	21	21	22	24	25	27	27	27	25	27	28
Sertoma Saturday Speech Clinic	14	14	14	18	22	22	22	22	21	23	24
Private	5	5	5	6	6	8	8	9	9	9	9
Parent enrichment					(4)			(2)	(2)	(2)	(2)
			3	2	2	2	2				
United Cerebral Palsy						1	1	1	5	5	5
Total	111	111	134	169	178	185	189	192	188	192	192
Pending placements		2	1	1	1	5	5	6	3	2	2
Refused services		7	7	7	10	8	9	11	8	8	8
Total unserved		9	8	8	11	13	14	17	11	10	10
Being evaluated		7	12	10	8	8	10	11	8	5	6

Duplicated counts are indicated in parenthesis.
Data were not collected in July when most programs are closed.

can assist the council in its planning and service delivery efforts.

Council Operations   The operation of the council can be most effectively evaluated by the council members themselves.

Examples of Evaluation Approach   Planning: The council assesses its operational effectiveness and efficiency on an ongoing basis. The council's continued development should be refined through a focus on its goals, the ability to identify and respond to needs, continuity of membership, and through an emphasis on collaboration and its viability as a vehicle to achieve its goals. The council should plan specific self-examination on a periodic basis.

Monitoring: The council reviews consistency of representation from agencies, development of action plans, case reviews, exchange of critical information, collaborative efforts, and progress toward council goals within the framework of its current development stage (i.e., cooperation, coordination, or collaboration). Monitoring by all members is important in keeping the council focused on its goals, objectives, and activities.

Appraising: The council appraises its operations to ensure that it is moving in desired directions. The appraisal may result in emphasis on new development and problem resolution.

Examples of Information and Data Levels   Documentation: Council meetings are doc-

Table 3.   Analyses of council minutes by level of information and data

Analytical questions	Level of information/data
OPERATIONS	
Do the minutes reveal basic information, rather than mutual problem solving and actual coordination of services?	Change
ACTIONS	
Do the minutes reflect discussion about identification of existing services, service gaps, strategies to resolve those gaps?	Documentation
Do the minutes reflect discussion and resolution of procedural or policy constraints to services with an intent to resolve those problems?	Change
Do the minutes reflect measurable or identifiable accomplishments or products (directories, flowcharts, brochures, collaborative parent programs, collaborative staff development opportunities, and action plans)?	Documentation
Do the minutes reflect measurable activities, products, or accomplishments of council subcommittees that have been assigned responsibilities?	Documentation
Do the minutes reflect consistent attendance of members and their continuity of representation?	Documentation
Do the minutes reflect regular or monthly meetings of the council rather than sporadic or occasional ones?	Documentation
Do the minutes reflect emphasis on the needs of children and their families rather than emphasis on operation of the council itself?	Documentation
Do the minutes reflect mutual decision making and problem solving?	Change
Do the minutes reflect action on the part of the council in response to agency announcements, such as loss of funding or staff, to re-create a balance in the service delivery system?	Change
Do the minutes reflect that agency personnel seek assistance or answers from other council members?	Satisfaction
Do the minutes reflect identifiable and measurable goals of the council?	Documentation
Do the minutes reflect actual coordination of cases through discussion and identification of agency roles and responsibilities?	Change
Do the minutes reflect resolution of case management problems, rather than simple discussion of them?	Change

umented through the minutes. Table 3 provides an overview of the use of council minutes to analyze and evaluate operations through documentation, satisfaction, and change. Accurate minutes are the key at all three levels of information and data compilation for monitoring and appraisal of council activities. The action plans are another vehicle for analyzing council operations.

Satisfaction: One of the most important

means of evaluating council operations is by assessing the perceptions of council members in relation to this subject. Figure 2 provides sample items that can be used to rate members' perceptions in the areas of council organization, attitudes toward collaboration, group dynamics, and council outcomes. These sample items are not exhaustive, but they provide a basis for assessing members' satisfaction with the council's operation.

Circle the number that best describes how you view the functioning of the interagency team on the following dimensions and the manner in which anticipated outcomes have been reached.

		Disagree			Agree

COUNCIL ORGANIZATION

1.	The council includes the primary agencies that serve preschool children with disabilities and those at risk and their families.	1	2	3	4	5
2.	Agency representatives consistently attend meetings to provide continuity of planning.	1	2	3	4	5
3.	Council members are committed to cooperation and the council goals.	1	2	3	4	5
4.	Group size is small enough to encourage free and open discussion by all council members.	1	2	3	4	5
5.	The council meets on a regular, monthly basis.	1	2	3	4	5
6.	Meeting locations are convenient.	1	2	3	4	5
7.	Meeting rooms are comfortable and facilitate necessary discussion and planning.	1	2	3	4	5
8.	Council members have authority to represent their agency, implement recommendations, and commit and secure resources.	1	2	3	4	5
9.	Council members feel an equal partnership in identifying and implementing goals.	1	2	3	4	5
10.	The council coordinator facilitates the meetings effectively.	1	2	3	4	5
11.	Sufficient notice is given for meetings.	1	2	3	4	5
12.	Meeting length is sufficient to accomplish the necessary agenda items.	1	2	3	4	5
13.	Meeting minutes are provided in a timely manner.	1	2	3	4	5

		Disagree			Agree

ATTITUDES TOWARD COLLABORATION

1.	My program/agency has benefited from participation in the council.	1	2	3	4	5
2.	Collaboration can lead to more complete services for preschool children.	1	2	3	4	5
3.	Programs/agencies gain from collaboration.	1	2	3	4	5
4.	Collaboration helps programs/agencies develop more positive relationships with other programs/agencies.	1	2	3	4	5
5.	The council improves communication between community programs/agencies.	1	2	3	4	5
6.	Collaboration decreases the amount of "red tape" encountered by programs/agencies.	1	2	3	4	5
7.	Time spent in council meetings actually saves time because of information learned, resources identified, and contacts made.	1	2	3	4	5

(continued)

Figure 2. Sample items for interagency collaboration rating scales. (From *Interagency problem solving,* 1989; reprinted by permission.) (Adapted with Permission of the Florida Department of Education, Bureau of Education for Exceptional Students, from *Interagency problem solving,* [1989], p. 99.)

Figure 2.   *(continued)*

	Disagree				Agree
8. The council has provided me with significant information and knowledge of resources.	1	2	3	4	5
9. I enjoy working with other agency personnel on the council.	1	2	3	4	5
10. Families are provided a more organized network of services because of collaboration.	1	2	3	4	5
11. Pooling resources for activities, such as parent education and staff development, is more effective than separate agencies developing these services alone.	1	2	3	4	5
12. There is no benefit in competition for children or funds between agencies/programs.	1	2	3	4	5
13. Agencies/programs can meet the needs of children and families more efficiently if agencies/programs work collaboratively.	1	2	3	4	5
14. The positive outcomes of collaboration outweigh the time and effort required.	1	2	3	4	5

GROUP DYNAMICS

	Disagree				Agree
1. Friendly and supportive relationships exist within the council.	1	2	3	4	5
2. Group size allows for easy discussion and interaction with the group.	1	2	3	4	5
3. The atmosphere is relaxed, open, and warm.	1	2	3	4	5
4. Sufficient trust exists for council members to disagree and offer different views.	1	2	3	4	5
5. Council members have a sense of "mission" that binds them together as a team.	1	2	3	4	5
6. The council is a cohesive group with a spirit of camaraderie.	1	2	3	4	5
7. Group atmosphere and procedures are stable and predictable.	1	2	3	4	5
8. Time is well-managed and not wasted.	1	2	3	4	5
9. The meeting style is flexible enough to allow for discussion and necessary deviations from the agenda.	1	2	3	4	5
10. The council coordinator facilitates and encourages input from all council members.	1	2	3	4	5
11. The council coordinator is high-task oriented as well as high-relationship (sensitivity to people's needs) oriented.	1	2	3	4	5
12. Discussions are thought-provoking and motivating, and encourage action.	1	2	3	4	5
13. A high level of respect among council members and for various agencies exists.	1	2	3	4	5
14. Meetings are characterized by good humor, laughter, and enjoyment.	1	2	3	4	5
15. Comments, beliefs, and suggestions of council members are treated equally.	1	2	3	4	5

COUNCIL OUTCOMES

The following section identifies the degree to which the council has had a positive impact on services to children and families, and whether anticipated outcomes have been achieved. Indicate the degree to which you disagree or agree with each of the following statements using the following:

  As a result of participating in the local interagency council . . .

	Disagree				Agree
1. I have an increased understanding of the agency programs and services.	1	2	3	4	5
2. I have an improved understanding of the eligibility criteria for various programs.	1	2	3	4	5
3. I am more aware of the location of the agency facilities and programs.	1	2	3	4	5
4. I know whom to contact (contact person, secretary, social worker, coordinator) in each of the agency programs if I have questions or need information.	1	2	3	4	5
5. I make more efficient referrals because of improved understanding of the agencies.	1	2	3	4	5
6. My respect for agencies and programs has increased.	1	2	3	4	5
7. My daily contacts and networking with agencies have increased.	1	2	3	4	5
8. General communication with the agencies and programs has increased.	1	2	3	4	5
9. Records and reports are exchanged with greater efficiency.	1	2	3	4	5

(continued)

Figure 2. (*continued*)

	Disagree			Agree	
10. The gap in time between referral of children to other agencies and the provision of services has been reduced.	1	2	3	4	5
11. Evaluation services to children have improved.	1	2	3	4	5
12. There is less duplication of effort with respect to screening and evaluation.	1	2	3	4	5
13. Acceptance of outside agency evaluations and reports has increased, resulting in faster eligibility determination and placement.	1	2	3	4	5
14. Individual educational and service plans have included increased participation by outside agency personnel in development of the plans.	1	2	3	4	5
15. Referral of children and families to my agency's program(s) has increased.	1	2	3	4	5
16. Coordination of services to preschool children has improved, resulting in more complete services.	1	2	3	4	5
17. I am better aware of changes in agency programs as they occur (staff, resource allocation, funding levels, procedures).	1	2	3	4	5
18. I utilize community resources more effectively.	1	2	3	4	5
19. Agency roles and responsibilities have been clarified.	1	2	3	4	5
20. My budget/funds stretch further due to increased information about other available funding sources (Medicaid, grant programs, other agency funding capability).	1	2	3	4	5
21. My program has increased the number of children served.	1	2	3	4	5
22. In-service opportunities for staff have increased.	1	2	3	4	5
23. Less duplication of effort and funding has occurred for staff training, workshops, and consultants.	1	2	3	4	5
24. My agency has entered into new contracts or written agreements to expand or refine services.	1	2	3	4	5
25. Budget planning (local, state, or federal grants categorical funding) is done based on consideration of the funding and resource capabilities of other agencies/ programs.	1	2	3	4	5
26. My agency has developed, refined, modified, or expanded programs based on identified community needs and planning rather than isolated planning.	1	2	3	4	5
27. Agency policies and procedures have been changed or modified to eliminate constraints to services encountered by families.	1	2	3	4	5
28. Agencies have appeared more willing to share information and resources.	1	2	3	4	5
29. Transition of children between agencies has improved.	1	2	3	4	5
30. An effective child tracking system has been developed, ensuring that children are not "lost" between the agency eligibilities and programs.	1	2	3	4	5
31. Individual case coordination of difficult-to-serve children has improved.	1	2	3	4	5
32. Services to parents (parent groups, workshops, parent training, support groups, information) have increased.	1	2	3	4	5
33. Coordination of parent programs (workshops, parent groups, parent training, newsletters) has resulted in less duplication of effort and in cost savings.	1	2	3	4	5
34. Parents feel less frustration and encounter fewer barriers to services for their children.	1	2	3	4	5
35. The continuum of services to children and families has become more complete.	1	2	3	4	5

Change: The continuity of council members and the refinement of council operations based on the perceptions of the council members are relevant change indicators. If the agency representatives change frequently or there are unresolved complaints about council operation, the council will find it most difficult to be creative and achieve its goal. In another dimension, analysis of case reviews reflects the council's operations by revealing whether the council's efforts have resulted in successful collaboration and problem solving or in something less effective. A sample of children might be considered for a case review analysis on an annual basis. Surveys or interview questions for agency representatives could supplement this information in order to assess council operations in effectively changing the focus to coordination and collaboration among agencies.

Specific Examples

Information Exchange   The sample action plan objective is to develop a standardized release-of-information form to facilitate exchange of information across agencies.

Example of Evaluation Plan Approach
Planning: The needs assessment indicates this to be a council priority. The action plan includes a review of existing forms, identification of common and critical elements, drafting of a common form, review of the form by the council, revision of the form based on critique, pilot testing of the form, and adoption of the form by the council. The use of the form by all agencies should reduce the number of forms in use, increase the sharing of information on a timely basis, and reduce the amount of time necessary to initiate services under an IEP/IFSP.

Monitoring: All of the action plan items are monitored through council minutes, which indicate progress for each item according to the timelines specified in the action plan. Each agency is asked to indicate when it adopts the form. Data concerning the increased sharing of information and the time necessary to initiate services are requested for a sample of two children and families from each agency on a quarterly basis.

Appraising: At the end of the first year of using the common form, the council reviews the quarterly results to determine if objectives have been achieved and if the action plan needs revision. Each member agency is asked to commit to continued use of the form. Commitment of the agencies indicates that the action plan has achieved its intended purpose and no further action plan is necessary.

Example of Information and Data Levels
Documentation: The action plan is developed, and copies of all agency release forms

are shared with the council members. This information is contained in the council minutes. A common release-of-information form is developed that incorporates all of the common and critical information items from each agency.

Satisfaction: Each agency submits a written statement that the common form is acceptable and will be utilized by the agency in place of its own referral forms.

Change: Records are now exchanged among agencies within one week, unnecessary agency forms have been deleted, and services are initiated for children and families in a more timely manner.

Public Awareness   The sample action plan objective is to educate the medical community concerning the need for early intervention and the availability of services for preschoolers with disabilities and those at risk and their families.

Example of Evaluation Approach   Planning: The needs assessment, through the completion of the community services matrix and the continuum of services matrix, reveals a lack of knowledge about available services on the part of the medical community and receipt of few referrals from this sector. The action plan is developed to create a council brochure that focuses on the need for early intervention and the services available for preschool children (birth through 5 years of age) with disabilities and those at risk and their families; to have council members review and approve the brochure; to mail this brochure to physicians, nurses, and hospitals, along with an offer to talk with them at their convenience; and to provide referral forms to all physicians' offices and hospitals. The impact of this action plan is to increase the referrals of appropriate children and their families for services.

Monitoring: The progress in completing the objectives for this action plan (development, review and approval, and mailing of brochures) is documented in the council meeting minutes. The impact is monitored by each agency's data on the number of referrals from the medical community and the percentage of referrals that are appropriate (i.e., for children with disabilities and those at risk and their families). These data are collected at the monthly council meeting.

Appraising: Twelve months subsequent to the initial mailing of the brochure, the council reviews the number of referrals and the percentage of appropriate referrals from the medical community, along with verbal and written feedback. The council determines if the brochure needs revising or updating based on continuing changes in programs, if it should be mailed periodically to members of the medical community (e.g., twice yearly), or if some new approach, such as personal contact, is necessary to stimulate appropriate referrals.

Examples of Levels of Information and Data Documentation: A brochure is developed for the medical community, reviewed and approved by council, and mailed to physicians, nurses, and hospitals. These actions are documented in the minutes of monthly council meetings.

Satisfaction: Notes received from physicians, nurses, and hospitals state the value of the brochure.

Change: Physicians, nurses, and hospitals increase the number and appropriateness of referrals to agency programs.

Screening and Identification The sample action plan objective is to develop effective screening and assessment procedures that minimize unnecessary duplication and result in accurate identification of preschool children with disabilities and those at risk.

Example of Evaluation Approach Planning: The needs assessment using the community services matrix reveals significant overlap for both screening and assessment procedures for all preschool children. An action plan is developed to compare screening and assessment procedures across agency programs, to determine the common and essential screening and assessment procedures for programs and agencies, and to collaborate in developing council screening

and assessment procedures that maximize the accurate identification of preschool children with disabilities and those at risk. Simultaneously, unnecessary duplication of screening and assessment services is eliminated; a child is screened and assessed only once.

Monitoring: Progress in completing the comparison of agency procedures, determining common and essential procedures, and developing council procedures is contained in the minutes of monthly council meetings. The recommendations for common and essential screening and assessment procedures are presented to the council members; the resulting action is also noted in the council minutes. The results of a pilot testing of the collaborative effort (e.g., three community-wide screenings per year with personnel from a variety of agencies in a common location) are shared with the council.

Appraising: Council members consider the results of the pilot testing based on accurate identification of preschool children who need services and verification that each child is screened and assessed only once. The council decides to implement the community-wide screening and assessment on a continuing basis, to revise the procedures in order to achieve better results, or to discontinue the effort because it is not perceived to be effective.

Example of Information and Data Levels Documentation: Existing screening and assessment procedures are reviewed and discussed by council members as indicated in the council meeting minutes. A written description of common screening and assessment procedures for all community agencies is developed, along with recommendations for eliminating unnecessary duplication, for council consideration.

Satisfaction: Each member agency endorses the common screening and assessment procedures and recommendations and commits to their implementation.

Change: Agencies collaborate in screening and assessment procedures by sharing personnel at community-wide "round-ups" conducted several times during the year. No child is screened or assessed more than once. The additional time resulting from more efficient and effective procedures is channeled into direct service activities by each agency, as indicated by the council representatives.

Case Management The sample action plan objective is to improve the services provided to children and their families as a result of case management efforts by the council.

Examples of Evaluation Approach Planning: The agency to which a child has been referred requests the council to consider the unique and complex needs of the child and family. The council discusses their needs and provides alternative services for consideration, as indicated in council meeting minutes.

Monitoring: The council receives an update from the agency representative regarding the actions, consistent with the IFSP/IEP process, that were taken by the parents and the appropriate agencies. The actions are listed briefly in the council minutes.

Appraising: The agency representative indicates which services were provided as scheduled and whether the needs of the child and family have been or are being met. The council reviews the final actions to differentiate between the effective and ineffective actions in order to improve alternatives under similar circumstances in the future.

Examples of Information and Data Levels Documentation: The child and family are discussed at the council meeting as indicated in the minutes.

Satisfaction: Council members agree to collaborate and provide multiple services across agencies that are consistent with the IFSP/IEP and approved by the family and the agencies. The parents express satisfaction that these services meet their needs, as indicated by signatures on the IFSP/IEP form.

Change: Services are provided as scheduled; unnecessary duplication is eliminated.

Referral and Transition The sample action plan objective is to develop and use a child tracking system to project transition needs.

Example of Evaluation Approach Planning: As a result of reviewing the problems associated with transition during June through September of last year, the council determines the need to improve transition services across agencies to ensure that all children who need services receive them during the summer months. The council designs an action plan to track all preschool children with disabilities and those at risk and emphasize the children who require transition to new programs or agencies because of age or changed needs. Each child and family who need transition services should receive them. No child or family should "fall between the cracks."

Monitoring: Updates on designing and implementing the plan are presented at council meetings during fall and winter. Council members learn what actions are necessary to ensure that children receive needed transition services. The tracking system is used during spring and summer to verify that these services are provided. Any problems are discussed by the council coordinator and the relevant agency representatives.

Appraising: The council reviews the results of the pilot test of the tracking system for transition services and determines if it needs refinement or if it works effectively. A new action plan is developed if the system needs refinement. A system that is working effectively will be implemented again in the coming year and a report provided to the council on its continuing effectiveness.

Example of Information and Data Levels Documentation: Council members develop and test a child tracking system across all agencies based on information in the action plan and in the council meeting minutes.

Satisfaction: Council members endorse the child tracking system for projecting transition needs. The council makes a commitment to work for the effective implementation of the system throughout the community.

Change: All children who will make transitions during June or September receive transition planning services during the previous March. No children will fail to receive appropriate services during the summer.

Program Delivery The sample action plan objective is to identify and eliminate sources of unnecessary duplication of effort and rechannel resources as appropriate in service delivery.

Examples of Evaluation Approach Planning: The completion of the community services matrix reveals areas of unnecessary duplication of direct services provided by multiple agencies. The council develops an action plan to review these services; provide recommendations for priority services, based in part on consideration of agency philosophies, histories, and expertise; and suggests redirection for unnecessary duplication into direct services that are needed in the community. Implementation of the recommendations should result in more effective services, the creation of new services, and the provision of services to a larger number of preschool children with disabilities and those at risk. This information is contained in both the action plan and the council meeting minutes.

Monitoring: The council receives periodic reports on progress toward the action plan objective at its monthly meetings. The reports are also briefly reviewed in the meeting minutes. Discussions among agencies to consider alternatives to recommendations and strategies are shared by the council members. The council reviews the final recommendations and determines which ones should be implemented according to specified timelines.

Appraising: The council reviews agency results in eliminating unnecessary duplication and enhancing direct service delivery following the period of implementation. The results are appraised in terms of new or improved services provided to preschool children with disabilities and those at risk

and their families. Based on the results to date, new action plans may be instituted. A new community agency services matrix is developed to reflect the elimination of unnecessary duplication and an increase in other services.

Examples of Information and Data Levels Documentation: The community agency services matrix is completed, areas of unnecessary duplication of effort are identified, and recommendations for rechanneling agency efforts are presented to the council. This information is contained in the action plan and council meeting minutes.

Satisfaction: Council members endorse the recommendations and commit to their implementation according to specified timelines.

Change: Member agencies implement the recommendations, reduce unnecessary duplication, and increase services in other areas. These actions are indicated by changes in the community agency services matrix, the continuum of services matrix, and the number of preschool children with disabilities and those at risk and their families who are served.

Parent Involvement The sample action plan objective is to provide knowledge and skill training to parents in serving their children.

Example of Evaluation Approach Planning: During September, a survey is distributed by the council to all parents of preschool children being served by council member agencies and other agencies in the community. The survey reveals that many parents want knowledge and skill training to work with their children at home, consistent with their IFSPs/IEPs. The council reviews these results and appoints an interagency collaborative team to develop an action plan for workshops to provide parents with the knowledge and skills they need. The council wants the workshops completed by the end of the current year with the dual results of increased knowledge and skills for parents and collaboration among agencies to avoid unnecessary duplication of staff time and resources. This information is contained in the action plan and in the monthly council meeting minutes.

Monitoring: The council reviews and approves the action plan in October with minor refinements. The council agrees that the workshops should be conducted during January through March with an appropriate follow-up of individual children and families by agency personnel. The parents should be contacted in October or November to determine their commitment to participate. Following the workshops in March, the council receives a report concerning the increased knowledge and skills demonstrated by the parents and the parent perceptions of the effectiveness of the workshops.

Appraising: The council reviews the final results, observes several parents demonstrating their skills to others, and determines the workshops to have been effective both in providing the knowledge and skills and in avoiding unnecessary duplication of staff time. Based on the information and data provided, the council suggests refinements and commits to continuing the parent workshops during the coming year if the survey in September shows significant need in these areas.

Example of Information and Data Levels Documentation: As an integral part of the IFSP/IEP, the needs for knowledge and skills for all parents are specified; however, parents may have other needs. A combination of the IFSP/IEP needs and parent perceptions is developed to design a parent training program that will provide the necessary knowledge and skills, and the program is offered to parents. The information and data are contained in the action plan statement and council minutes.

Satisfaction: Parents are surveyed and asked whether they think the training program met their needs. Staffs from the various agencies are also surveyed to determine if they think the training was effective.

Change: The parents demonstrate the knowledge and skills they learned by show-ing other parents how they serve their children. Based on information provided in April, the council decides that the knowledge and skills learned and the satisfaction with the training are sufficient to continue the workshops if the parent survey and IFSPs/IEPs indicate a continued need. A new action plan is developed for the coming year.

Staff Development The sample action plan objective is to conduct an interagency needs assessment regarding in-service staff training and to provide community wide in-service training based on common needs to improve staff knowledge and skills and the quality of programming for preschool children with disabilities and those at risk.

Examples of Evaluation Approach Planning: The council members realize a continuing need to improve the knowledge and skills of agency staffs, but they recognize the considerable expense involved in high-quality staff development. Based on these factors, the council develops an action plan to conduct an interagency needs assessment for community-wide agency staffs. After identifying the needs and targeting the common needs, the council plans an in-service training opportunity for all those who are interested. The in-service training program is to be sponsored by the council membership.

Monitoring: The council reviews the results of the needs assessment, the common needs, and plans for the in-service training and provides recommendations for improvement. Council members approve the plan. They commit to joint sponsorship by providing resources available to each agency and by encouraging their staffs to participate.

Appraising: The council reviews the results of the training experience, including the perceptions of the participants, and determines that the training met the needs identified in the needs assessment. The council recommends that a similar activity be established by action plan for the coming year.

Examples of Information and Data Levels
Documentation: An interagency needs assessment regarding staff training needs is conducted by a subcommittee of the council. Common needs across agencies are identified, and a program is designed to provide the training for staffs from all agencies. The program is to be conducted through collaboration of the agencies. This information and data are contained in the council minutes and the action plan.

Satisfaction: The participants are asked if they think the training was helpful to them in providing services to children and their families.

Change: The participants demonstrate increased knowledge and skills in the areas of identified needs. The council commits to developing an action plan for staff training during the coming year.

Additional Resources

Councils that determine a need for more sophisticated methods to answer complex evaluative questions should refer to Popham (1988), Smith (1990), Wolf (1990), and Worthen and Sanders (1987). Personnel resources include research, development, and evaluation specialists at local agencies; university professors in the areas of administration, leadership, early childhood education, and program evaluation; and doctoral students who are completing dissertations on such topics as the effectiveness of interagency councils.

REFERENCES

Huberty, C.J., Quirk, J.P., & Swan, W.W. (1973). An evaluation system for a psychoeducational treatment program for emotionally disturbed children. *Educational Technology, 13*(5), 73–80.

Huberty, C.J., & Swan, W.W. (1977). Evaluation of programs. In J.B. Jordan (Ed.), *Handbook of exemplary practices in early childhood special education* (pp. 256–281). Reston, VA: Council for Exceptional Children.

Interagency problem solving. (1989). Tallahasse: Florida Department of Education, Bureau of Education for Exceptional Children.

Popham, W.J. (1988). *Educational evaluation* (2nd ed.). Englewood Cliffs, NJ: Prentice Hall.

Smith, M.J. (1990). *Program evaluation in the human services.* New York: Springer Publishing.

Swan, W.W. (Ed.). (1989). *The resource manual for preschool handicapped in Georgia.* Atlanta: Preschool

Handicapped Task Force for the Division for Exceptional Students, Georgia Department of Education.

Swan, W.W. (1990). Needs assessment for special programs. In C.T. Holmes (Ed.). Athens: *Monographs in Education,* No. 11, University of Georgia, Bureau of Educational Services, ERIC Documentation Reproduction Service Abstract (Requested).

Travers, J.R., & Light, R.J. (Eds.). (1982). *Learning from experience: Evaluating early childhood demonstration programs.* Washington, DC: National Academy Press.

Wolf, R.M. (1990). *Evaluation in education: Foundations of competency assessment and program review.* New York: Praeger.

Worthen, B.R., & Sanders, J.R. (1987). *Educational evaluation: Alternative approaches and practical guidelines.* New York: Longman.

Section IV

Financing Early
Intervention Services

In an attempt to expand early intervention services to children with disabilities and conditions of risk from birth through age 5, the local interagency council must find solutions to the limitations that plague service providers. Collaboration, in its most sophisticated form, is characterized by the development of contracts and written agreements among providers (*Interagency problem solving*, 1989). Contracts permit purchase of needed services, solutions to personnel shortages, and compensation for lack of sufficient facilities and transportation. Written agreements can creatively combine agency resources in a manner previously unknown through shared decision making and co-location of services.

Chapter 17, "Financing," discusses local financing of early intervention services—a formidable task requiring flexibility and innovative use of available resources. Although state-level efforts to finance services focus on written agreements among primary federal and state programs, local providers must examine more immediate resources and avenues of community support.

Chapter 18, "Contracts and Interagency Agreements," focuses on contracts and written agreements. Components of agreements are discussed, along with key principles for successful implementation. Sample contracts and agreements are shown in the appendices.

REFERENCE

Interagency problem solving. (1989). Tallahassee: Florida Department of Education, Bureau of Education for Exceptional Students.

Chapter 17

Financing

Tight economic times, paired with increasing needs for services, create greater competition for available dollars to support early intervention services. Both state and local agencies are challenged to secure sufficient levels of funding and to eliminate the current duplication of services and other wasteful procedures that exist within the system. Multiple funding sources and collaborative agreements are particularly important to local providers in sustaining or expanding the quality of services to young children with disabilities and conditions of high risk.

STATE FINANCING OF SERVICES

The passage of the Education of the Handicapped Act Amendments of 1986 (PL 99-457), now referred to as the Individuals with Disabilities Education Act (IDEA), created a new impetus for the development and provision of services for children (birth through 5 years of age) who have disabilities or conditions of risk. PL 99-457 created a policy and authorized additional federal assistance to the states for educational and related services for children with disabilities from infancy to school age. Title I of PL 99-457 established Part H, providing for the development and implementation of a statewide system of comprehensive, coordinated, multidisciplinary interagency programs of early intervention services for children from birth to 3 years of age. Title II amended Part B of the Education for All Handicapped Children Act of 1975 (PL 94-142) to expand special education and related services to children, ages 3 through 5 years.

Key provisions of PL 99-457 require payment for services to be made from identification and coordination of all available federal, state, local, and private sources (including public and private insurance coverage) at no cost to families (Title I, Part H, §676[b]9[B]), except where federal or state law provides for a system of payment by families, including a schedule of sliding fees (§672[2][B]). Funding under the act is designated to expand existing services and to develop currently unavailable services. Agencies other than educational agencies are not absolved of any obligations to pay for some or all of the costs of a free and appropriate public education for children with disabilities, ages 3 through 5 years. Furthermore, the act clearly states that all such funds must be accessed before federal funds are used. Congress appropriated funds under Part H of the legislation to develop and implement the system of services; facilitate the coordination of payment; and enhance, expand, and improve the capacity of the states to serve eligible children and their families.

The identification of appropriate public and private funds is particularly vital to the success of a state's Part H program and financing is a significant responsibility of participating states (Fox, Freedman, & Klepper, 1989; Peterson, 1991). Comprehensive surveys by the Carolina Policy Studies Program (CPSP) revealed that the states have been slow to implement the major financial provisions of the law. Of the 14 components required under Part H, the states have made the least progress in developing, approving, and implementing the requirement to assign financial responsibility for services (Harbin, Gallagher, Lillie, & Eck-

211

land, 1990) and in establishing state-level interagency agreements (Harbin, Gallagher, & Lillie, 1989). Development of procedures for contracting services, however, was the sole financial area in which substantial progress was demonstrated.

Local coordinating groups have been facilitating systems to finance services for children and their families; state-level coordination has proceeded more slowly. Although efforts are under way to improve financial coordination at the state level, it is premature to determine whether the normal turf battles that exist in bureaucracies will permit states to accomplish the desired goals (Clifford, 1991).

Sources of State Funding

The Part H program is intended as the payor of last resort, with primary funding to be identified through "assignment of financial responsibility to the appropriate agency" (PL 99-457 ($676[b][9][C]). The program specifically identifies Medicaid, Maternal and Child Health block grants, and private insurers as funding contributors in early intervention services.

A case study of funding used in six states (Clifford, 1991) found that major sources of funding under Part H are Medicaid, state or interagency health programs, Chapter I (disabilities), state education programs, private insurance, parent fees, and local funds. Only one state revealed that its major sources include more than two of these seven sources. The study suggests that securing significant commitments from various agencies is a substantial undertaking. States that have been successful in moving toward adequate financing systems for services to infants and toddlers with disabilities have focused their efforts on a small number of fund sources. They have avoided any attempt to access all possible sources but have generally concentrated on maximizing the use of two or three funding mechanisms. The following three funding approaches were among those utilized by the states in the study:

1. Unit rate financing, in which standard rates of payment for specified services are established; typically involved when insurance is used for payment
2. Contracting for services, in which services are purchased from a provider through a request for proposals that describes expected services and state controls
3. State core financing, involving some substantial source of state funds used for a large share of the financing, with a possible intent to build a broader financial base of less dependable sources through use of these funds (e.g., state appropriations supplemented by private insurance reimbursements, state appropriations to match Medicaid)

Third-Party Billing

Education agencies and community providers have accessed Medicaid and other third-party sources in seeking alternative funding for special education and related services and other early intervention programs. State and local education agencies have sought third-party funding in direct response to provisions in federal and state laws that require public agencies to seek funding sources other than those available under Part B or Part H of IDEA (O'Brien, 1991; White & Immel, 1991).

Medicaid is a national health services program that brings federal matching money to the states to assist in providing certain medically necessary services to eligible low-income children. This public insurance program is a potential resource to service providers, including schools, for enhancing the quality and quantity of Medicaid-eligible services based on an individualized family service plan, individual education program, or treatment plan. Medicaid does not pay any claim until all other sources of private insurance have been billed (*School-related services and medicaid*, 1991). Parent permission must be secured before Medicaid is billed.

The Medicare Catastrophic Coverage Act

of 1988 (PL 100-360) clarified the use of Medicaid to pay for services provided in the schools (Wolf, 1991). Although this act was subsequently repealed, Section 1903, which amended the Social Security Act, remained in effect. This amendment states:

> Under PL 94-142, children with handicaps are entitled to a free and appropriate public education with conformity with an individualized education program (IEP) which describes the educational and "related services" necessary to meet the child's unique needs. While the State education agencies are financially responsible for educational services, in the case of a Medicaid-eligible handicapped child, State Medicaid agencies remain responsible for the "related services" identified in the child's IEP if they are covered under the State's Medicaid plan, such as speech-language pathology and audiology, psychology services, physical and occupational therapy, and medical counseling and services for diagnostic and evaluation purposes.

New Medicaid mandates have had special significance for the expansion of early intervention services; it is estimated that 30%–35% of children in programs for children with special health needs are eligible for Medicaid (Van Dyck, 1991). Beginning April 1, 1990, all states had to cover any of these children (from birth up to age 6 years) whose family income was less than 133 percent of the poverty level. In addition, changes in the Early Periodic Screening, Diagnosis, and Treatment (EPSDT) program mandated that all abnormalities requiring medical care identified during screenings must be covered by the state Medicaid agency. This new mandate has at least doubled, and in some states tripled, the number of Medicaid-eligible children served in Part H programs (Van Dyck, 1991).

Private health insurance plans may provide coverage for early intervention services, and they represent a largely untapped funding source. The option of private insurance is less than ideal because it is inaccessible to many families and, when it is available, it designates limits on the amount of treatment. Private plans also have lifetime caps and specify the total dollar amount that they will pay during an individual's life. Billing the third-party payor for early intervention services provided by schools, clinics, or private health care professionals may either deplete the specific coverage or exhaust the lifetime cap. The child could be left without health care coverage for the rest of his or her life. Program personnel should obtain informed written consent from parents and provide an explanation of the possible risk to the lifetime cap before billing private health insurers. Because of this risk to future benefits, using private health insurance must remain voluntary for the family.

LOCAL FINANCING OF SERVICES

The dilemma posed by the need to secure sufficient funds for a range of early intervention services at the local level for children from birth through age 5 is not easily resolved. No single funding source exists, and local program administrators are challenged to identify and maintain a multiple-source funding base. Again, no single agency (including the lead agency) can provide all of the Part H services needed by individual children and their families. Federal legislation in the form of PL 99-457 clearly envisions coordinated and extensive involvement by noneducation agencies and the use of noneducational sources of funding. Imagination, creativity, and strong organizational skills are needed in financing the range of local services. Many alternatives and options must be considered.

Government Sources

Local Educational Agencies Public school programs provide special education and related services to children with disabilities, ages 3 through 5 years. Funding levels vary by state and are based on a general funding formula with an adjustment for the provision of special education (e.g., unit funding, weighted funding, personnel funding, excess costs, percentage formula, differentiated) for eligible children. Types of early intervention services to eligible children from birth to 3 years of age and their families also may be provided under state funding formulas (e.g., special education, parent training, speech therapy, occupational therapy, physical therapy). These funds should be utilized before federal funds, such as the Education for the Handicapped grant program (PL 94-142), preschool entitlement grant program (PL 99-457), Part H grant program, or flexible nonprofit funds are spent.

Local Taxing Boards and Commissions
Local taxing authorities may exist by virtue of referendum for the purpose of generating additional revenue for community programs. Early intervention agencies should consider requesting these taxing commissions to fund services that the agencies are unable to provide through existing operating budgets. Such requests may include funds for parent services, specialized equipment or materials, transportation, day care, glasses, and hearing aids.

State-Funded Programs Local programs funded through state-operated agencies, including health and human resources, developmental disabilities, and children's medical services, serve eligible children in a manner similar to public education programs. Funding levels and formulas may not be consistent with the entitlement formulas used for educational programs by the state. A straight-sum formula may be used, or annual legislative appropriations may set funding levels.

Federal Entitlement Funds Special education programs in schools or public-funded agency programs may be financed through a combination of federal, state, and local funds. Federal funds may be provided through an entitlement program that authorizes money in accordance with a specific formula relating to the number of children served. These funds are provided under the Individuals with Disabilities Education Act (IDEA) (PL 94-142), preschool entitlement grants provided in PL 99-457, and

Chapter I (handicapped). Funds flow through the state education agency to the local education agency. The amount of the entitlement varies from year to year, depending on the fiscal authorization of Congress.

Federal or State Competitive Funds
Federal or state funds are made available in the form of grants that are awarded on a competitive basis to local agencies. The Handicapped Children's Early Education Program (HCEEP) projects are model demonstrations funded by the Office of Special Education Programs, United States Department of Education. States grants for various early intervention initiatives may be funded by a flow-through of federal dollars or by state revenue.

Nonprofit and Private Sources

Nonprofit Community Agencies Nonprofit agencies, such as United Cerebral Palsy, The Arc, and Easter Seal Society, have long provided early intervention services for young children and their families. Funding has been historically derived from a number of sources that include donations, fund-raising events, telethons, bequests, United Way contributions, and foundations. Because of their long-standing community status, widespread public awareness campaigns, and a strong sense of community ownership, nonprofit agencies will continue to be vital in the provision of early intervention services. The availability of their personnel, expertise, and facilities may provide excellent opportunities for contracting. Nonprofit agencies offer alternative placement options for children whose families will not accept public programs that require categorical labels as a condition of funding. Some also provide year-round or extended day care.

Hospitals, Clinics, and Rehabilitation Centers Hospitals and other healthcare centers, both public and private, provide such services as medical, speech therapy, occupational therapy, physical therapy, evaluation, and counseling that are funded by

Medicaid, private insurance, county or local government, or private fees. These sources frequently offer opportunities for schools and other public agencies to contract for therapy services that may be in short supply because of recruitment problems and shortages of available personnel.

Private Practitioners Therapists, counselors, specialists, psychologists, and staff development trainers can be found in every community. They provide services through agency contracts, foundation support, Medicaid, third-party payment, and private fees. Under contractual arrangements or written agreements, they can alleviate staff shortages (e.g., speech, occupational, or physical therapists) and fiscal constraints of schools and community agencies. A contract between the school system and a speech therapist, for example, might provide services and generate state funding for eligible children in a subsidized day care setting or a nonpublic program, such as The Arc center. A contract with a clinical psychologist who serves on the school interdisciplinary evaluation team at a flat fee per evaluation may be more cost-effective than employment of an additional staff psychologist requiring a salary, fringe benefits, office space, supplies, and travel expenses.

United Way Agencies These nonprofit agencies provide funding opportunities in the form of community grants or annual allocations to local programs in need. Fundraising drives receive widespread public and business support and result in substantial discretionary funds.

Volunteer Organizations Church groups, support groups, and other community organizations provide volunteer services, fundraising activities, and assistance to families. Babysitting and respite care services may be funded or organized through the efforts of retired nurses, Girl Scouts, or church groups. Clerical and secretarial assistance, classroom volunteers, and interpreters can be found. Volunteers may assist with transportation of families to therapy or medical appointments, or they may organize donations of items needed by families (e.g., infant supplies, clothing, cribs, car seats, toys). Adopt-a-family programs for holidays or in times of special need may prove to be excellent projects.

Parent Groups Parent-teacher organizations, parent resource centers, and parent support groups can help in developing a continuum of services for families of children with disabilities. Generally unfunded and organized by parents, rather than professionals, these groups provide a means for parents to become involved and contribute to children's programs. Parents' knowledge and support are critical to the successful operation of programs, and their insights into needs of children and families must be considered in program planning. These groups can organize babysitting cooperatives and respite care, in addition to developing formal support and education activities for parents. Parent-to-parent organizations can establish outreach programs that include visits to mothers who have just given birth to premature babies and those who have children with disabilities. Packets of parent materials, such as brochures, parenting tips, child find information, developmental checklists, and agency telephone numbers, can be given to new mothers at local hospitals. Armed with facts and figures, parent groups are often powerful advocates for needed changes in legislation, policy, and funding.

Foundations and Nonprofit Organizations The March of Dimes, Epilepsy Foundation, Muscular Dystrophy Association, Multiple Sclerosis Society, Spina Bifida Association, United Cerebral Palsy (UCP), and other organizations often provide specialized equipment, instructional and parent materials, medical supplies, diapers, and family services. They serve as valuable resources for individual children and families in need.

Community and Civic Groups Members of local civic groups, such as Kiwanians, Sertomans, Lions, Elks, Jaycees, and Shriners, seek ongoing projects for their service requirements and fund-raising efforts. Because the established priorities of their parent organizations often include services to children with disabilities, civic groups represent excellent resources for early intervention programs. Funding may support field trips, equipment and supplies, equestrian therapy programs, purchase of playground equipment, and home-based therapy. Other target groups include local chapters of national organizations with specific membership, such as retired nurses, university women, and retired persons. The members have special skills, knowledge, and expertise and can be substantial assets to local programs.

Private Business The role of the business community in the support of education and human service programs has been increasingly evident. Business partnership programs, utilizing the particular skills and resources of local business ventures, can make effective contributions to early intervention services. In addition, the participation and interest of the business community can result in strong advocates and promoters of early intervention programs. Members of the business community often have strong ties to the political and legislative community.

Universities, Community Colleges, and Vocational Programs Regional university and community training programs may be underutilized sources of services and staff development opportunities. Additional resources obtained through collaborative programs with universities may include direct services for children and families, research projects, internship opportunities, and consultation. Students often volunteer for babysitting, extended day care programs, and classroom duties.

Institutes and Research Centers These organizations may serve as resources for programs seeking innovative and creative service delivery options. A research center, for example, may furnish consultation, funding, personnel, and other assistance in providing services to children and their families while it collects data relevant to the establishment of best practices.

Tools for Collaboration

Interagency Agreements Agreements among community agencies can facilitate the combination of available resources to improve or expand services for children and families. As a result, a program could be co-located in one facility in order to coordinate the educational program (e.g., schools), therapy services (e.g., UCP), and after-school care (e.g., subsidized child care). Formal or informal agreements should specify the role and responsibility of each participating agency with respect to the types of services and the conditions under which they are provided.

Contracts and Purchase of Services Contracts between agencies are often necessary in order to provide intended services. Contracts may offer a more cost-effective means of providing early intervention or allow agencies to compensate for personnel shortages or transportation limitations. For example, the school district may compensate for a shortage of classroom space by contracting to place children in other settings. Therapy services, in short supply due to a personnel shortage, might be purchased from a local clinic and provided in the school setting. To avoid transporting young children long distances to a center-based program, home-based services could be purchased from another agency.

Local Interagency Coordinating Councils Local councils provide a mutual strategy for agency personnel to design the community system of services and identify the most appropriate funding sources for individual children and their families. Although they do not constitute a separate funding source, local councils are vital in promoting contracts and written agreements among community providers, developing grants and projects, and coordinating the roles and responsibilities of agency programs to ensure the most cost-effective use of available funds.

REFERENCES

Clifford, R.M. (1991). *State financing of services under PL 99-457, Part H.* Chapel Hill: University of North Carolina at Chapel Hill, Frank Porter Graham Child Development Center, Carolina Policy Studies Program.

Education for All Handicapped Children Act of 1975, PL 94-142 (August 23, 1977). 20 U.S.C. 1401, et seq: *Federal Register, 42*(163), 42474–42518.

Education of the Handicapped Act Amendments of 1986, PL 99-457 (September 22, 1986). 20 U.S.C. Sec. 1400, et seq: *Congressional Record, 132*(125), H 7893-7912.

Fox, H.B., Freedman, S.A., & Klepper, B.R. (1989). Financing programs for young children with handicaps. In J.J. Gallagher, P.L. Trohanis, & R.M. Clifford (Eds.), *Policy implementation and PL 99-457: Planning for young children with special needs* (pp. 169–182). Baltimore: Paul H. Brookes Publishing Co.

Harbin, G., Gallagher, J., & Lillie, T. (1989). *States progress related to fourteen components of PL 99-457, Part H.* Chapel Hill: University of North Carolina at Chapel Hill, Carolina Institute for Child and Family Policy, Frank Porter Graham Child Development Center, Carolina Policy Studies Program.

Harbin, G., Gallagher, J., Lillie, T., & Eckland, J. (1990). *Status of states' progress in implementing Part H of PL 99-457: Report No. 2.* Chapel Hill: University of North Carolina at Chapel Hill, Carolina Institute for Child and Family Policy, Frank Porter Graham Child Development Center, Carolina Policy Studies Program.

O'Brien, M.A. (1991). Third-party billing for school services: The school's perspective. *Asha, 33,* 43–48.

Peterson, N.L. (1991). Interagency collaboration under Part H: The key to comprehensive, multidisciplinary, coordinated infant/toddler intervention services. *Journal of Early Intervention, 15*(1), 89–105.

School-related services and Medicaid. (1991). Tallahassee: Florida Department of Education, Bureau of Education for Exceptional Students.

Van Dyck, P.C. (1991). *Use of parental fees in PL 99-4577, Part H.* Chapel Hill: University of North Carolina at Chapel Hill, Carolina Institute for Child and Family Policy, Frank Porter Graham Child Development Center, Carolina Policy Studies Program.

White, K.R., & Immel, N. (1991). *Medicaid and other third-party payments: One piece of the early intervention financing puzzle.* Bethesda, MD: National Center for Family-Centered Care, Association for the Care of Children's Health.

Wolf, K.E. (1991). Third-party billing for school services: The healthcare provider's perspective. *Asha, 33,* 45–48.

Chapter 18

Contracts and Interagency Agreements

The Education of the Handicapped Act Amendments of 1986 (PL 99-457) state that interagency cooperation, coordination, and collaboration must occur to reduce duplication of services and to use existing resources effectively. The infants and toddlers program (Part H) represents a clear intent to finance early intervention services through coordination of the respective funding sources of various community agencies. This requires the agencies to focus on interagency planning, coordination, contracts, and agreements in meeting the service delivery needs of these children and their families.

Traditionally, attempts at service coordination have been focused on state-level written agreements that have minimal impact at the local level (Clifford, 1991; Hodge, 1984). Contracts and written agreements, however, are critically important at the local level. Each community has a unique assortment of agencies that provide a combination of educational, medical, therapeutic, parent, and social services. The agencies vary according to mission, personnel expertise, delivery models, community location, target populations, policy, procedures, funding methods, and constraints. Development of interagency contracts and written agreements is necessary for a complete range of coordinated services. Written agreements are important not only in funding but also in achieving successful outcomes, such as effective transition.

In order to expand and improve services, agency limitations in overall funding, personnel, facilities, and therapy services must be overcome. Barriers to expansion or qual-

ity services include inadequate facility space; least restrictive environment options; transportation needs; rural and geographical spread; personnel shortages and lack of staff development; fragmented parent education activities; and insufficient occupational, physical, and speech-language therapy.

Contracts and cooperative agreements will play a critical role in the development of a comprehensive array of community services under PL 99-457. Local interagency councils have the potential to develop the trust required among agency personnel to implement contracts and agreements that provide solutions to minimize constraints and improve the quality and quantity of services.

CONTRACT VERSUS WRITTEN AGREEMENT

A contract and a written agreement differ in their intent and actual content. A *contract* between agencies describes the purchase of services and specifies the cost of those services. For example, a school district program may enter into a contract with a local rehabilitation center for the purpose of purchasing occupational and physical therapy services. The cost for those services (e.g., $60 per therapy hour) and the terms and conditions are agreed upon by both agencies and formalized in writing. A contract is a legal document.

A *written agreement* does not specify the purchase of services, but it may delineate the financial responsibilities of the agencies by clarifying which agency pays for what service. The primary purpose of agreements is to describe in writing the collaborative elements that have been developed in the form of policy, procedures, and working relationships among agencies (Elder, 1980).

By analyzing the array of existing community services and the gaps in services, local interagency councils are in a position to identify potential interagency partnerships that can be formalized by contracts and agreements. Each local council should facilitate the development of an interagency agreement that delineates the respective roles and responsibilities of the agencies to young children with disabilities and conditions of risk within the community. A cooperative agreement among agencies may describe the adoption of uniform procedures for referral, transition activities, and standardized forms; identification of the role and responsibility of each agency for payment or provision of specified services; identification of the primary payor and the payor of last resort; shared use of personnel for such activities as screening and evaluation; shared use of facilities, equipment, and materials; co-location of programs and services; adoption of uniform calendars; coordination and shared funding for staff development and parent education; integration of a data base or registry information; and cooperative development of grants and program budgets (Audette, 1980).

CONTRACTS

Components of Contracts and Agreements

Eight important elements or components of a contract or agreement can be identified (Elder, 1980); however, all of them may not be required for every agreement:

1. Statement of purpose
2. Definition of terms
3. Description of service or focus
4. Financial responsibilities of each agency
5. Roles and responsibilities of each agency
6. Designation of responsible positions

7. Administrative procedures and contract duration
8. Evaluation procedures

A well-written contract includes a clear statement of the purpose for the agreement between the parties. Terminology, definitions, and acronyms must be clarified to avoid ambiguous or unfamiliar terms. For example, the school day may be defined differently by agencies, with varied implications for the cost of services. The type of services, such as speech therapy, physical therapy, transportation, parent services, or the use of a classroom, must be clearly described, along with the cost of the services. The sections on specific roles and responsibilities, including funding and timelines, should spell out the agency responsible for each aspect of the services. There should be no confusion as to who does what, where, and when. Staff members with designated responsibilities for certain provisions of the contract should be identified. Details of administrative procedures should include effective date, termination date, procedures for modification, confidentiality issues, nondiscrimination clauses, and other assurances. Evaluation procedures for periodic review of implementation of the contract and the effectiveness of its provisions also should be defined.

Readiness for Contracting

The ability of agencies to engage in written contracts depends on several factors, as shown in Table 1. Contracting, a complex relationship between two (or more) agencies, is based on identification of a need to combine

Table 1. Prerequisites for agency contracting

1. Need for purchase of services
2. Agency/program self-assurance
3. Belief that contracting is advantageous
4. Trust between the contracting parties
5. Willingness to exercise trade-offs
6. Understanding of program funding
7. Understanding of state board rules
8. Understanding of contracting procedures

resources and requires trust and respect, knowledge of statutory regulations and constraints, and the ability to engage in shared decision making.

Principles of Successful Contracting

Successful contracting is a relationship between two or more agencies. It places six demands on each agency:

1. To share a common goal that is within the scope of the general goals of each agency
2. To share commitment to the goal
3. To invest agency resources through contribution of time, personnel, materials, or facilities
4. To exceed the simple act of endorsing an idea
5. To share decision making and leadership
6. To make a joint evaluation and judgment of the effectiveness of the project and the quality of the collaboration

Principles of successful contracting have been identified by several authors (Elder, 1980; Morgan & Swan, 1988; Peterson, 1991) and are described below. Contracts are legal documents and require careful investigation and preparation before execution. A carefully prepared contract for the purchase of services is one of the most effective ways to expand the quality and quantity of local early intervention services in a relatively short period of time.

Understanding State Regulations Criteria for approval of nonpublic school programs are described in statutes and state board of education rules. They usually address areas of certification, qualified personnel, conditions under which contracting is permitted, administrative responsibilities, curricular and program requirements, compliance with civil rights regulations, and the contents of the contract. Agency personnel must thoroughly understand the state's audit and monitoring procedures for review of these contracts and establish agency pro-

cedures for developing and implementing them in accordance with state law.

Understanding the Program Understanding the policies, procedures, guidelines, personnel qualifications, and administrative structure of a program facilitates attempts to bring together two or more agencies through a mutually advantageous contract. Services provided under the contract must be acceptable to all parties.

Conducting a Pre-Contract Review of the Program Site All parties should review the program site before entering into a contract. They should verify that the program meets the established standards under which it must operate and determine that it will offer high-quality preschool services (Schweinhart, 1988). A standards or criteria checklist, as shown in Figure 1, that includes all legal and program requirements is a useful review tool (see Appendix A at the end of this chapter). Areas needing modification should be identified before execution of the contract and so noted within the contract.

Building Mutual Respect and Trust Bringing together two or more independent agencies into a contractual arrangement is a challenging endeavor. Complex collaborative efforts require agency personnel to share a common goal, a commitment to that goal, and a belief that expansion of existing resources and the development of new resources can be effectively accomplished if the agencies work as a team. Teamwork requires confrontation of procedural and philosophical differences among agency programs and consensus on resolution. For example, issues relating to the exchange of student information and confidentiality will emerge. Trust among the agencies is important in creating a fair and safe climate for resolution of problems encountered during the contract period.

Disclosing the Reason for the Contract Agencies must honestly disclose the reason for the purchase of services and any related conditions that affect the terms or duration of the contract. For example, an agency may wish to enter into a brief or temporary

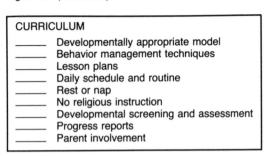

```
┌─────────────────────────────────────────┐
│          Contracting Checklist          │
│                                         │
│ PROGRAM ORGANIZATION                    │
│ _____  Calendar year                   │
│ _____  Attendance requirements and procedures │
│ _____  Hours per day                   │
│ _____  Before- and after-school care   │
│ _____  Transportation                  │
│ _____  Dress code or standards         │
│ _____  Field trips                     │
│ _____  Adult to child ratio            │
│ _____  Class size                      │
│ _____  Absence of prayer in classroom  │
│ _____  Meal and snack procedures       │
│ _____  Registration forms and enrollment proce- │
│ _____  dure                            │
│ _____  IEP/IFSP procedures             │
│ _____  Program eligibility             │
│ _____  Income eligibility              │
│ _____  Fees or special assessments     │
│                                         │
│ STAFF                                   │
│ _____  On-site administrator           │
│         Supervision procedures and extent of │
│ _____  supervision                     │
│ _____  Qualifications                  │
│ _____  Personnel practices             │
│ _____  In-service training for teachers │
│ _____  Paraprofessional training       │
│ _____  Provisions for substitutes      │
│ _____  Multicultural/bilingual         │
│ _____  Therapists                      │
│ _____  Social workers, nurses, and specialists │
│ _____  Parent/teacher partnerships     │
│ _____  Teaming                         │
│ _____  Experience and training with disabled │
│         Policies on planning time, including break │
│ _____  and lunch                       │
│ _____  Evaluation procedures           │
│                                         │
│ SERVICES PROVIDED                       │
│ _____  Speech-language therapy         │
│ _____  Occupational and physical therapy │
│ _____  Medical                         │
│ _____  Dental                          │
│ _____  Counseling                      │
│ _____  Parent education and support    │
│ _____  Social worker or service coordinator │
│ _____  Nurse                           │
│ _____  Psychologist                    │
│ _____  Transportation                  │
│                                         │
│ FACILITY                                │
│ _____  Air conditioning/heat           │
│ _____  Accessibility for physically impaired │
│ _____  Size/square footage             │
│ _____  Playground space and equipment  │
│ _____  Bathrooms and access to sinks   │
│ _____  Safety standards                │
│ _____  Materials and equipment         │
│ _____  Absence of religious symbols    │
│                              _____    │
│                          (continued)    │
└─────────────────────────────────────────┘
```

Figure 1.   Sample checklist of interagency contract issues.

Figure 1.   (continued)

```
┌─────────────────────────────────────────┐
│ CURRICULUM                              │
│ _____  Developmentally appropriate model │
│ _____  Behavior management techniques  │
│ _____  Lesson plans                    │
│ _____  Daily schedule and routine      │
│ _____  Rest or nap                     │
│ _____  No religious instruction        │
│ _____  Developmental screening and assessment │
│ _____  Progress reports                │
│ _____  Parent involvement              │
└─────────────────────────────────────────┘
```

contract for a program site until new facilities are constructed. The contracted agency should clearly understand the situation, particularly if it must expand staff or modify its program to accommodate the contract. Agencies should never place others in a situation that may potentially harm them, financially or otherwise.

Understanding the Formulas for Program Funding   School systems are often reluctant to contract with nonpublic programs for occupational, physical, or speech therapy services because of the high hourly cost. Program administrators must understand the formula by which state funding is generated in order to determine if contracting costs are reasonable. Calculating the hourly rate of funding indicates the equivalent cost of purchased services. For example, if state funding for speech-language therapy programs provides $14.50 per hour to the district for each child served and the nonpublic agency charges $24 per hour for the service, children must be scheduled in groups of two to generate sufficient state funding to cover the cost of the services. Approximately 20% of the amount generated remains in the district to cover administrative and indirect costs.

Identifying Mutual Trade-Offs and Advantages   A successful contract provides mutual benefits for all parties. If the contract benefits only one party, the other parties may not be motivated to execute, continue, or renew it. Contracts should not be used to force other agencies into compliance with procedures.

Using Specific and Descriptive Contract Language A vague contract that fails in clearly defining roles, procedures, terms, responsibilities, outcomes, and exclusionary factors results in problems, questions of contract interpretation, and a potential negative impact on services to children and families. Each party must precisely understand the terms and expectations. See Appendices B and C at the end of this chapter for examples of carefully prepared contracts.

Having an Attorney Review All Contracts Contracts are legal documents and, as such, should always be reviewed and approved by an agency's attorney. The contents and method of implementation must be consistent with state statutes, regulations, and agency policies and procedures.

Recognizing Indirect Benefits When a school district program enters into a contract with a nonpublic school program, for example, many indirect benefits become apparent. Guaranteed and steady income to the nonpublic school program may enhance its budget and permit higher salaries that attract more qualified or certified personnel. Such indirect benefits as increased staff development result in services of higher quality for all children in the program, not just the children enrolled under the contract. These types of benefits are important to all parties. Sample advantages of collaborative programs are listed in Table 2.

Recognizing New Areas of Need Created by Contracting As contractual arrangements are implemented, other needs may arise. For example, contracting with The Arc center may have implications for an expanded staff development program or assistance to teachers who need to reactivate their certification. For a successful outcome of the contract, these situations should be recognized early and resolved in a timely manner.

Engaging in Joint Evaluation A contract implies a partnership between agencies that is built on trust, shared decision making, and joint evaluation. In a contractual situation, both parties have ownership. The

Table 2. Benefits of contracting for services

1. Secures needed therapy services to compensate for staff shortage
2. Secures needed classroom space to expand services to children
3. Reduces overhead costs (facility, utilities, maintenance)
4. Results in greater cost-effectiveness for low-incidence populations
5. Results in cost sharing and minimizes costs to individual agencies
6. Minimizes duplication of effort and inefficient spending
7. Decreases time required for transporting children to distant centers
8. Adds options for extended-day and extended-year programs
9. Reduces number of children waiting for program slots
10. Minimizes time lag in placement and delivery of services
11. Expands program and service options (location, delivery model)
12. Facilitates integration of children with disabilities
13. Increases options for family focused services
14. Provides steady income for nonprofit and community programs
15. Increases income of nonprofit programs and enables them to raise staff salaries and to require certified teachers
16. Increases standards and quality of care for all children

contracted arrangement provides a newly created collaborative venture and partnership that did not formerly exist. Establishing procedures and guidelines, as well as evaluating the operation of the venture, must be accomplished through the process of shared decision making.

Using "Gentlemen's Agreements" in Place of Formal Contracts Agencies may be reluctant to enter into formal written contracts that commit them to promises they cannot keep later. If a contract is written too tightly, without sufficient "wiggle room," an agency may simply refuse to consider it. For example, a contract may be developed between children's medical services and United Cerebral Palsy for the provision of occupational and physical therapy in a home-based setting for infants and toddlers. The contract stipulates that children's medical services will pay one half of the cost of therapy for each eligible child. The agency may be reluctant to sign such an agreement because its budget is typically overspent before the end of each fiscal year and it is forced to cut back temporarily on nonemergency services. Children's medical services may be quite willing, however, to fund such services under a verbal "gentlemen's agreement," with the understanding of both contracting agencies that their ability to do so may fluctuate during the year. Such a verbal agreement between agency personnel may be adequate until the agencies are able to accept a formal commitment.

WRITTEN AGREEMENTS

Written agreements, in contrast to contracts that specify purchase of services, delineate policy and procedures that describe the working relationships among agencies. Examples of written agreements are:

A school district agrees to provide speech-language, occupational, and physical therapy services to children enrolled in Head Start and a federally subsidized child care program. The school district sends staff to the centers and generates state funding for services provided to eligible children. Head Start and the child care center provide space, materials, transportation for children, and medical and dental services and agree to comply with school board procedures for the provision of therapy services (e.g., evaluation, placement, individualized education program, confidentiality, records).

A written agreement is developed by the school district, United Cerebral Palsy, The Arc preschool program, the Easter Seal Society, and the human resources parent training program. Consistent procedures and standards are adopted for referral, screening, evaluation, and provision of services. The agencies agree to survey staff

development needs jointly and to fund in-service and training activities jointly.

A written agreement among the school district, a local rehabilitation center, and the federally subsidized childcare program provides for co-location of services. The school district agrees to provide evaluation, case management, education, and transportation services for preschool children with disabilities. The rehabilitation center agrees to send therapists to the school centers to provide all therapy (speech, physical, and occupational) and to bill Medicaid and private insurance carriers for the cost of services. The child care program provides staff at the school facility to care for the children before and after school.

The school district, United Cerebral Palsy, Easter Seal Society, and county public health department enter into an agreement to provide a community screening program for the early identification of children needing special services. A team consisting of staff members from each agency organizes bimonthly screenings at the local shopping mall. The agencies agree to provide evaluations to all children identified in the community screening program.

The school district, the county public health department, a parent-to-parent group, and the human resources program enter into an agreement to co-locate staff members and create an interagency intake team. The team provides a consolidated application process for families. Standardized forms and procedures are adopted, and program eligibility is determined simultaneously. The agencies resolve the issues of confidentiality and the use of tracking data.

Agencies serving preschool children (birth through 5 years of age) with disabilities and conditions of risk enter into an agreement to specify their respective roles and responsibilities. A matrix of services is developed, eligibility criteria are examined, and financial responsibilities are described for various populations of children. Educational, therapeutic, economic, family, case management, mental health, and medical services are described. Procedures are established for modification of responsibility when designated agencies suffer budget cutbacks or funding deficits.

Appendix D at the end of this chapter presents a sample agreement among four agencies for the development of a coordinated early intervention program.

REFERENCES

Audette, R.H. (1980). Interagency collaboration: The bottom line. In J.O. Elder & P.R. Magrab (Eds.), *Coordinating services to handicapped children: A handbook for interagency collaboration* (pp. 25–44). Baltimore: Paul H. Brookes Publishing Co.

Clifford, R.M. (1991). *State financing of services under PL 99-457, Part H.* Chapel Hill: University of North Carolina at Chapel Hill, Frank Porter Graham Child Development Center, Carolina Policy Studies Program.

Elder, J.O. (1980). Writing interagency agreements. In J.O. Elder & P.R. Magrab (Eds.), *Coordinating services to handicapped children: A handbook for interagency collaboration* (pp. 203–242). Baltimore: Paul H. Brookes Publishing Co.

Hodge, R. (1984). *Interagency cooperation: Related issues and concerns.* A CASE Research Committee Report. Bloomington: Indiana University, School of Education, Division of the Council for Exceptional Children.

Morgan, J.L., & Swan, W.W. (1988). *Local interagency councils for preschool handicapped programs: An effective strategy to implement the mandate.* Bloomington: Indiana University, Council for Administrators of Special Education, Inc. (CASE) (A Division of the Council for Exceptional Children).

Peterson, N.L. (1991). Interagency collaboration under Part H: The key to comprehensive, multidisciplinary, coordinated infant/toddler intervention services. *Journal of Early Intervention, 15*(1), 89–105.

Schweinhart, L.J. (1988). *A school administrator's guide to early childhood programs.* Ypsilanti, MI: The High/Scope Press.

Sample Site Review
Checklist for Contracted Settings

Preschool Program Quality Checklist

Center:_____Date:_____
Observers:_____

Directions: This checklist identifies the three primary components of a high quality preschool program:
1. A well-defined and developmentally appropriate curriculum
2. Highly qualified and competent staff
3. Involved parents

Indicate the presence of the program characteristics and descriptors listed below with a check.

I.   A WELL-DEFINED CURRICULUM

_____ The classroom is divided into clearly identifiable learning areas or centers.

_____ An age-appropriate environment is provided (i.e., play areas for free play, dramatic play, art, stories, and music; toys for manipulation; equipment for large and small muscles).

_____ Learning areas include *at least* all of the following: art area, block area, quiet/language area, house area, toy area, circle/music area.

_____ Learning areas are clearly marked by labels, pictures, signs, and/or colors.

_____ Lesson plans describe the particular unit, concepts, key experiences, etc. that have been included in these activities; the lesson plan does not simply reveal the daily schedule.

_____ The classroom is well organized, bright, colorful, stimulating, and enhances learning.

_____ Teaching activities are preplanned by the teacher and the teacher aide; there is evidence that the classroom environment is frequently changed or varied (art materials, interest centers, pictures, posters, etc.) to maintain interest and stimulate learning.

_____ There is evidence that all legal and regulatory requirements are met for local day care standards.

_____ There is adequate bathroom space for the number of children; a sink and running water are accessible.

_____ An abundant array of age-appropriate toys and materials and manipulatives are available; materials are in good repair.

_____ Toys, manipulatives, and art materials are readily accessible to children and arranged on low open shelves to promote independent use.

_____ Toy areas, shelves, bins, and storage containers are labeled with pictures, outlined drawings, words, colors, etc.

_____ Classroom space is sufficient for the number of children enrolled in the classroom (30 to 35 square feet per child).

_____ An abundance of materials can be found in the learning areas:

Block Area/Building Area

_____ Variety of wooden blocks, shapes

_____ Large cardboard blocks

_____ Transportation toys, such as small trucks, trains, tractors, cars, etc.

_____ Variety of accessories including toy animals and people

_____ Large cardboard blocks
_____ Large Tinkertoys, plastic or wood
_____ Interlocking train tracks
_____ Carpet pieces, boards, old sheets, cardboard pieces

House Area

_____ Housekeeping furniture (stove, sink, refrigerator, cupboard)
_____ Outside house area accessories (pots, pans, dishes, glasses, silverware), table, chairs
_____ Assorted food cans, boxes, play food
_____ Dish towels, pot holders, napkins, place mats, tablecloths
_____ Assorted dolls and doll clothes, mixed races
_____ Dress-up clothes, assorted jewelry, hats, shoes
_____ Storage for dress-up clothes
_____ Doll bed
_____ Doll buggy
_____ Iron, ironing board
_____ Play telephones
_____ Play shopping cart
_____ Play cash register
_____ Real electric frying pan (for cooking activities)
_____ Real toaster oven
_____ Popcorn popper

Art Area

_____ Easel (2+)
_____ Tempera paints, assorted colors
_____ Variety of brushes, brush sizes
_____ Assortment of drawings and painting paper; easel-size paper
_____ Large crayons, assorted colors
_____ Colored chalk
_____ Pencils
_____ Felt tip markers
_____ Scissors (8–10 pairs)
_____ Glue
_____ White paste
_____ Glue sticks
_____ Assorted string, yarn, ribbon
_____ Assorted Styrofoam items (egg cartons, packing material, trays)
_____ Craft supplies, glitter, craft sticks, pipe cleaners, cotton balls
_____ Assorted magazines, catalogs, postcards, pictures
_____ Needles and thread
_____ Soap flakes, liquid starch for fingerpaints
_____ Ink pads and stamps, printing trays

Quiet/Language Area

_____ Large assortment of books
_____ Assorted puzzles (wooden, foam, knobbed, cardboard)
_____ Pegboards and pegs
_____ Beads and laces, pattern cards
_____ Legos
_____ Bristle blocks
_____ Listening center with earphones
_____ Design cubes, parquetry blocks, picture dominoes
_____ Lotto games

Music/Circle Area

_____ Record player
_____ Variety of age-appropriate records
_____ Rhythm instruments

_____ Puppets
_____ Flannel board
_____ Flannel board accessories
_____ Cassette recorder
_____ Assortment of tapes

Outdoor Area

_____ Access to an appropriate outdoor space that is fenced and safe
_____ A wide variety of appropriately sized equipment that allows for development of physical skills and large muscles
_____ Outdoor equipment that is safe and in good repair
_____ Playground swings
_____ Playground slide
_____ Playground equipment for climbing
_____ Equipment for hanging
_____ Balance beam
_____ Sand and water table
_____ Accessories for sand and water play (buckets, scoops, funnels, shovels, measuring cups, molds, etc.)
_____ Tricycles
_____ Wagons
_____ Wheelbarrow
_____ Scooter
_____ Irish mail
_____ Jump ropes
_____ Variety of balls, large and small
_____ Hula hoops
_____ Bean bag and ring toss

Construction/Wood Working Area

_____ Wood working bench
_____ Tool chest
_____ Hammers and nails
_____ Saw
_____ Screwdrivers
_____ Hand drill
_____ Wood scraps
_____ Wood glue
_____ Wooden tools, materials, and so forth
_____ Safety glasses and ear protectors
_____ Nuts, bolts, washers

Discovery/Science

_____ Scales and measuring sets
_____ Play clock
_____ Shells, rocks, other natural substances
_____ Plants
_____ Caged pets
_____ Aquarium
_____ Prisms and kaleidoscopes
_____ Magnifying glass
_____ Magnets
_____ Mirrors
_____ Timers, egg timers

II. HIGHLY QUALIFIED AND COMPETENT STAFF

_____ The teacher and teacher aide listen to the children with attention and respect; speak with children in a friendly, positive, and courteous manner.

_____ The teacher and aide provide verbal support.

_____ The children engage in activities, ask open-ended questions, and facilitate language learning.

_____ The teacher and aide set appropriate classroom limits, clarify classroom rules for the children, and manage classroom behavior effectively.

_____ The teacher and aide abstain from corporal punishment or other inappropriate behavior management techniques.

_____ The High/Scope curriculum is implemented in this classroom.

_____ Lesson plans are well written and describe a particular unit, concepts, vocabulary, working experiences.

_____ The teacher has arranged the classroom environment and learning tasks to facilitate key learning experiences.

_____ A developmental profile or observation record is maintained and current for each child in the classroom.

_____ The teacher coordinates classroom activities with other child care or with therapeutic services the children receive.

_____ There is evidence of planning meetings or conferences with therapists or other specialists who work with the child and family.

_____ The teacher knows the procedure for making referrals to social agencies for families in need.

_____ The teacher ensures that the appropriate sensory screening (vision and hearing) is completed for each child early in the year and that the necessary follow-up is done.

_____ Medical, vision, hearing, dental, evaluation services, and so on are appropriately recorded in cumulative folder.

_____ The teacher is able to recognize children's disabilities, special needs, behavior problems, and respond appropriately.

_____ The teacher is aware of the procedure to refer a child to the child find specialist.

_____ Confidential information and reports on children are kept in a safe, secure place out of the view of others.

_____ The teacher and teacher aide have passed the security screening.

_____ The teacher has teacher certification in early childhood.

_____ The teacher is certified in another area (   ) but will have early childhood certification within 2 years.

_____ If the teacher has an AA degree or the Child Development credential, she is supervised by an early childhood teacher at least one half-day per week.

_____ The teacher aide has completed the required 20-hour minimal training component.

_____ The teacher and teacher aide have a designated planning period each day when they are not in contact with children.

_____ The teacher has attended in-service training during the past year.

_____ The teacher/aide desk and work area is well organized, clean, and clutter free.

_____ Attendance records are accurate and properly maintained.

III. INVOLVED PARENTS

_____ Teaching staff responds to parents in a friendly, supportive, respectful, and nonjudgmental manner.

_____ Staff members are responsive to parents' needs, questions, and concerns.

_____ Staff members provide appropriate referral information to parents as needed.

_____ There is a well-defined system of parent involvement.

_____ There is evidence of daily and/or weekly informal discussions with parents about their child.

_____ There is evidence of conferences to discuss the progress of each child.

_____ There is evidence of meetings or parent workshops.

_____ The teacher makes home visits.

_____ There is evidence of written progress notes or a positive feedback to parents.

_____ There is a bulletin board or wall area where notices to parents are posted.

_____ There is evidence of scheduled parent conferences when concerns arise about children (illness, suspected hearing/vision problems, excessive fatigue and need for sleep, feeding and nutritional problems, behavioral problems, etc.).

There is evidence that parents are involved in the daily operation of the classroom as
____ visitors, volunteers, field trip chaperones, and so forth.

The teacher regularly sends suggestions or materials home to the parent including art
____ papers, drawings, reading materials, and/or suggestions for home activities.

IV. SPECIAL SERVICES

____ Transportation services are provided to and from school.

____ Social work services are provided.

____ Speech-language therapy services are provided.

____ Occupational therapy services are provided.

____ Physical therapy services are provided.

____ Mental health services are provided.

____ Vision and hearing screenings are provided to all students.

____ Health and dental screenings are provided.

Bilingual staff members are employed to communicate with non–English speaking fam-
____ ilies.

____ The program has an active parent education component.

____ The program employs visiting teachers.

____ A kitchen or cafeteria is on site and prepares daily meals.

____ The center participates in the USDA School Lunch Program/Child Care Food Program.

V. SUMMARY

The classroom has well-organized, well-defined learning areas needed in a high quality
____ preschool program.

____ Equipment and materials are in abundant supply and in good condition.

____ A developmentally appropriate curriculum model is implemented.

____ Classroom space, both indoor and outdoor, is sufficient for operation of the program.

____ All legal and regulatory requirements are met for local child care standards.

____ The staff meets certification and minimum training requirements.

____ Security clearances have been completed for all teacher aides.

The staff organizes the environment, facilitates activities, develops lesson plans, and re-
____ sponds to the children in an effective manner that enhances learning.

Vision, hearing, and other screening is done on all children early in the year; follow-up
____ is completed on children needing referral or medical attention.

____ Staff responds to parents in a friendly, supportive, and respectful manner.

There is evidence that parents are actively involved in their child's program, serve as
____ volunteers, and are included in conferences, parent meetings, and groups.

____ Transportation is provided when necessary to and from school.

Special services such as social work, speech-language, and occupational therapy services
____ are available at the school for students with impairments.

____ Food services are available on site.

Apparent areas of deficiency/noncompliance with high quality standards:

Recommendation:

Sample Contract

1992 CONTRACT
between the
Scott County School Board
and
Parent to Parent of Scott County, Inc.

I. PARTICIPATING AGENCIES

The Scott County School Board, hereinafter called the School Board, and Parent to Parent of Scott County, Inc., hereinafter called Parent to Parent, are the participating agencies of this agreement.

II. DEFINITIONS

Developmentally Delayed	As defined by the Department of Education under the state. Infants and Toddlers Program and local School Board policy.
Interagency Intake Team	A team comprised of service coordinators from Human Services, Scott County Schools, Public Health Department, Children's Medical Services, and Parent to Parent that meet to simultaneously review and determine program eligibility; establishes a single point of intake into agency services avoiding the need for a parent to visit individual agencies separately and complete multiple application and consent forms.
Parent Service Coordinator	The position funded under this contract, responsible for serving as a member of the Interagency Intake Team and providing organization of parent support/education activities.

III. PURPOSE

In order to provide appropriate parent education and support activities under the goals of both state and federal legislation, the School Board enters into a contractual agreement with Parent to Parent.

Under this contract, the School Board hereby contracts with Parent to Parent for parent education and support services up to 20 hours per week and a maximum of 600 hours for the fiscal year. Parent to Parent will be responsible to provide a part-time position referred to·as the Parent Service Coordinator. In addition, Parent to Parent will provide the expertise and services of other support parents necessary for development and implementation of parent education and support activities. Activities include: 1) assisting in the establishment of a referral process designed to refer families of infants and toddlers with disabilities and at-risk to a single point of intake, 2) participation in the Interagency Intake Team, 3) preparing parents for participation in the IFSP, 4) assisting in the development of the Individual Family Service Plan process, and 5) development of activities for parent education and support.

IV. DURATION

This contract shall be effective July 1, 1992, and cover the period consistent with the fiscal year. The expiration date shall be June 30, 1993.

V.   GENERAL PROVISIONS OF THE CONTRACT

Each party, in consideration of the agreements to be performed by the other, agrees to the definitions and conditions of this contract as stated:

1.   Services are designed to expand services and are nonsupplanting in nature.
2.   Parent to Parent will be responsible for the employment and supervision of a part-time Parent Service Coordinator funded under this contract. This person shall not be considered an employee of the School Board. Selection will be made with the approval of the Early Interventon Program Coordinator and the Preschool Interagency Council.
3.   Development of parent activities is an interagency effort and guided by the principle of shared decision making and involvement of the local Preschool Interagency Council.
4.   Activities of the Parent Service Coordinator funded under this contract will be consistent with the attached job description, objectives, and timelines.
5.   Funds in the amount of $500 will be provided for necessary supplies, parent materials, daily travel, postage, and printing.
6.   Travel reimbursement may be provided, upon prior approval, for out-of-district travel for the Parent Service Coordinator to attend meetings, conferences, and workshops. In such cases, travel forms submitted must conform to policy and procedure of the School Board. Travel is reimbursed at a rate of $0.20 per mile.
7.   Parties will meet at least three times during the contract period to evaluate accomplishment of the objectives and to recommend any necessary modifications.
8.   Identifying trademark and logos developed for the School Board and the Preschool Inter-agency Council will be used in conjunction with the Parent to Parent logo on locally developed materials.

Specific Responsibilities of Parent to Parent

1.   Monthly invoices and corresponding time sheets will be submitted for reimbursement for salary and fringe benefit costs of the Parent Service Coordinator.
2.   Office space, furniture, equipment, access to telephone, and other necessary work areas will be provided.
3.   Assistance in the transition of children, birth to 2, to programs serving 3-year-old children (with disabilities and at risk) will be provided.
4.   Adoption and use of all standardized application, consent, service, and IFSP forms as required by the School Board.
5.   The Parent Service Coordinator will represent Parent to Parent by attendance at all Preschool Interagency Council meetings.

Specific Responsibilities of the Board

1.   The School Board will work in conjunction with Parent to Parent, the community agencies, and the Preschool Interagency Council in development of a coordinated system of parent education and support services.
2.   Upon monthly receipt of an invoice and time sheet, the School Board will initiate payment to Parent to Parent for services provided. Payment shall be made at the rate of $15.00 per hour for a maximum of $9,000.00 for the contract period.
3.   Upon receipt of the required travel reimbursement forms for authorized out-of-district travel, the School Board will initiate payment consistent with School Board policy.

VI.   MODIFICATION OF THE CONTRACT

Modification of the contract shall be made by mutual consent of both parties or the contract may be terminated by either of the two parties upon a sixty (60) day notice.

Dated this _____ day of June, 1992.

_____   _____
President   Superintendent
Parent to Parent of Scott County, Inc.   Scott County Schools

_____   _____
Coordinator   Chairman
Preschool Interagency Council   Scott County School Board

_____   _____
Coordinator   Director
Early Intervention Programs   Exceptional Student Education

Sample Contract for Student Placement in a Hospital-Based Program

1992-1993 CONTRACT
between
Scott County School Board
and
Scott Memorial Hospital

Agreement made and entered in Scott County, Florida, this first day of July 1992, by and between the Scott County School Board, hereinafter referred to as the School Board, and Scott Memorial Hospital, hereinafter referred to as the Hospital.

PURPOSE

The purpose of this agreement is to specify procedures and fees which will be charged to the School Board for students who are placed in the Scott Memorial Hospital Preschool Speech and Language Program.

RESPONSIBILITIES

The Hospital agrees:

1. To provide services at a rate of $13.00 per hour (per child) for speech-language therapy and $21.20 per hour (per child) for occupational therapy for children enrolled under contract in the Preschool Speech and Language Program. Only direct therapy services will be billed. Therapy will be provided to eligible students following the proper authorization by the Director of Exceptional Student Education or designee and consistent with the objectives specified in the student's Individualized Education Program (IEP).
2. To provide a monthly statement to the School Board itemizing speech-language and occupational therapy (OT) charges on students enrolled. Speech-language and OT services will not exceed a part-time program with combined billing not to exceed 12 hours per week per child.
3. To provide services rendered by qualified, certified speech-language pathologists and occupational therapists. A current copy of the certificate of registration or the state license to practice in Florida will be provided for all staff members working with the children under contract.
4. To designate a program contact person who shall work cooperatively with the Coordinator of Early Intervention Programs or designee in matters relative to placement, provision of services, re-evaluation, and annual revision of the IEP as well as contract issues.
5. To ensure participation of the speech pathologist and, when appropriate, the occupational therapist in placement and IEP meetings.
6. To provide consultation, information, education, and training to parents as a required program component.
7. To provide semester progress reports for each child. Copies will be provided to the parents, the School District, and other professionals or agencies (e.g., pediatrician, Children's Medical Services [CMS], Health and Rehabilitative Service/Developmental Services [HRS/DS]) as appropriate.
8. To maintain daily attendance records and to submit weekly attendance reports to the Coordinator of Early Intervention Programs.

9. To assist in re-evaluation of students in April/May and to provide all necessary student records at the time the student is transferred or reassigned to another school program.
10. To provide an adult–child ratio of no greater than 1:5.
11. To provide daily administrative and supervisory activities for the operation of the program, appropriate facilities, and sufficient instructional materials in the provision of a high-quality program.
12. To ensure staff participation in relevant staff development activities provided by the School District.

The School Board agrees:

1. To provide the necessary student information and reports on each child recommended for placement and to arrange for evaluation, placement staffings, development and revision of the IEP. Determination of program eligibility will be the responsibility of school district personnel.
2. To designate the Coordinator for Early Intervention Programs as the contact person; to provide necessary supervision to ensure quality of programming and consistency of procedures.
3 To provide a written contract for each student which specifies fees, conditions, and duration.
4. To provide transportation for students placed under contract when specified in the IEP.
5. To initiate payment of bills rendered by the Hospital within thirty (30) calendar days of receipt of billing statement.

NONDISCRIMINATION ASSURANCES

The Hospital assures the School Board of Scott County, Florida, that it does not discriminate on the basis of race, sex, marital status, national origin, religion, handicap, or age in the operation of its business or provision of services.

DURATION

This agreement shall be effective July 1, 1992, and shall continue in effect until June 30, 1993. It may be cancelled by mutual agreement of the parties or until either party cancels it by giving to the other party a notice thirty (30) days in advance of the desired date of cancellation.

Dated this＿＿＿day of＿＿＿1992.

_____
Superintendent
Scott County Schools

_____
Administrator
Scott Memorial Hospital

_____
Chairman
Scott County School Board

_____
Director, Speech Department
Scott Memorial Hospital

_____
Coordinator
Early Intervention Programs

_____
Director, Occupational Therapy
Scott Memorial Hospital

Sample Agreement

1992-1993 COOPERATIVE AGREEMENT
between the
Scott County School Board, United Cerebral Palsy,
Child Care Services, and Kiddie Care Preschool

This Cooperative Agreement, entered into this first day of July 1992, between the Scott County School Board, United Cerebral Palsy, Child Care Services, Inc., and Kiddie Care Preschool, sets forth the terms and conditions pursuant to the development of a coordinated program of early intervention services for 3- through 5-year-old students with disabilities in an integrated setting.

WHEREAS, Public Law 99-457 has mandated services to preschool children with disabilities beginning with their third birthday; and

WHEREAS, the above listed agencies are committed to serving young children with disabilities in the least restrictive setting and integrated settings with nondisabled peers; and

WHEREAS, Public Law 99-457 has required payment for early intervention services from coordination of all available federal, state, and local funding sources (private and public); and

WHEREAS, Public Law 99-457 has declared that agencies other than educational agencies are not absolved of any obligation to pay for some or all of the costs and that all funds must be accessed before federal funds are used.

NOW THEREFORE, in consideration of mutual covenants herein contained and other good and valuable consideration, the receipt of which is hereby acknowledged, the parties agree as follows:

I. **PURPOSE**

   This agreement between the stated parties relates to provision of coordinated, co-located services for children with disabilities, age 3 through 5 years, in an integrated setting. Under this agreement, the School Board hereby agrees to place an estimated five to eight children with disabilities in Kiddie Care Preschool for a 180-day school year. United Cerebral Palsy agrees to provide speech-language, occupational, and physical therapy consistent with the individualized education program (IEP). Child Care Services, Inc., agrees to provide before-school care, after-school care, as well as child care on days (holidays, summer) that school is not in session.

II. **DURATION**

   This agreement shall cover the period from July 1, 1992, through June 30, 1993.

III. **GENERAL PROVISIONS OF THE AGREEMENT**

   All parties agree:
   1. Funding of early intervention services is the joint responsibility of the named agencies and designed to serve children in an integrated community setting.
   2. Program curriculum utilized will be developmentally appropriate according to current nationally recognized standards for high-quality preschool programs.
   3. Appropriate parent education and support services will be provided by program personnel.

4. Provision of adaptive equipment (e.g., wheelchairs, standing frames) will be coordinated among the providers and determined by numerous funding sources.
5. Each agency shall be responsible for recruiting, hiring, and supervising its respective personnel. Personnel shall be selected based on their ability to work with children with disabilities, as well as nondisabled children, and their ability to work cooperatively as a member of a teaching team.
6. Preschool children with disabilities shall be distributed across the two classrooms at Kiddie Care Preschool in order to maintain an appropriate balance and a successful environment.
7. Mandatory staff development activities will be provided during the year to ensure the development of a high-quality integrated setting.
8. Agency staff will comply with policy and procedures of the Scott County Schools with respect to confidential and cumulative student records and reports.
9. All parties agree to meet on at least a quarterly basis to evaluate program accomplishments and needs. Program evaluation will be jointly done by the Director of Child Care Services, Inc., the Preschool Program Coordinator of Scott County Schools, the Director of Kiddie Care Preschool, and the Director of United Cerebral Palsy. Review of program accomplishments will also be made by the Scott County Preschool Interagency Council relative to future recommendations for expansion and modification.

IV. AGENCY RESPONSIBILITIES

The School Board agrees to:
1. Provide one full-time teacher, certified in early childhood/special education, to serve as a member of the teaching team and provide consultation and services for children with disabilities enrolled in Kiddie Care Preschool.
2. Provide supplementary equipment and general instructional materials in an amount not to exceed $600 for the school year.
3. Provide round-trip transportation for children with disabilities, as indicated by the IEP.
4. Schedule all placement and IEP meetings.
5. Provide student records to Kiddie Care Preschool for each child approved for placement.
6. Provide itinerant vision, orientation, and mobility training to eligible students.
7. Report students as appropriate for generation of state (FTE) funds and on the December 1 child count for federal funds (PL 94-142; PL 99-457).
8. Enter student data and daily attendance in the Student Information System consistent with school board policy and procedures.

Child Care Services, Inc., agrees to:
1. Provide staff for before-school (6:30 A.M.–8:30 A.M.) and after-school care (3:30 P.M.– 6:30 P.M.) for a total of 5 hours per day.
2. Provide two staff members for child care services to permit the children with disabilities who are enrolled to remain at Kiddie Care Preschool on days that school is not normally in session (holidays, teacher in-service days, record days, summer) for a total of 80 days per year.
3. Provide staff who meet all the requirements and qualifications for child care workers and who work effectively with children with disabilities.

Kiddie Care Preschool agrees to:
1. Enroll children with disabilities, as identified by the School Board, across the two preschool classrooms in the center.
2. Provide a high-quality, developmentally appropriate curriculum in an environment that provides adequate equipment and learning materials.
3. Provide adequate facilities, custodial services, utilities, and outdoor play equipment.
4. Provide one teacher (certified in early childhood) and one teacher aide per classroom, maintaining a ratio of no greater than 1:10.
5. Provide daily breakfast, lunch, and an afternoon snack at no cost to the families of the enrolled children with disabilities.
6. Provide bimonthly field trips for students, including transportation and fees.
7. Arrange vision, hearing, health, and dental screenings for all students.

8. Meet screening and training requirements required by law, and maintain satisfactory child care licensing standards.

United Cerebral Palsy agrees to:

1. Provide speech-language, occupational, and physical therapy consistent with each child's IEP.
2. Process Medicaid and private insurance billing, when possible, or provide all services at no cost to the family.
3. Provide therapy at Kiddie Care Preschool by personnel who are properly licensed or certified to practice within the state.

V.   RELEASE OF LIABILITY

1. Kiddie Care Preschool, United Cerebral Palsy, and Child Care Services, Inc., hereby agree to purchase such insurance, including but not limited to professional liability and public liability insurance, and keep such insurance in force during the entire term of this agreement.
2. Kiddie Care Preschool, United Cerebral Palsy, and Child Care Services, Inc., hereby agree to indemnify and save harmless the School Board from and against any and all claims, suits, damages, liabilities, or causes of action arising during the term of this agreement arising out of, related to, or in connection with the negligent performance or non-performance of any provision of this agreement required of them including personal injury, loss of life, or damage to property and from and against any orders, judgment, or decrees that may be entered hereon, and from and against costs, attorney's fees, expenses and lawsuits incurred in and about the defense of any such claim and investigation thereof to the extent of the insurance purchased by the agencies. However, nothing herein shall be deemed to indemnify the School Board for any liability or claim arising out of the negligence, performance, or nonperformance of the School Board or as a result of the negligence of any unrelated third party.

VI.   NONDISCRIMINATION ASSURANCES

Kiddie Care, United Cerebral Palsy, and Child Care, Inc., assure the School Board of Scott County, Florida, that they do not discriminate on the basis of race, sex, marital status, national origin, religion, handicap, or age, in the operation of business or provision of services.

VII. MODIFICATION OF THE CONTRACT

Modification of the contract shall be made by mutual consent of all parties. Termination of the contract may occur by any party upon a 60-day notice.

Dated this_____day of_____, 1992.

_____   _____
Director   Superintendent
Child Care Services, Inc.   Scott County Schools

_____   _____
Director   Chairman
Kiddie Care Preschool   Scott County School Board

_____   _____
Director   Witness
United Cerebral Palsy

Index

Page numbers followed by a "t" indicate tables; those followed by "f" indicate figures.